Radical Connecticut

People's History In
The Constitution State

by Andy Piascik and Steve Thornton

HARDBALL

PRESS

Radical Connecticut — People's History in the Constitution State

Copyright 2024 by Andy Piascik and Steve Thornton

Published by Hard Ball Press.

Library of Congress Cataloging-in-Publication Data:. Hartford - History 2. Connecticut - History 3. Shoeleather History 4. Labor - history 5. Progressive movements 6. Black Panther Party

Book design by Matthew Tallon

Set in Times New Roman 11 font.

ISBN: 979-8-9898025-0-0

To contact the authors for a book talk: info@hardballpress.com

Hard Ball Press

415 Argyule Rd., 6A

Brooklyn, NY, 11218

DEDICATION

To my brother Tom: stay the course, bro. – **Andy Piascik**

For my comrade, friend and teacher Peter Kellman. – **Steve Thornton**

"*Radical Connecticut* offers a vast array of dissenters and issues that have perhaps been forgotten. As such it is a valuable antidote to the mythology that often clouds our understanding of the past... the topics covered are varied and fascinating... For the concerned but casual reader troubled by the notion of Connecticut staidness, the book is a delightful eye-opener." —**New York Labor History Association**

"Connecticuters have a long tradition of making history 'from the bottom up'... Enlightening and just plain fun to read, *Radical Connecticut* belongs in every library in the state." —**Priscilla Murolo, co-author of From the Folks Who Brought You the Weekend: An Illustrated History of Labor in the United States, and a Connecticut resident**

"Andy Piascik and Steve Thornton tell the stories of everyday people and well-known figures whose work has often been obscured, denigrated or dismissed. The book provides fascinating narratives of Connecticut social movements and popular organizations that have changed the state and the country for the better." —**Counterpoint, Between the Lines radio news magazine**

"A young Connecticut public school student once described her Connecticut history class as "the story of great white men and their great inventions." *Radical Connecticut* tells the other side of the story." —**Jeremy Brecher, author, documentarian, activist and a Connecticut native**

"While most history books focus on momentous events with widely-known, prominent people, *Radical Connecticut* strives to tell stories about lesser-known everyday people and well-known figures. With 22 chapters, the 93 short stories continue to grab the reader's attention by focusing on the important aspects of each event... Even for non-history buffs, *Radical Connecticut* keeps readers well informed and delivers history in a unique way. Why not take a travel through time?" —**Kaily Martinez, West Hartford News**

"*Radical Connecticut* contains a wealth of elucidating commentary on a number of important women: Olympia Brown, America's first ordained woman minister, muckraking journalist Ida Tarbell, Wobbly and later UAW organizer Matilda Rabinowitz (later Robbins), the radical thinker Helen Keller, who lived in Connecticut from 1939 until she died in 1968, and suffragist Josephine Bennett... Yes, this is a quirky book, but saturated with rich content. It reminds me of the Federal Writers Project during the New Deal when unemployed writers were hired to research and write books about each state's history. May this book spawn at least 50 more in its wake!" —**Eric Gordon, People's World**

"For people who actually lived in Connecticut, the factories could be grim, struggles for unionization fierce. Activists of every kind faced threats from the vested interests, yet fight they did, leaving their mark on progress in so many ways." —**Paul Buhle, American historian, retired Senior Lecturer, Brown University**

"While Connecticut has long been known as "the land of steady habits," it has also been the setting for a wide array of "radical" thinkers and movements…They are highlighted in a book by Connecticut-based political activists Steve Thornton and Andy Piascik, Radical Connecticut: People's History in the Constitution State. Thornton says a radical should not be "stigmatized," but instead praised as someone who is not bound by traditional ways or beliefs. He prefers "progressive, unorthodox or innovative." —**Randall Beach, Connecticut Magazine**

"Unlike a traditional history that focuses on the actions of politicians, generals, business moguls and other elites, this volume features workers, the poor, people of color, peacemakers, women, students, artists and others who joined the never-ending struggle for justice and freedom… a fresh look at history that can spark young people to engage in social justice work in an increasingly complex and dangerous world. It can also be used as a guide for strategy and tactics useful to those who are engaged in today's social struggles. Whether you are a veteran or a novice, Radical Connecticut reminds us that today—and down through the years—organizing is always worth the effort." —**Progressive Area Roundtable, New Haven**

"It seems to many Americans that this is the worst of times. That's where a new Hard Ball Press book comes in. *Radical Connecticut: People's History in the Constitution State…* is designed to inspire ordinary people by illuminating past struggles for social change. They introduce us to stories of union workers, peace activists, civil rights campaigners, feminists, environmentalists and many more. Their "history from below" comes to life with almost 100 stories that span decades… While the book's focus is Connecticut, the lessons are universal." —**Texas Socialist Network**

"This is people's history at its best…a monumental work of scholarship that is also loads of fun to read…they inspire all of us to see that we too live in places alive with radical history." —**Kristin Lawler, Professor of Sociology, Mount Saint Vincent, New York**

"Needed insight and perspective on the History of the Constitution State… Should be required reading in every school." —**Yohuru Williams, Professor of History, Founding Director of the Racial Justice Initiative at the University of St. Thomas and a Connecticut native.**

TABLE OF CONTENTS

Foreword by Paul Buhle

Connecticut, like New England at large, slipped downward in prestige and influence as the nation expanded. Many New Englanders felt somehow left behind, and for good reasons. But industrial, social, political and cultural life did not end here, quite the contrary. In many ways, the development of intellectual and artistic circles continuously found new life. So we say for Connecticut's radical, leftwing, avant-garde, feminist and anti-racist movements and their personalities.

This is a big story to tell, and two hundred and fifty pages cannot encompass it all. However, the saga that follows is rich, meaningful and told in a very lively manner. We might say, at risk of drastic oversimplification, that the Yankee Radical phase preceded the sophistications made possible by the proximity of Connecticut to Greater New York. For theater and movieland, Connecticut was a kind of Neverworld of gorgeous winters and jolly bumpkins. For people who actually lived in Connecticut, the factories could be grim, struggles for unionization fierce. Activists of every kind faced threats from the vested interests, highlighted in a series of Red Scares. Yet fight they did, leaving their mark on progress in so many ways.

As a cultural historian, I am inclined to emphasize the great contributions of Connecticut to the world of social satire, Mark Twain to Walt Kelly. To see the world as the world does not necessarily want to see itself: this is the highest form of criticism as well as the most accessible to ordinary folks.

Paul Buhle is retired Senior Lecturer of Brown University and author or editor of many histories of social movements, as well as editor of more than twenty non-fiction graphic novels.

Introduction

This book is a collection of stories written over a period of years about people's history. As the book's title implies, the stories are about people who were history makers connected in one way or another to the state of Connecticut: workers, farmers, slaves, labor activists, community organizers, prisoners, high school and college students, journalists, artists, political figures, writers, soldiers, veterans and others who defy easy categorization. Some of the stories profile specific individuals. Others describe events, strikes, campaigns and organizations.

Some of those profiled, like Malcolm X, Elizabeth Gurley Flynn, Hellen Keller and Arthur Miller, were quite famous in their time and remain so today. All were "of the people" and were regarded as controversial and even reviled for at least part of their lives by the powerful for precisely that reason. That they are more highly regarded today than while they were alive is a testament to both the impact of their work and the fight successfully waged ever since by their supporters to document their importance.

People's history is a direct outgrowth of the popular upheaval of the 1960s. As a result of that upheaval, some academic historians began to put everyday people at the center of this country's history. Their efforts were not very well received at first because history to that time had overwhelmingly been told from the vantage point of the most powerful: industrialists, conquerors, generals, slave owners and politicians. The most important figures in that telling of history are almost always white men.

One early example of people's history was Staughton and Alice Lynd's *Rank and File: Personal Histories by Working Class Organizers*. The truth of the new approach was confirmed by the enthusiasm with which *Rank and File* was received by both a large number of everyday people and even a number of the intelligentsia. Not too many years later, Howard Zinn published *A People's History of the United States*, one of the most important history books ever written. That 40 years later, none other than Donald Trump singled Zinn's book out for attack is perhaps all that is needed to appreciate its value.

The years since Zinn's book have seen the flowering of people's history authored by an incredibly wide array of outstanding writers. There are far too many to list, but some are worthy of mention, in addition to Zinn and the

Lynds: Roxanne Dunbar-Ortiz, Priscilla Murolo, Judson Jeffries, Jama Lazerow, Paul and Mari Jo Buhle, Yohuru Williams, Linda Gordon, Herbert Aptheker, Nell Irvin Painter, Jeremy Brecher, Peniel Joseph, Richard Moyer and Herbert Morais, Philip Foner, Jane LaTour and Harvey Wasserman.

The authors of this book are not professional historians, and we would never compare ourselves to any of the writers mentioned above. We do believe, though, that people's history can be told by others besides academics. Many people have spent much, if not all, of their adult lives participating in organizations, movements, campaigns and other efforts such as those described in this book. This accumulated wealth of experience and knowledge is of the utmost value and should be considered a vital contribution to historian Eric Foner's concept of a "usable past."

We especially encourage those from marginalized groups whose voices are the most often ignored to tell their stories. While our book covers a range of subjects, it is no way comprehensive. The gaps come from the limitations of our experience and knowledge. Of particular note is our unfamiliarity with Indigenous history in the centuries both before and after the European invasion. Some of those stories have been told. We encourage people to tell the stories that have not been told and to better re-tell some that have, including those in this book.

1. Early Connecticut: The 1776 Revolution To the Civil War

Caleb Brewster and the Culper Spy Ring

Like many children raised at a time when traversing the world's oceans was the ultimate adventure, Caleb Brewster dreamed of going to sea. It's not difficult to imagine young Caleb standing on the shore near his childhood home in Setauket, New York, looking north across Long Island Sound to Connecticut. He undoubtedly dreamt, too, of sailing the far greater expanse of the Atlantic Ocean to the east, out of sight at that distance but alive nonetheless in the imagination of a young boy. Brewster eventually realized his dream and, in so doing, helped shape the destiny of the new United States of America.

Brewster was born in Setauket in 1747 and signed on to a whaling boat as a young man. By the time hostilities between colonial revolutionaries and the British Crown escalated in 1775, he was an expert seaman. He was especially familiar with the many intricacies of the northern Long Island coastline, as well as the 18-mile stretch north to Connecticut, particularly Fairfield and what is now Bridgeport.

Among Brewster's acquaintances when he was a young man were members of the Tallmadge family, also of Setauket. Benjamin Tallmadge was a graduate of Yale who became General George Washington's chief intelligence officer and eventually rose to the rank of colonel. Tallmadge was a college classmate of Nathan Hale and, in the early years of the Revolutionary War, helped organize the Culper Spy Ring.

Brewster's friendship with the Tallmadges and his expertise as a seaman made him a natural for recruitment to the Culper Ring. (Culper was the phony name used by Abraham Woodhull, another Setauket native, who was one of the ring's agents). New York City was a strong British base of operation during the war, and the Culper Ring proved instrumental in securing information of vital importance to the revolutionary cause. According to some historical accounts, the Ring even played a role in uncovering the spy work done by Benedict Arnold on behalf of the British.

With Tallmadge stationed in Connecticut and most of the spy work transpiring in New York City, Brewster's role was to transport information across the Sound from Long Island. Information secured in New York passed to several members of the Ring and eventually to Brewster in Setauket. Brewster then sailed to Connecticut and delivered the information to Tallmadge. Frequently, Brewster then sailed back to Long Island to deliver whatever reports and supporting documents Tallmadge gave to a courier, who relayed them to General Washington via a network of other couriers.

The security of New York City and western Long Island were of critical importance to the British and they had a highly developed counterintelligence force throughout the area. On one occasion, a British officer discovered Brewster while he waited to receive information from another member of the Culper Ring. Brewster knocked the officer from his horse and forcibly took some of the man's possessions before fleeing, thus making it appear that the confrontation was simply a robbery rather than a matter of espionage.

Despite all the precautions they took, some of those involved in the Culper Ring fell under British suspicion. In Brewster's case, the British knew his name, they knew he lived and operated in and around Setauket, and some accounts indicate they knew he was the primary courier between Long Island and Connecticut. The British never captured him, though. Brewster had a reputation for being extremely brave, and some accounts indicate several occasions where he effectively battled British ships far larger than his whaling boat. Of equal importance were his resourcefulness, his seamanship and his familiarity with every cove and eddy on both sides of the sound. In combination, these enabled him to carry out his work aiding the revolutionary cause.

After the Revolutionary War, Brewster settled in Connecticut and became a blacksmith and a farmer. He was also, for many years, an officer in the United States Revenue Cutter Service, forerunner of the Coast Guard. He died in 1827 at the age of 79 in a section of Fairfield that is now part of Bridgeport. There is a street named after him in the Black Rock section of Bridgeport near where he lived.

Thomas Skidmore, Fairfield County's Forgotten Revolutionary

Thomas Skidmore's name does not appear in many history books. Certainly not mainstream ones. There are no schools or parks named after him, and while historian Mark Lause for one has done an excellent job of documenting Skidmore's life's work, it is unlikely there ever will be a book about Skidmore. Though he wrote with great insight about freedom and other weighty subjects, finding any of his published works is difficult. Yet Skidmore deserves to be remembered—celebrated even—for his lifelong belief that the ideals of the American Revolution were important ones. Important enough that they be extended not just to an elite few, but to everyone.

Skidmore was born in Newtown, Connecticut, on August 13, 1790. A voracious reader and extremely bright, he was appointed to the position of teacher at the Newtown district school when he was just twelve years old. At 18, he took a teaching job at a military academy in Weston.

As Skidmore came of age, the contradictions of the American Revolution continued to blaze. The elite class of propertied white males had won the day, but their hold on power in the decades after the Revolution did not go unchallenged. Skidmore was influenced, for example, by tales he heard growing up of Shays Rebellion in neighboring Massachusetts. He saw the limits of the Revolution as well as its promise and possibilities.

Skidmore was strongly influenced by the international radicalism of the time. Foremost among his literary influences were the English revolutionaries Mary Wollstonecraft and William Godwin. As a young man, Skidmore also admired Robert Owen, the social reformer who founded several utopian communities in the United States. Eventually, Skidmore soured on Owenism. He agreed with the value of building alternative institutions to foreshadow how human beings might live more freely, but felt Owen placed too much emphasis on this and not enough on engaging society as it is in order to transform it. He also believed the Owenite communities replicated many of the hierarchies of mainstream society.

Skidmore was appalled by the twin holocausts of U.S. history: the genocidal war against Native Americans and the African slave trade. In his writings and in the organizations he joined, he worked for full rights for people of all colors. His calls for liberation and equality for women were similarly unequivocal and visionary.

The foundation of Skidmore's work was his linkage of human freedom

9

to cooperative economics. He called for the producers, Black and white, slave and wage-slave, male and female, to seize the means of production. This put him at odds not just with the ruling class, but with liberal abolitionists and others who did not share his view that tyranny was inextricably connected to the concentration of wealth in a few hands.

While still a young man, Skidmore moved to New Jersey. He eventually settled in New York City, and all available evidence indicates that he never again lived in Connecticut. In 1829, he published *Rights of Man to Property*, in which he critiqued the limited vision of human freedom of Thomas Jefferson and other leaders of the American Revolution. It was the best known and most influential of his works and served as an inspiration to labor militants throughout the 19th century.

The Workingmen's Party

In 1829 Skidmore was part of a group that founded the Workingmen's Party in New York City. They envisioned an organization led by workers and farmers working to build a society where land and industry would be cooperatively owned and goods would be shared based on need. Though the Workingmen's Party lasted only several years, the dream of Skidmore and the other founders has taken shape in many organizations in the decades since, from the Industrial Workers of the World to the Mississippi Freedom Democrats to groups of our own time.

Thomas Skidmore died in 1832. He is very much in the tradition of Harriet Tubman, Frederick Douglass, John Brown, Geronimo, Victoria Woodhull and other great 19th century American revolutionaries. His visionary call for liberation, his recognition that no one can be free if their neighbors are not, his critique of the totalitarian essence of capitalism, all ring as true today — perhaps truer — than in his time. When we get to higher ground, his life will be celebrated in the manner it deserves.

The War Criminal and the Patriot

On the west side of the State Capitol in Hartford, one statue stands as a reminder of Connecticut Civil War soldiers who died in Southern prisoner of war camps. The memorial's subject, unarmed and with his army cap in hand, is known as the Andersonville Boy. Thirteen thousand captured Union soldiers perished under horrible conditions in the Andersonville, Georgia, military prison from 1864 to 1865.

The sculpture was created by Norwich-born artist Bela Pratt. In 1907 the original piece was dedicated at Andersonville, Georgia, now a national historic site. A copy of the figure was installed two years later in Hartford. The subject is meant to honor all the men, Black and white, who died as Confederate captives. But the Andersonville Boy could just as well have been Casper Young of Hartford.

In 1862 Casper Young lived on Front Street at a hotel he managed called the German Republic House. The hotel was originally known in the 1840's as the Deutsches Gasthaus, located on Hartford's East Side around Sheldon and Grove Streets in the area known as "Little Germany."

At one point Young befriended Heinrich Wirz, a Swiss national, and invited him to room at the hotel. They became friends.

A year after the Civil War began, Young enlisted as a Union soldier. Germans made up a significant number of the Northern army: 516,000 served, with about 60% having been born in the United States. Many Germans emigrated to the U.S. around 1848, after the failure of their liberal revolution, bringing their democratic ideas with them.

These facts alone are not exceptional; at least 360,000 Union soldiers died in the war to halt the South's secession and to abolish slavery.

Heinrich Wirz also participated in the war as a volunteer. But unlike Casper Young, Wirz joined the Confederate Army. After leaving Hartford, Heinrich (later known as Henry) Wirz traveled, moved to Louisiana, and practiced medicine. He was also the overseer of hundreds of slaves. He joined the South at the start of the national conflict because, as he testified, "I was carried away by the maelstrom of excitement." Wirz was promoted to captain and then assigned to run Andersonville. He forced slaves to build the camp's stockades and bury dead prisoners.

Casper Young was a prisoner of war at Andersonville while Wirz was commandant. Young and a total of 45,000 of his comrades suffered in the Georgia prison camp. Young was one of the 13,000 soldiers – including 291 from Connecticut – who died under the watch of Heinrich Wirz. All Union

11

deaths at Andersonville were recorded by fellow prisoner Dorence Atwater of Terryville, Connecticut.

Another Union soldier imprisoned at Andersonville was Robert H. Kellogg of Wethersfield. Kellogg survived the camp and was later a witness at Heinrich Wirz's court-martial trial. His daily journal (which he later published) recorded the disease, starvation and atrocities committed against the Union prisoners. Kellogg called Wirz a cold blooded, cowardly, cruel fellow.

Walt Whitman had an even more severe judgment. The poet, who served as a nurse during the war, wrote that while "there are deeds, crimes that may be forgiven, this is not one of them. [Andersonville] steeps its perpetrators in blackest, escapeless, endless damnation." (Jon Royce, *The Execution of Henry Wirz)*

After the South's defeat, Heinrich Wirz was captured and convicted of war crimes in a military court, based on the testimony of a hundred eyewitnesses, like former prisoner, J.H. Burns of Connecticut, who testified he had seen Wirz order a guard to kill a captive. Fellow Confederates also testified against him. Wirz was hanged on November 10, 1865. Confederate president Jefferson Davis called Wirz a "martyr" (Davis was named an unindicted co-conspirator at the court martial). As late as 1981, modern-day apologists for the Confederacy lamented that Wirz was merely an unfortunate victim of circumstance.

The Wirz case was closely followed and fiercely argued across the entire country. Advocates for Wirz and other Confederate leaders triggered the growth of the "Lost Cause," so named because they could not admit defeat, nor could they own up to the horrors of the enslavement of millions of Black people.

Far right "historians" (see the pernicious Institute for Historical Review, written by the world's leading Holocaust denier) and groups such as the United Daughters of the Confederacy (UDC) have spent the last one hundred years attempting to rehabilitate Heinrich Wirz, Nathan Bedford Forrest, Jefferson Davis, and many more as noble heroes. The monuments to their crimes are being taken down, one at a time.

An obelisk commissioned by the UDC was erected in the town center at Andersonville, a short distance away from the Andersonville Boy. According to Douglas Kirby , co-author of Roadside America, the Wirz memorial is the only U.S. monument to a war criminal.

2. Working Class Life

Labor Family Beats Garment Boss

This is the story of two Hartford families: one that rose to the top of the economic and social ladder by cheating their employees and putting them in danger every workday; the other, an extended "family" united by their work, their union, and their determination to survive.

The Kolodney family lied to the government to avoid paying millions in taxes and repeatedly broke the law. They intimidated and assaulted workers and denied them the right to freely organize. This is a story of class struggle that spans almost fifty years. Neither the Kolodneys nor the garment workers they employed emerged unscathed. But the workers maintained dignity and solidarity, and the Kolodneys went to prison.

The history of Connecticut working people, and especially immigrant workers, holds many unrecorded examples of persistence and courage. This is especially true with the garment and textile workers, who, in Hartford, numbered in the thousands during the first part of the 20th century.

Many of these girls and women who worked in the "needle trades" were foreign-born or first-generation European immigrants searching for better lives. They were not strangers to hard work, but in return they expected fair wages, decent hours, and safe workplaces. Garment workers, and in fact, the entire working class, faced employers who had more money, more power, and more influence in the business and political world. The workers' livelihoods depended on the whim of the boss.

At the turn of the 20th century, workers were also battered by the boom-and-bust cycles of the capitalist system; they were hit hard by a stock market crash, followed by yet another economic downturn (there had been twenty-four recessions and depressions during the previous one hundred years). When a boss suffered losses, immigrants were the first to suffer layoffs.

Hartford garment workers' pleas for better conditions, however, fell on deaf ears. These women (and a smaller number of skilled male cutters) decided that joining a union was the best way– the only way– to achieve better lives.

The First Strike

On January 30, 1919, hundreds of garment workers from seven Hartford factories walked off their jobs in coordination with a massive garment strike in New York City. One of the businesses affected was owned by the Kolodney family: the Elite Shirtwaist Company on 52 Union Place.

The women worked fifty-two hours, six days a week in unsanitary

15

conditions for as little as $6.50 a week. In contrast, the average weekly wage in the U.S. at the time was $25.60 for a 45-hour workweek for men.

On the first day of the job action, the strikers challenged the appearance of newly hired replacement workers. At closing time on Friday, February 7th, they gathered to confront the scabs to stop them from their jobs. It was especially galling that co-owner George Kolodney gave scabs free cab rides home. Police were present when Kolodney struck one of the strikers but was not charged.

Seven strikers, including union organizer Sam Rosen, were arrested. They were accused of hitting a scab, throwing beans, "attacking" a cop and knocking off his hat. The group appeared the next day in Police Court, accompanied by a crowd of supporters. Also present was Josephine Bennett, a prominent Hartford suffragist and labor activist, who brought her brother, attorney George H. Day.

As the two sides argued, fifteen-year old Constance Corvo entered the court and joined the strikers gathered at a table, drawing the attention of Jo Bennett. It turned out that young Connie felt she had been left out of the legal proceedings and turned herself in. These women had become her family, Bennett said.

Some of the scabs had been recruited from New York City to break the strike. They were kept in the dark about the Hartford conflict. When one Manhattan cutter arrived by train, he quickly realized that he had been duped by the scab recruiter. He promptly told the boss he would not work. Instead of being sent home, the Hartford police kept the worker confined overnight. The next day he was forcibly escorted to the Union Place railroad station and put on the return train to New York.

Two days later at a mass meeting in the Labor Lyceum on Park Street, Rose Kaufman from the International Ladies Garment Workers Union (ILGWU) of New York pledged full support for the Elite Shirtwaist workers. Also speaking was Josephine Bennett, who had already earned a reputation as a skilled organizer against child labor, for the liberation of Ireland and India from British domination, and in support of union efforts in the city. She told the crowd:

"Even in the courts, which are supposed to be tribunals of justice, the rich and poor are not treated alike. I have just lately realized what Dr. Anna Shaw meant when she said that the courts 'dispensed with justice,' not dispensed justice. In the trial in Hartford of these boys and girls accused of intimidation there was no justice done. The boss appeared and praised the girl who was working against the strikers and the girls on trial were convicted almost without evidence. If the judge of that court had seen the inside of my mind he would have sentenced me to five years for contempt of court." (Thornton, Steve, Shoeleather History Online, July 23, 2017)

Ultimately, the strike was short-lived and did not succeed. George

Kolodney's brother Ralph became sole owner of the factory. He moved Elite Shirtwaist in 1920 from 52 Union Place to a building he purchased for $160,000 at the corner of High and Allyn Streets and ultimately to a larger building on Capitol Avenue. By this time the Elite workforce numbered 250 workers.

First Evidence of Kolodney's True Nature

Ralph Kolodney was a man on the way up. He was elected president of the Hartford chapter of Zionist Organization of America in 1921. He performed high-profile charity work, like ordering his employees to knit socks for the poor of Europe. His family could be regularly found in the Society pages. He was a fixture in his synagogue, a good, moral man.

But in 1936 there was a crack in the façade. Kolodney was found guilty of forcing women in his shop to work overtime. He received a paltry fine. A few subsequent attempts at unionization were thwarted. Kolodney insisted his workers were happy; ILGWU organizers said the workers were being intimidated.

A few years later the U.S. Labor Department charged him with violations of wage and hour laws, including illegally withholding overtime pay. But what no state or federal investigators knew at the time was the magnitude of Kolodney's criminal activities.

A New Generation Organizes

March, 1941: It was an extraordinary sight. Women in prison uniforms marched back and forth in front of the Kolodney & Meyers Company, as Elite was now known. Heading up this parade was a uniformed "prison guard," wearing sunglasses and carrying a police baton. The "prisoners" carried signs reading "Don't be chained to your machine for less than you deserve," and "Join the ILGWU."

Feigel Levine, 21, portraying the guard, had staged this colorful protest to draw attention to the ILGWU's re-appearance. The young organizer was later arrested for driving a sound truck up and down Capitol Avenue in front of Kolodney's business.

On April 22, a new generation of Kolodney workers were again on strike. There were now 500 workers employed at his Hartford and New Britain plants. On this first day, 200 strikers were looking like an army without guns, dressed in smart strike uniforms with overseas caps that read ILGWU, and "Kolodney Striker" sashes over their shoulders. Two days later, Lucille Uccello was arrested, accused of hitting a scab. She and her brother Salvatore had come from Italy in 1920 when she was fourteen years old.

On April 29th, 25,000 leaflets were distributed in downtown Hartford by strikers. They were all dressed in homemade peasant costumes and were unmistakably union women. Two of the workers handing out leaflets were brought in for questioning by police.

The Connecticut state board of mediation and arbitration attempted to settle the strike on May 7th. The ILGWU announced it had a majority of workers signed up on union "intent" cards which they would turn in to the labor board. In Manhattan, David Dubinsky, the diminutive but larger than life president of the ILGWU, contacted Hartford Mayor Thomas J. Spellacy to request a meeting.

Kolodney was active too. He had four strikers arrested for assault and battery. Two of them, Mort Goodman and Ann Mascariella, were found guilty, based on accusations made by scabs. In July, Kolodney sued to limit the number of pickets in front of his plant. His motion was denied in Superior Court.

Feigel Levine attended to the strikers' needs and kept them in constant motion. She announced to the press that the strikers were doing quite well despite not receiving paychecks. In fact, Levine said, they were gaining weight. Photos of very healthy children on the picket line seemed to confirm that strikers' families were not suffering malnutrition.

Picketing took place every workday, so the Union bought new shoes for all strikers. After 5 weeks, weekly strike pay increased from $10 to $20, along with a transportation stipend and a daily two-meal allowance.

One photo of the picket line showed the strikers dressed in their Sunday best. They were reading PM, a daily news periodical not unlike Life magazine. PM, however, was a progressive publication and very pro-labor, so the strikers were anxious for sympathetic coverage.

During this period, two Manhattan garment factory owners came to town. The union announced the men were checking out locations where they might expand their business. But why did the Union care? On June 9th, the answer was revealed: Lady Youth Dresses Company moved to Hartford, filing incorporation papers in Connecticut.

When it looked like Kolodney planned to weather the strike – and even lose profits to keep the union out – the ILGWU announced that Lady Youth Dresses would soon be opened near his plant. This new company would compete with Kolodney. All the strikers, the new employer announced, were welcomed to take jobs at this union-friendly business. And they did, effectively ending the strike.

Kolodney's Dismal End

In 1957 Ralph Kolodney, pillar of the community, was charged by the federal government with tax evasion. The tax fraud case was the "biggest in Connecticut," the authorities boasted, with 35 agents having been assigned to his misdeeds. Kolodney's son was also found guilty. The tax men said Ralph

Kolodney's misdeeds reached back decades. His supposed 1951 salary was listed as $33,000, when it was actually $155,000 that year (in today's dollars, $1.5 million). He had shortchanged the public over $5 million during the course of 32 years.

Kolodney had branched out into real estate, purchasing properties that included a four-story Garden Street apartment building in 1956 for $1.4 million ($12 million today). Ironically, the IRS office rented offices in Kolodney's building when it started the investigation against him.

The 69-year old Kolodney was convicted of tax fraud and began a two-year prison sentence in March 1957. Five months later, he was sued by his sister-in-law, who accused him of cheating her.

Kolodney was scheduled to be released on October 1, 1958. The release would have been sooner, but he was caught trying to smuggle mail out of prison by bribing a guard.

Kolodney's son was also convicted and imprisoned for the tax schemes. He earned a short sentence after convincing the judge that he had been coerced into the illegal business by his father.

In 1960, Ralph Kolodney paid $2.8 million in back taxes, fines, and penalties. In 1962, the Feds took possession of his 460 and 470 Capitol Avenue buildings, where his garment factory had been. Today they are State of Connecticut office buildings, filled with several hundred state employee union members. Kolodney died at 91 in 1979.

The ILGWU eventually merged with other unions to become UNITE HERE and today represents 270,000 workers, mostly women and people of color who consider decent treatment and fair wages as important today as did the 1919 Elite Shirtwaist strikers.

"We Irish Are A Working Race"

A cold morning in March, 1849. The angry Irish laborers marched from Hartford to East Hartford across the covered bridge that spanned the Connecticut River. They converged at the home of their boss, a contractor who had hired the immigrants to help build the Hartford/ Providence railroad. The Irishmen were immigrants escaping the Great Hunger (also known as the Famine) in their country that had claimed 1 million lives. They had finished their work and they expected to be paid. But with no warning the contractor declared he was bankrupt and closed his business, failing to pay the men he hired.

When the workers arrived at the contractor's home they demanded their back pay. The boss refused to meet them. He would wait them out, sure that the police would soon arrive. They didn't.

The workers surrounded the house. If the boss wouldn't come out to them, he wouldn't be allowed to leave at all. Finally, after three days, the police escorted the contractor from his home.

History does not record the end result of this siege. Take into account that it took *three days* before the authorities arrived. They were clearly in no hurry to interfere with the laborers' cause. When the sheriff finally showed up, he removed the boss without a fight from the men who had formed the blockade. Most certainly, some sort of deal had been struck for the workers' wages. These Hartford laborers would not be starved again.

Widespread ethnic and religious prejudice taught the Hartford Irish to rely on themselves. That prejudice ran from Connecticut's "Know Nothing" party, which actually elected a governor in 1855 based on hatred of the Irish, to the *Hartford Courant*, which for fifty years called the Irish neighborhood on Hartford's east side "Pigville."

Michael Davitt of the Land League

Just as they built their churches, schools, and social clubs in Hartford, the transplanted Irish also formed their own unions. A week-long strike of journeymen horseshoers, dominated by Irish blacksmiths, took place in 1906. The strike affected 17 shops in the city. Their demand was a nine-hour workday and a minimum daily wage of three dollars. The master horseshoers finally submitted to the new wage and hour standards and agreed to hire union men when there were vacancies.

"We Irish are a working race," Michael Scanlon told Connecticut's Irish in 1874. "Labor is our pride and privilege." (Shoeleather History Online, November 15, 20214) A well known poet and Irish nationalist, Scanlon exemplified the link between the Irish American working class and their homeland. For Hartford's immigrants, the first priority was feeding the family, but running a close second was the liberation of Ireland from British domination.

In the 1880's, tenant farmers in Ireland formed the Land League to wrest control of farms from the landlord class. The League's primary founder (along with Charles Stewart Parnell) was Michael Davitt from County Mayo. Davitt was born at the height of the Great Hunger. His family was evicted when he was four years old. At age nine he worked in a cotton mill where his right arm was mangled in a machine, resulting in an amputation.

In 1882 Davitt spoke to an enthusiastic Hartford crowd of 1,200 at the Opera House. He was wildly popular in Hartford and well known to Irish communities across the country. Hartford could boast that at the time of Davitt's public appearance, the Ladies Land League had 2000 members and 3 branches. The British had effectively suppressed the male-dominated League, but the women soon won the reputation for running bigger, more effective, and more militant boycotts and protests on behalf of their people back home.

Slowly, methodically, the Irish worked their way into leadership positions in Hartford's labor unions and in politics. In 1902, with a third party called the Economic League, they elected the union man Ignatius Sullivan as mayor of Hartford.

Between the Hills and the Sea: A Novel of Working Class Bridgeport

Bert Gilden was born in Los Angeles in 1915 and moved to Bridgeport with his family when he was a boy. His family moved a number of times and Bert attended Shelton, Barnum and Elias Howe Schools. He graduated from Central High School in 1932 and then from Brown University in 1936.

Katya Alpert was born in 1914 in Bangor, Maine. She graduated from Radcliffe College in 1935 and was the first woman to publish in the *Harvard Advocate*. The couple met, married and settled in Bridgeport in the 1940's after Bert was discharged from the U.S. Army, where he saw heavy combat action during the Second World War. At some point during this period, both joined the Communist Party.

Union Activism

The Gildens embarked on a joint literary career and co-authored articles for *Collier's*, *Liberty* and other magazines. Bert also worked in a number of factories in Bridgeport, including General Electric, Remington Shavers and Singer Sewing Machines. He was involved in workplace organizing and union activities during a particularly tumultuous time in American labor history.

Those activities included the 1946 nationwide strike of 175,000 workers by the United Electrical, Radio and Machine Workers of America (UE), of which Bert was a member, against General Electric and Westinghouse. Begun in the middle of winter, the strike coincided with other nationwide strikes by 500,000 members of the United Automobile Workers against General Motors, 800,000 members of the United Steelworkers of America against the steel conglomerates, and 300,000 meatpackers of the United Packinghouse Workers of America. Later in the year, there was also a large strike by coal miners from the United Mine Workers and general strikes in Pittsburgh, Rochester and Oakland.

In Bridgeport, Bert and Katya walked the picket lines with thousands of others at the massive GE plant on Boston Avenue. The workers were out for nine weeks, during which they endured blizzards, court injunctions, police violence and strike breakers before they won a significant victory.

Virtually all of the other labor actions of 1946 were also victories for workers, and the labor left in Bridgeport and the country as a whole seemed on the rise. As the titans of Capital regrouped, GE head Charles Wilson gave voice to the Cold War strategy the business class would follow when he said simply, "Russia abroad, labor at home."

The UE Under Attack

With the passage of the Taft-Hartley Act and the launching of raids by unions opposed to the labor left in general and the Communist Party specifically, the UE was soon on the defensive. Bert Gilden experienced these attacks first-hand as both a CP member and an occasional officer in his Bridgeport UE local. In 1949, the UE cut its ties with the Congress of Industrial Organizations (CIO). Its local at the GE plant in Bridgeport was decertified from representing workers at GE because UE leaders were seen as too close to the CP. Both were big blows for labor. The ousting of the International Union of Mine, Mill and Smelters Workers (IUMMSW) from Bridgeport Brass was another nail in the coffin of militant Connecticut trade unionism.

The People's Party

During this time, Bert also served as the executive director of the People's Party, the Connecticut chapter of the Progressive Party, which had been created in 1948 as a vehicle for former Vice President Henry Wallace's bid for the Presidency. Bert ran for local office on the People's Party ticket on several occasions at a time when the party was being viciously red-baited, just like the UE and IUMMSW. Katya was also active in various organizations and campaigns in Bridgeport while giving birth to and being primarily responsible for raising their three sons. When the House Committee on Un-American Activities held hearings in Connecticut, Bert was called and grilled about his political and union activities. Katya was not called, perhaps because the Committee was concerned how it would look to grill the mother of three small children.

Hurry Sundown

Amidst all this activity, the Gildens continued to make progress with their joint writing career. By the early 1960s they were working on a novel, *Hurry Sundown*, that was accepted for publication by Doubleday. The book sold in excess of 300,000 copies and Paramount Pictures purchased the movie rights for $800,000. Released in 1967, the movie was directed by Otto Preminger and featured Jane Fonda, Burgess Meredith, Diahann Carroll and Faye Dunaway. A short time later, the Gildens began work on a novel about life in Bridgeport in the years after World War 2 that would become *Between the Hills and the Sea*.

The Gildens truly did work in tandem. A profile in *Life* magazine published during the time they were working on *Between The Hills and The Sea* includes a photo of the couple in the room where they worked, which they referred to as their "writing center." The accompanying text states that the couple lived a Spartan life style for years as they spent 12 hours a day writing, while another photo shows them outside the 16-room house they purchased with some of the proceeds from *Hurry Sundown*.

Between the Hills and the Sea

Between The Hills and The Sea is set in the fictitious Connecticut industrial city of Shoreham in 1956. Throughout, the novel shifts between 1956 and the beginnings of the romance between the story's protagonists, Priscilla and Michael "Mish" Lunin, in 1946. Mish is a production worker at United Vacuum, or UV, caught up in union factionalism and the workers' resistance to an increasingly aggressive factory management. Priscilla is raising the couple's children while organizing tenants at the housing project where the family lives and assisting Mish in his union activities.

Anyone reading *Between The Hills and The Sea* who has some inkling that the story is based on Bridgeport is likely to recognize and easily identify certain people and places in the book. The UV factory where Mish works, for example, is drawn on the General Electric plant on Boston Avenue. The GE plant was at its apex during the time covered in the novel, with in excess of 10,000 workers.

There are a number of references to Mayor Rod Kearnsey, who bears a strong resemblance to Jasper McLevy, the Socialist mayor of Bridgeport from 1933-57. Like Mc Levy, Kearnsey came out of the labor movement and became mayor in the 1930s. And like McLevy, he is seen by those on the left like the Lunins as having betrayed the working class. The Tidal Flats Park housing project where Mish and Priscilla live also bears some resemblance to Yellow Mill Village, later known as Father Panik Village.

Factory Work

The description of work at UV is one of the book's strongest features. In those sections, the reader gets a very real sense of the unrelenting pressure of factory life as the company uses every means to get workers to produce more, with little regard for their well-being and no intention of willingly compensating them accordingly. Compounding matters is the weak, collaborationist inclination of a part of the leadership of the Electrical Workers International Union (based on the union that was created to drive out the UE), which is intent on proving its patriotism and not on defending workers. The Gildens vividly bring to life the destructive impact the anti-communist witch hunts had in curtailing the rights of workers in the workplace and negating any chance they had of increasing their control of their work.

Alongside stirring moments of solidarity, the Gildens are also brutally honest in their depiction of the jealousies, betrayals, opportunism and just plain meanness of *Between the Hills and the Sea's* many working class characters. In a culture so thoroughly imbued with the notion of getting ahead no matter the damage to anyone else, it is perfectly reasonable for some workers to try and eke out an advantage for themselves at the expense of others. One of the great accomplishments of the novel is that the link between this aspect of working class life and a society based on profits over everything is clearly drawn, even though it is never drawn didactically.

Prominent in the book's flashbacks are scenes of the 1946 picket line where Mish and Priscilla first meet. Mish is a strike leader who, while always pragmatic and somewhat guarded the way pragmatists tend to be, also embodies the optimism of the labor left of the time. Priscilla is a recent college graduate who brings her guitar to the picket line and plays and sings labor songs. The scenes serve to contextualize both the rapid changes in the fortunes of the labor movement between 1946 and the 1950s as well as the relationship between Mish and Priscilla: Priscilla, the upper middle-class idealist who takes "going to the working class" as seriously as she takes life and Mish, the worker who's all too familiar with the myriad difficulties of working class life.

Between The Hills and The Sea frequently puts the strains in Mish and Priscilla's marriage front and center. While those strains are linked to the harsh chill of Cold War repression, the Lunins experience the inter-personal difficulties that most couples go through. Their dreams are somewhat different and the way they live their lives and envision the future reflect that. Still, the shattered dreams of an earlier time and the very real political pressures of the McCarthy era *are* a major factor in their marital difficulties, and the way the two of them occasionally tear at each other's vulnerabilities rings true even as it is sometimes makes for difficult reading.

Bert Gilden died in 1971 at age 55 just months before *Between The Hills and The Sea* was published. Katya died in 1991, age 77. *In Between The Hills and The Sea*, they eschewed the glamor of New York, Los Angeles and San Francisco for the gritty, blue collar city of Bridgeport. They depicted Bridgeport as only those who lived it from inside-out and the bottom-up can, with the degrading nature of factory work and, mainstream narratives notwithstanding, the not quite so Wonder Bread wonderful nature of life in the 1950's. In so doing, they captured an era that, while certainly gone, nonetheless provides important insights about who and where we are these many years later.

Hartford Federal College, Experiment in Democracy

People have long believed that free public education is the bedrock of democracy. Thomas Jefferson believed an educated citizenry was vital for our survival as a free people, famously saying "Light and Liberty go together."

History, however, tells us otherwise. Access to high school or college has often been in dispute; education has been seen by some as the exclusive privilege of the elite, a way to groom the future leaders of business and politics. Free schooling has been a defining line of class differences throughout U.S. history.

Beginning in the 1700s, voices for subsidized education included President John Adams, who wrote in 1785 that "the whole people must take it upon themselves the education of the whole people and be willing to bear the expense of it."

Labor unions were among the first groups to make free education a demand. *The Workingmen's Advocate* reported on an 1829 Boston meeting of working people who declared: "Our public system of Education, which so liberally endows those seminaries of learning, which are only accessible to the wealthy, while our common schools are so ill provided for. . . Thus even in childhood, the poor are apt to think themselves inferior." (Workingmen's Advocate, 1829)

At the famous 1848 congress of women at Seneca Falls, the Declaration of Sentiments argued that men created an "absolute tyranny" over women by denying them "the facilities for obtaining a thorough education—all colleges being closed against her." (Seneca Falls Declaration of Women's Rights, 1848)

It's true that 19th century industrialists encouraged schools to produce a docile workforce for their factories. But pioneering educators sought to construct systems that, according to Horace Mann (1837), should be universal, non-sectarian and free, which in John Dewey's words (1897), would foster a social consciousness for social reconstruction.

Union leader and socialist presidential candidate Eugene Debs in 1908 insisted that we should be "teaching for American Democracy rather than American aristocracy." The Hartford Socialist Party took as one of its election planks the provision of free books to all students, since those costs were a barrier for many.

The 1948 UN Declaration of Human Rights, ratified by the United States and 47 other countries, includes in Article 26 that "Everyone has the right to education," and that "higher education shall be equally accessible to all on the basis of merit."

The 1955 Supreme Court decision in Brown v. Board of Education overturned the "separate but equal" basis for official segregation. The Court decided that segregation violates the Constitution's Fourteenth Amendment (equal protection), stating that "education is perhaps the most important function of state and local government."

By 1961, civil rights legend Septima Clark established thirty-seven Citizenship Schools in the Deep South as the racist system continued to fight the Brown decision. "Literacy is liberation," she declared. Clark's work influenced the Freedom Schools organized by the Student Nonviolent Coordinating Committee (SNCC).

Today, two-thirds of Americans believe college tuition should be free and supported by public funding, according to several recent polls.

Not Everybody Agrees

"When asked in 2016 about tuition free education, Sam Clovis, policy director of Donald Trump's presidential campaign, asked how would it be paid for, declaring it "absurd on its surface," Unfortunately, this belief has its historical roots.

In 1924, Professor Edward F. Humphrey of Trinity College expressed support for a very different higher education system. Speaking at a meeting of the Daughters of the American Revolution (DAR), Humphrey praised the radical changes recently made by Italian dictator Benito Mussolini:

Under the old regime, thousands of young men who would have made excellent working men loafed through free public schools and at the end of their educational career were forever spoiled for any useful occupation. Mussolini decided that the state ought to educate only those worthwhile. He did not attempt to deprive parents of the right to make loafers out of their own children; they were allowed to send them to private schools if they could afford it.... the number of those to receive free education was rigorously reduced. This applied, of course, to secondary and higher schools. (Thornton, Steve, *"Hartford Federal College Experiment in Democracy,"* (Shoeleather History Online, August 26, 2018)

The president of Yale University used the specter of fascism to warn against "collective control of" (publicly funded) education. Charles Seymour wrote in 1944 that financial help would mean "ultimate control from the outside. When that happens, liberty will have disappeared and authority will be supreme. We know what happened in Germany... the basis of totalitarianism was laid." (Thornton, August 26, 2018 op.cit.)

Hoping to put the issue of debt-free education permanently to rest, the U.S. Supreme Court during the Nixon/Reagan years declared that education was not a "fundamental right" of the people, and the poor could be forced to pay for public education (San Antonio v. Rodriguez, 1973).

Trump's dismissal, Seymour's hyperbole, Humphrey's slavish admiration of Il Duce, and the Supreme Court's edict were all arguments diametrically opposed to the first principles of Jefferson and Adams.

Hartford's Landmark Experiment

At the start of the Great Depression, this country's worst economic crisis, 3.5 million young people were unable to attend high school. Supporting their meager family income was the first priority. Aubrey Williams, head of the National Youth Administration, argued in 1937 that education was only the privilege of those who are economically able to afford it,

As part of Franklin Roosevelt's New Deal efforts, an extraordinary experiment in higher education was tested in the 1930s in Connecticut with the Federal Colleges.

The Depression hit every job category hard, teaching included. At one point, the state of Georgia closed all its public schools. Through Roosevelt's Federal Emergency Relief Administration (FERA), thousands of teachers were put to work to the benefit of a half million students, both young and old.

The Federal College succeeded beyond all measure, demonstrating that a free system of public education could be built, providing learning, jobs, and outstanding graduates with the means to advance in life. The backers of the Hartford Federal College and its sister schools also reinforced the concept of higher education as a right, not a privilege, despite those who wished to see it fail.

Besides Hartford, a total of 1,400 students attended Connecticut's federal colleges in New Haven, Winsted, Bristol and Farmington. New Haven was the largest project, serving 500 students through Yale University, the YMCA and YWCA. Also called "emergency junior colleges," these schools were also established in Michigan, Texas, Ohio, New Jersey and Kansas.

Dr. Richard K. Denlinger was chosen to lead the local effort. Denlinger had for 12 years been the head of the University of Connecticut history department. Hartford Federal College first started admitting students in 1934 with a grant from FERA. Control of the school was maintained by the Hartford Board of Education, which appointed the superintendent and faculty. The College operated six days a week, with most of the classes held at the Hillyer mansion.

The Hillyer property at 2471 Main Street was purchased for $26,000 in 1924. It had been a fifty-acre site owned by Charles T. Hillyer; parcels were developed over the years, leaving only the mansion and a few acres. Originally seen purely as a relief effort (by keeping the unemployed off the streets), the Hartford experiment demonstrated the deep need adults felt for skills, knowledge, and self-improvement. They elected a student government, scheduled debates, held proms, organized baseball and basketball teams, and even created a popular orchestra. All this while picking up paying jobs where they could.

Eligibility for college entry was a high school certificate. But "mature adults" unable to meet that requirement and "competent to handle the work of college rank," could audit courses.

The college offered language classes in English, French, German, Italian, and Russian. Economic courses included "Labor Problems." Other available courses were mathematics, law, philosophy, psychology, art, and music. Some, but not all course credits were transferable to four-year schools.

The Community Chorus practiced at Hartford High School. The basketball team held its games at the Vine Street School. The school hosted the revival of an all-Negro chorus that had previously disbanded. In August of 1938, the J. Wesley Coffey WPA Chorus was born. As with all New Deal programs, participants earned wages through their program participation.

The College proved to be quite successful; it began to offer summer school courses in 1937, where regular semester classes were compressed into a summer schedule with full college credit. The next year, night courses were added to the school's schedule; two hundred students attended– after their day jobs – from 7:20 pm to 9:50 pm.

Tuition was free; students had to buy their own books ("no more than $4 a course"); there were attendance and grade standards that had to be met in order to remain at the school.

A student at Hartford Federal College pointed out that the program raised their standard of living and led toward better government. It enabled the next generation to understand fully and carry out the principles of democracy.

Students and Teachers

Considering its relatively modest resources, Hartford Federal College attracted exceptional talent and produced some outstanding graduates. Hartford-born Jerome Stavola (1904-1984) joined the faculty as an art teacher in 1938. Stavola had studied at the New York School of Design. His first mural for the Work Projects Administration was painted at Weaver High School. In 1934 he opened an art gallery on Allyn Street which showed the works of male and female artists. Stavola also helped lead a statewide group of Italian Americans opposed to Mussolini.

Young Kenneth Shaker of Love Lane finished his freshman year at the

Federal College in August 1937. But instead of returning to school, he spent 16 months fighting in the Spanish Civil War as a machine gunner for the Republican forces against Franco. He had joined 1,500 other Americans of the Abraham Lincoln Battalion, part of the International Brigades. Shaker was captured behind enemy lines but escaped with two companions by swimming across the Ebro River; he was wounded and hospitalized during his time in Spain. Shaker volunteered at the start of World War II, serving as a paratrooper and cited for exceptional bravery.

The End and a New Beginning

The Federal College closed its doors on September 22, 1939. Revised federal regulations limited WPA workers to 18 months of wages and by that time most of the Hartford faculty exceeded the maximum. The new rule went into effect on July 1, but the College received permission to finish its summer semester.

This cut-off was part of a Republican backlash against New Deal programs. All WPA workers still on the job had their hours doubled (from 60 to 120 a month) for exactly the same pay. Workers were required to sign loyalty oaths, and employees who volunteered for any political party were fired.

The Depression was not over, but the experiment was. The Hillyer building was demolished to make way for new Nelton Court public housing, the first of its kind in Hartford. Despite its closure, graduates held annual class reunions.

The College's student senate lobbied for permanent status in December 1938. They gathered 4,000 petition signatures in support of the effort. The 1939 General Assembly considered a proposal to award Hartford Federal College a junior college charter, but the state attorney general stated that they would lose their federal funding (which they did anyway).

It wasn't until 1961 that Connecticut opened the first of its community colleges in Norwalk. Today, the system serves 50,000 students at its twelve campuses.

Housatonic Community College: A Bridgeport Gem

This Fall marks 50 years since the establishment of Housatonic Community College. The school has come a long way in that time, from facilities scattered throughout Stratford to an old industrial building on Bridgeport's East Side to a lovely downtown campus. More importantly, enrollment has grown from 378 in the very first semester to almost 6,000 students and is likely to grow larger with new facilities and a continued commitment from the state of Connecticut.

Housatonic's origins can be traced to the dramatic increase in the need for higher education in the early 1960s. The empire of the United States was at its apex and there was a great demand for a better-educated workforce to fill the many professional and technical jobs of an expanding economy. As the first of the baby boom generation reached college age, new universities were constructed, state college systems expanded and many community colleges were established.

Despite its small-ish population, Connecticut was very much in the forefront of this development, and nowhere was this more apparent than in the growth of the state's community college system. Nine community colleges opened in Connecticut during the 1960's, including Housatonic, and a tenth opened in 1971. The state's community college system today includes twelve schools with a total enrollment of about 90,000 students.

Housatonic was originally established in 1966 as a branch of Norwalk Community College. The school's offices were located in Stratford and classes were held throughout that city, including at Bunnell High School, the Stratford United Methodist Church and the Stratford Public Library. Tuition that first year was $50 for a state resident attending full time, with additional fees ranging from $25 to $45.

A First Rate Art Museum

Housatonic became an independent school the following year and one of the institutions it's best known for, the Housatonic Museum of Art, opened. The driving force behind the museum was Burt Chernow, an art professor at the school. The first exhibit in 1968 featured works from the museum's collection by Elaine de Kooning, Robert Rauschenberg, Larry Rivers, Andy Warhol and many others.

Over the years, the museum's collection has grown as artists and collectors donated and bequeathed works, and the permanent collection includes paintings

31

by Pablo Picasso, Marc Chagall, Henri Matisse and other masters. After Chernow's death in 1997, the museum's collection has been maintained by Director Robbin Zella and continues to grow.

First Bridgeport Location

With a growing enrollment and the need for more space, HCC moved into the Singer Sewing Machine factory on Barnum Avenue in 1971. Located several blocks east of Washington Park and just north of the New York-New Haven railroad viaduct, the Singer plant had been a fixture on the city's East Side for decades. The company began phasing out production at its sprawling factory in 1965 and Housatonic moved in after the company closed up shop for good for what was said at the time to be a temporary stay.

Housatonic's enrollment continued to grow steadily in the years following the move. It was especially important that such a school be located in Bridgeport, where there were many young people for whom the costs of a four-year college were out of reach. A majority of the students came from working class families and the school, like Bridgeport, was ethnically diverse.

From the outset Housatonic also featured many students who were older than standard college age seeking training that would better position them to get professional or civil service employment. With many students working full-time, classes are held days and evenings to accommodate busy schedules. We can imagine any number whose parents or relatives had worked in the very same building during Singer's heyday, and perhaps more than a few who had worked there themselves.

In addition to the art museum, HCC regularly features films, forums and lectures that are open to the public. The school also makes meeting space available to local community organizations. And for a while in the 1970's, HCC fielded very competitive men's basketball and baseball and women's softball teams that featured many standout players from area high schools.

New Downtown Campus

By the 1990s, Housatonic was bursting at the seams and functioning in a space that was outmoded. In 1994, the state of Connecticut purchased property at State Street and Lafayette Boulevard which for several decades had been home to the Hi-Ho Mall (originally the Lafayette Shopping Mall) for a new HCC. Re-configuration of the building was completed during the 1996-97 school year and students returned to class on January 27, 1997, after winter break for the beginning of the Spring Semester in the new facilities. In addition to marking the 50th anniversary of the origins of the school this Fall, the Housatonic community is preparing to celebrate the 20th anniversary of the move to its current location.

With the opening of the new campus, the Burt Chernow Galleries of the Housatonic Museum of Art opened and had for its first exhibit a collection of photographs by Ansel Adams. The new college building, known as Lafayette Hall, also features expanded classroom space and a spacious library. With enrollment still growing, the state took control of the empty Sears building just to the south of the school and restructured it into a second building, Beacon Hall, that opened in September of 2008. At the center of the campus is a large green where students gather and study during warm weather.

As it enters its sixth decade, Housatonic offers Associate Degrees in 42 programs of study, ranging from Graphic Design to Paramedic Studies to Theater Arts. The school also offers credit certificate programs such as Early Childhood Education and Advanced Manufacturing Machine Technology. Also available are a wide variety of Continuing Education courses for those seeking new job market skills or knowledge enhancement.

Challenges

There are, of course, challenges and difficulties for Housatonic and its students. Despite a demonstrated need, schools like HCC face regular attacks from those who object to public education and seek to reduce and even eliminate valuable social institutions. Tuition and school fees for a Connecticut resident for two semesters at Housatonic total $4,188, while part-time enrollment costs $155 per credit. At the University of Connecticut, by contrast, in-state tuition and fees for two semesters total $13,366 at the Storrs campus and $11,324 at the regional sites. State budget cuts like those of recent years, however, imperil Housatonic's affordability.

In recent years, Housatonic and the Connecticut State Universities have established a partnership so that HCC students who achieve a grade point average of 3.0 or higher and an associate's degree in certain programs are guaranteed admission to the Universities and have equal access in the selection of majors. That ensures fluidity for HCC graduates who seek a bachelor's degree, while making it easier for them to do so in-state. It's also an important move to strengthen public education at a time when there is ongoing hostility to the very nature of a public sector. With continued popular diligence and a collective progressive vision, people from throughout the Bridgeport area will continue to have access to quality, affordable education at Housatonic.

3. The Industrial Workers of the World

Original Wobbly

The daughter of Pierce T. Wetter, known to her friends as "Bobbie," was remembering her father, an original member of the Industrial Workers of the World (IWW or Wobblies). Wetter was arrested in 1917 in a nationwide roundup of more than one hundred IWW activists for opposing the U.S. entry into the first World War. He and many others were imprisoned; Pierce served five years in the Cook County Jail in Chicago and the Leavenworth, Kansas Penitentiary. His brother Telfair ran the Baltimore office of the IWW during this period.

As soon as her father was mentioned, Bobbie launched into a chorus of *The Internationale*: "Arise you prisoners of starvation / Arise you wretched of the earth / For justice thunders condemnation / There's a better world in birth!"

Her dad taught her the song. This was the first time she had sung it since she was a young girl. Now, living in a Hartford-area retirement community, Bobbie began to remember more. She knew he wrote an article on behalf of those still imprisoned. "It's in Joyce Kornbluh's book [Rebel Voices]," she recalled.

Pierce Wetter led an amazing life, before and after his five-year act of conscience. Besides being a Wobbly, he was a Quaker and a pacifist. He was born on April 4, 1895, in Madagascar, the son of the American consul. Wetter and his siblings were raised in Georgia and Ohio, mostly by his aunt. His daughter remembers that Pierce was effectively abandoned at 12 years old, and with his brother they tramped around the country. He eventually inherited some family property. Pierce could trace his ancestry back to a member of the Revolutionary War Continental Congress and President Franklin Pierce.

In 1916, Pierce was an officer of the IWW's Coal Miners Industrial Union in Great Falls, Montana. He wrote to Bill Haywood of the workers' enthusiasm for "sabotage" as a tactic in their organizing campaign, but Big Bill did not approve, writing back that "there is nothing the enemy would like better" than to publicize the tactic. The letter was used against Pierce at his trial.

The federal government simultaneously raided sixty-four IWW offices in September, 1917, arresting Wetter and many of the union's most well-known leaders. The charges included interfering with the war effort and violating the Espionage Act. Their trial began on April 1, 1918. He and 114 other Wobblies — as IWW members were called — were charged with one hundred separate crimes each. Over 10,000 criminal acts.

Historian Melvyn Dubofsky writes in his history of the Wobblies: "The Justice Department was indeed fortunate that public hysteria had convicted the Wobblies before the jury heard the prosecution's evidence, for the prosecution, in fact, had no evidence." (Steve Thornton, *A Shoeleather History of the Wobblies)*. Wetter served his full five years; some of the defendants received twenty-year sentences.

Immediately after he was released from prison in 1922, Pierce Wetter was threatened with deportation by the federal Immigration authorities. He was charged with being an illegal alien, even though the government had his citizenship records on file. With the help of the ACLU, Wetter was able to stay in the United States. A Kansas newspaper called the government's attempt "a legal kidnapping."

After Leavenworth, Wetter continued to fight for the remaining Wobblies in prison. He wrote "Men I Left at Leavenworth," a passionate plea for their release that focused on the personal stories of a number of the inmates. His article emphasized that they were jailed for their beliefs and nothing more.

"War hysteria prevented a fair trial," he told a group of college students after his release. "When newspapers like the *Chicago Tribune* advocated that we should be shot without trial, when ten tons of [our trial defense] material was held up at the Post Office, when funds for the defense were not permitted to reach us, the handicap was too great." With a sense of humor that must have helped keep him sane in prison, he added: "I was rather fortunate when Judge Landis parceled out the sentences, for I only got only five years, though I don't know why." (Steve Thornton, *A Shoeleather History of the Wobblies)*

In 1923 Pierce worked to organize a massive IWW mobilization at Port Arthur, Texas. The union had announced its intention of organizing longshoremen and sailors there. Wobbly James Holland and two other unidentified fellow workers were murdered after being arrested by police and turned over to the Ku Klux Klan. The *New York Times* reported that Wetter's plan was to overrun the town with jobless I.W.W.s and create a problem for local authorities. At the same time, resolutions of protest would be forwarded to the Mayor.

Pierce Wetter had moved to Brooklyn by 1923 and studied to become a mechanical engineer. He and his family lived on Washington Square in Manhattan with Robertson Trowbridge (who had adopted Pierce at a late age). There he continued to "fight the power," challenging Robert Moses, the controversial "master builder" of New York City.

Moses wielded great control that he used to build highways and parks, willfully ignoring the consequences to residents and their neighborhoods. (He was also the reason the Dodgers left Brooklyn). When Moses wanted to put an encircling double roadway around Washington Square in 1939, Pierce organized community opposition to successfully stop the plan.

He faced Moses again in 1942 when the power broker planned to eliminate a waterfront complex in the Battery Park section of Manhattan. Before Ellis

Island opened, Fort Clinton had been the first stopping point for eight million immigrant families coming to America. Moses cared little about that kind of history and began demolition. Pierce led a campaign to halt its total destruction, saving the immigrant building.

Wetter felt the rage of Moses when the mogul used red-baiting and ad hominem attacks against the activist during this fight. Moses, referring to his IWW membership, publicly called Pierce "one of a gang of thugs and saboteurs who interfered with the military and civil works of the United State government during the World War." Pierce Wetter "did not have a single characteristic of a Quaker," Moses sputtered, and he deserved "a good public sock in the jaw." Fort Clinton is now a national monument.

Pierce Wetter was pardoned for the 1918 charges by Franklin D. Roosevelt in 1933. He died on May 10, 1963. He was 68 years old.

"Take Away Their Clubs and Give Them Shovels"

Arturo Giovannitti was invited to address the Italian Socialist Federation in New Haven on January 24, 1913. He had just come from Lawrence, Massachusetts where he was being prosecuted on trumped up charges during the successful "Bread and Roses" strike of 20,000 textile workers. Giovannitti, Joe Ettor and Joseph Caruso were all acquitted after a sensational trial that much of the world was watching.

As usual, the New Haven police were in the audience to monitor the organizer's speech:

"Within the next year the United States will face a great labor crisis which will be unlike any previous labor trouble. Discontent has been sweeping rapidly all over the country and it is a very significant fact, the strike of the 150,000 tailors in New York City and the waiters strike there, also.

"The next thing which we expect to see in this country is a terrible strike in the steel industries of Pennsylvania, which will be the greatest labor war that the world has ever known. The men employed in this industry and in the great steel foundries will rise and protest against the treatment which they are now receiving.

"To secure our rights in this country we must work together. Craft unionism has outlived its usefulness, and with this we cannot expect to cope with the present day situation and defeat the great capitalists of this country. The place which craft unionism once occupied will be taken by industrial unionism, one big union of all workers.

"Recently they accused Ettor of having advised the striking waiters in New York to place poison in the soup which they were to serve in the fashionable New York hotels. This is untrue. If we are anxious to do away with the capitalists we'll simply refuse to work for them and starve them out. Then we'll make a pair of good longshoremen out of Mr. Morgan and Mr. Rockefeller.

"They kept Ettor and I in jail during those long ten months but they couldn't do anything to myself nor to Ettor. It was not the fault of the judge who released us, or the work of the jury nor was it the fine work of our lawyers. But it was the protests of the working class of the country that secured us our liberty. We had the press, the capitalists, and all of the monied people against us, but they could not convict us." (Thornton, Steve. *A Shoeleather History of the Wobblies: Stories of the Industrial Workers of the World (IWW) in Connecticut)*

40

As Giovannitti finished, he surveyed the room. He knew he was being watched by the law everywhere he spoke. He could have riled up the crowd against the police. He decided to teach a lesson to the cops instead:

"I see three officers of the law standing in the rear of the room at the present time. The time will come, however, when we will take the uniforms and clubs away, place shovels in their hands, and set them to work." (Steve Thornton, A *Shoeleather History*)

Storm Center of Labor Unrest

On the morning of June 27, 1905, Bill Haywood used a piece of wood as a gavel to open the founding convention of the Industrial Workers of the World (IWW) in Chicago. Later that same day in Hartford, Connecticut, the State Senate voted to build an Armory for the protection of businesses located in "storm centers for anticipated riots or strikes."

The timing was pure coincidence. The two events, however, signaled a coming collision. As Jeremy Brecher wrote in his labor history *Strike!*, state governments built armories as fortresses in American cities "not against invasion from abroad but against popular revolt at home."

Certainly, Connecticut's lawmakers could not see into the future. They had no idea how threatened they would become by the IWW's organizing efforts throughout the state. Instead, the legislators made their case for the massive arsenal by invoking the great nationwide railroad strike of 1877, the recent labor unrest in Waterbury, and earlier union strikes right nearby on Capitol Avenue. Acting in the interest of local industrialists, the elected officials argued not *if* the armory should be built, but *where* it would do the most good. Some favored a location near the state house; others said it should be built near the Colt Firearms factory. A former Hartford mayor testified he wished he had the use of an armory to protect public order in 1901 when striking machinists took over Hartford's streets (and won the nine-hour day).

By 1919, the Connecticut General Assembly had approved funding for armories across the state and passed laws designed to curb union organizing efforts. By that time, the radical IWW was shaking the very foundations of the nation's economic system. And although the union officially shunned the political arena, the Wobblies threatened capitalism's hold on the electoral system as well, with battles in the workplace that spilled over into the voting booth, particularly in support of the Socialist Party's presidential candidate Eugene Debs. Many Connecticut workers, impoverished, suffering, and powerless, would find the IWW's appeal to take control of their own destinies very compelling.

More emphasis on property than on life

At the turn of the 20th century, it was a dangerous proposition for a worker to join a union. You could be fired and there was no law to protect you. You could be blacklisted, and no other company would hire you. And worst of all, being a union supporter could get you beaten by employer-hired vigilantes, private detectives, the police, or even the military, as workers and organizers throughout American history had already discovered. Retaliation was frequent from employers who feared losing control of their property, which meant workers as well as machines. Their prerogatives as captains of industry were also threatened. Why should they give up their wealth, status, leisure, and power to a bunch of ragtag foreigners?

Here is what workers faced every day on the job in Connecticut during the first half of the 20th century:

The Blacklist: Companies quickly learned that union organizers, when identified by supervisors and then fired, could move to another shop. The bosses maintained a list of workers they considered troublemakers and shared what they knew through their employer associations. The state legislature banned company blacklists in 1911. The bosses objected and appealed. In 1912 the Connecticut Supreme Court upheld the lawmakers' ban. The law was of no use to blacklisted workers: that same year it was revealed that the Connecticut Manufacturers' Bureau kept tabs on discharged workers and communicated this information to businesses across the state. The list included the reasons for dismissal, including "wanted an undeserved increase" and "misunderstanding with the boss." Once on the blacklist, a worker found it impossible to find new employment. Scovill Manufacturing Company in Waterbury had a formidable spy system, as did Winchester Arms in New Haven. They both kept detailed files on every worker who seemed "suspicious."

Discrimination and Exploitation: Women, immigrant workers, children, and African Americans, who were growing as a significant part of the state's workforce, were ignored by the traditional labor unions. They had no representation and no power. These groups comprised a significant percentage of the working class, but they were rebuffed when they knocked on the door of the American Federation of Labor (AFL), the country's largest union coalition. They could not turn to the political system either; most of these workers didn't even have the right to vote. A study done by a special state commission in 1913 on the status of women workers found that most factories had no first aid resources even though accidents were epidemic. Toilets didn't work and changing rooms didn't exist. Connecticut working women totaled 49,000. More than 5,000 workers were minors. Almost 80% of the women were not married and supported themselves on pay that the commission said was "barely a living wage."

Long hours, poverty pay: The workday ranged from 10 to 16 hours for at least six days a week. Parents and their young children worked in mills together. And still, for millions of unskilled workers, take-home wages barely fed most families. The Quidnick Mill in Willimantic was one example. Like Walmart workers today who must count on government-subsidized health care, the Quidnick workers in 1912 had to rely on public assistance even though entire families worked there full time.

Deadly jobs: Matilda Cevitti worked at American Hatter and Furrier in Danbury. No effective state or federal laws required safety devices on factory machines. On April 6, 1906, Matilda was standing near a revolving machine shaft that generated static and caught her hair. The shaft ripped off her scalp and caused serious injuries to her face, hearing, and eyesight. "This is a great country for liberty, but we lay more emphasis on liberty of property than we do on liberty of life," declared a safety expert from Hartford-based Travelers Insurance Company. He reported that across the country, two million workers were injured each year and one hundred workers a day died from industrial accidents.

Speed ups: Always looking for methods to increase the pace of work and thereby increase profits, Connecticut employers such as the Yale & Towne Company utilized the "scientific management" method known as the Taylor system. Workers' smallest movements were carefully measured in order to eliminate delays and speed up production. It wasn't just efficiency the boss was after. Taylorism also had the effect of stealing the trade secrets that workers had developed to perform their jobs. By studying the job, the boss could appropriate a worker's techniques – actually, his property – and replace him with an unskilled worker or a machine. In 1912, Congressman John Q. Tilson of New Haven spoke out against Taylorism, citing a study that found it gave employers a "dangerously high level of uncontrolled power."

Poor housing: Living conditions were so bad in Hartford that a "sweeping investigation" was done in 1904, resulting in modest reforms. A decade later, little had changed: tenement apartments still had no running water or indoor toilets, insects infested the dwellings, garbage filled the yards, and children died from the polluted water of the Park River (known as the Hog River because it was so polluted). Landlords easily got around the zoning laws, causing overcrowding which fostered the spread of diseases such as tuberculosis and diphtheria. A local minister complained that "industries are parasites and are taking lives from the country [local farms]" without creating adequate housing in the cities. Where industry did provide housing, like the Moosup textile mill, employers used it as leverage against union organizing. In March, 1906, the mill boss issued eight hundred eviction notices after the Moosup weavers went on strike.

Why would Connecticut workers join the IWW?

These conditions can certainly explain why workers would join a union to improve their conditions. But why the IWW? The Wobblies were condemned by clergymen, outlawed by politicians, lied about by the press and attacked by the police. Even the term "Wobbly," a nickname with an unclear origin, seemed strange.

There were at least two reasons workers were attracted to the IWW. First, unskilled workers were largely ignored by the traditional craft unions. The dominant voice of labor was the AFL and its president Sam Gompers, who ran the coalition for thirty-eight years. The federation was composed of craft union members, skilled white males who jealously guarded their own benefits to the exclusion of all others. The IWW called the AFL the "American Separation of Labor" because the group could not even get its constituent unions to cooperate with each other against common employers.

Workers turned to the organization that had as its principle "one big union" of all working people. The IWW projected "a vision of a really democratic society," not one where plutocrats ruled the economy, according to historian Paul Buhle. "Decentralized democracy, democratic decision-making at all levels, is the most radical idea ever hatched in North America and the only one with real lasting appeal."

There was another reason the IWW attracted unorganized workers, less tangible but just as important. The Wobblies offered the workers a new labor culture, one that included them and respected their own languages and traditions. It was a culture that sang to them.

The Wobs had their own celebrities, brazen figures like Elizabeth Gurley Flynn, who could mesmerize thousands at a mass rally. They had their own troubadours, like Joe Hill, who lampooned hypocrites in high places and cut them down to size. The IWW had its own sound track, with scores of tunes sung from the "Little Red Songbook" that kept up workers' morale in dark times. Songs like *Solidarity Forever* are still sung at union meetings, even though many workers don't know it came first from the Wobblies.

Immigrants didn't have to change their names and lose their accents to join the Wobblies. They were welcome to join as themselves, and the union adapted to them with newspapers in a dozen languages, interpreters at meetings, and organizers like Joe Ettor, who looked and dressed as if he could be an a Italian cousin who just landed at Ellis Island.

The Wobblies communicated through "silent agitators," small stickers with pithy ideas. They could boil down big concepts into highly potent weapons. "An Injury to One is an Injury to All," they declared. "We will build a new society within the shell of the old." "One Big Union for all workers." IWW organizers were ready to sacrifice their comfort, safety, and even their lives to make those slogans a reality.

Workers discovered strength in themselves when they joined the Wobblies, even as they endured harassment and violence in order to become IWW members in Connecticut's mill and factory towns.

Despite the destruction of records from police raids and unfortunate internal splits, much of the IWW's history has been documented. Still, very little research on Wobbly organizing has been done in Connecticut. According to the Hartford Trade Board, Hartford had "wholly escaped the contagion [of] any rash agitator who should attempt to disturb the harmony" of the city. Historians have quoted this business group's glib assurance as proof of labor peace, but history tells a different tale.

The Rebel Girl on May Day

In 1912, on the heels of the historic "Bread and Roses" strike in Massachusetts, textile workers on the east coast of the United States were inspired to take action as well. In and around Willimantic, the IWW won a number of victories within a short time. The union's dynamic young organizer Elizabeth Gurley Flynn visited the Thread City on May 1st – International Workers Day – to congratulate workers there. She urged them to maintain a strong internal organization and counseled vigilance against employer retribution:

"Fellow workers, your victorious strike has been a grand one. You are here this evening to organize. Your victory must be backed up. Unless you keep up your organization you will sooner or later fail.

"It was unity on your part that ended the difficulty. It was the quickest settlement I ever heard of. The stockholders of the American Thread Company who live in Boston, Chicago, New York and other places had no other decision but grant the ten percent raise asked. They were forced to it by a just demand. They did not care to stop their mills because of the fear of losing big dividends and in this respect their pocketbooks would be touched.

"On this beautiful May Day you operatives of the American Thread Company have much to be thankful for. You have won a moral as well as a labor victory in your strike for better wages and conditions. May 1 is recognized all over industrial Europe as the real labor day. By your action you have added a new spirit of independence to your lives.

"There is a new era beginning for textile workers in this country. There is no reason why you should not share in the good things in life. It is a certainty that the mill owner makes as much from the labor of this class of operatives as the mine owner, the brewers and other lines of business who have raised wages and lessened working hours.

"The day is coming when there will be an eight-hour working day and a $3 daily wage for the textiles worker. Then the real cause of broken homes will be cured. Little children can attend the schools instead of stunting their lives in the mills. Mothers will have a chance to perform what the Almighty allotted them, the care of the homes instead of trying to eke out an existence under present conditions. The bread-winner, the father, will then perform the work and the homes will be more like heaven and there will be a contented lot of people.

"When the strike committee waited on Mr. Boss [the plant manager's actual name] and when a settlement was reached he was asked if he or the

47

company would hold any grievance against the leaders of the strike. He stated there would be none. There were men and women in this fight and at some time there may be an attempt to weed them out. You must defend those who fought the battle." (Steve Thornton, *A Shoeleather History of the Wobblies)*

4. Movements of the Unemployed

"Something to Show for Our Work:" The Unemployed Organize

Brainard Field may well be the country's first municipal airport. Located in a former cow pasture in southeast Hartford, Brainard opened in 1921. The era's greatest aviators – Amelia Earhart and Charles Lindbergh – landed there to great acclaim.

For its first decade, the field was used primarily for passenger flights. But in 1933, as the Great Depression tightened its grip, city officials decided Brainard should accommodate commercial traffic to spur the economy. This would require expansion, and the grass airstrip runways needed to give way to blacktop pavement.

How could the work be done on the cheap? With the city's ever-growing number of jobless workers, of course. City employees who drove ash wagons had already been replaced by jobless men. In August 1933, the city's public welfare department advertised for the Brainard project. One hundred workers were hired. Most were family men, now desperate for jobs. They had worked in local factories as machinists, assemblers, laborers and office clerks before the massive layoffs occurred.

The unemployed men had heard they were to be paid 40 cents an hour. Unfortunately for them, they found there were no wages, only food and partial rent subsidies.

Work started at 7:30 am. Most of the men had to walk three or more miles to reach the airfield. They were told that if they did not have sufficient food to eat for lunch they should try to get a private charity to assist them. Married men without children were restricted to working a maximum of 2 1/2 days a week. Men with four or more children were allowed to work 5 1/2 days a week.

Relief as Punishment

The jobs were "compulsory," announced Hartford welfare superintendent William J. Ryan. If any of the men were hired but then refused to work, and later applied for public assistance, they would be arrested for nonsupport. This program would give the men "the opportunity to regain their self-respect," Ryan declared, with no apparent irony.

The men had a different view. Many complained they could not work for

51

nothing, they had to make payments on furniture, insurance premiums, doctor bills and clothing for the children. One man suggested all they needed was a ball and chain…and striped work clothes.

"Conditions like that are enough to turn anyone into a radical," another worker said.

Federal relief programs were still several years away. Most welfare, as meager as it was, came from local sources. The popular theory was to make public assistance as difficult as possible to obtain, to discourage dependence. Welfare violated the American spirit of pride and self-sufficiency, according to policy makers.

Outright refusal to provide government support wasn't necessary, the noted sociologist Frances Fox Piven has written. If receiving aid was made degrading enough, recipients would become outcasts. Early in the dispute, Hartford Mayor Walter Batterson warned that if the men were paid wages, they would buy alcohol instead of providing for their families.

The Men Fight Back

The day after the project had begun, as word spread there would be no wages at all, dozens of men threw down their picks and shovels. A strike was on.

The action was led by former railroad man Martin Meaney and by Will Thomas, an African American mechanic. They were supported by a multiracial committee and quickly met with Mayor Batterson. "We like to feel that no matter how small the wages, we have something to show for our work," one committeeman told him.

The dispute was settled when the mayor guaranteed that no one would be arrested for refusing the outdoor work. The men agreed to $1.00 a day plus their food and rent assistance. Two buses from Main and Gold Streets would transport them to and from the job site each day.

In the first years of the Depression, the Hartford Open Hearth shelter gave out 10,000 meals to unemployed men – mostly donuts and oatmeal – twice a day. The Hartford Association of the Unemployed (HAU) formed in 1932 in response to the substandard meals, demanding and winning better nutrition. The group also opposed "conscript labor" like the original no-pay airport jobs.

HAU established seven chapters in the city, including one at Brainard Field. The members initiated free speech fights in order to protest publicly about their poverty conditions. HAU organizer Morris Yousman frequently made the connection between local poverty and the need for a comprehensive federal response to the upheaval of the Great Depression.

Believing that neither big business nor local government would answer their needs, the militant organizing of the unemployed grew, fostered by socialist and communist groups. During this period, unemployed "hunger marchers" demonstrated at the General Assembly in Hartford, and thousands of army veterans descended on the nation's Capital to increase the pressure begun by small efforts like those at Brainard Field.

Bonus Veterans: An Army Without Guns

It was a warm Sunday night in Hartford on August 7, 1932. Several dozen men and women–exhausted, dirty, hungry–trudged into the city after a hard trip from Washington, DC. They had just made history. Along with 45,000 other military veterans and their families, they camped for several months to press the government for aid. Specifically, they wanted the immediate release of cash payments (the Bonus) promised to them after World War I. They failed: the so-called Bonus Army could not compel Congress to vote for the pay. But the fight was far from over.

These were the Depression years, with a 25 percent jobless rate and two million men and boys walking the roads or hopping the freights in search of work. Many of the unemployed were workers-turned-soldiers who had expected jobs when they returned from European battlefields.

It's a historical fact we don't care to acknowledge: when workers are hurt by economic crises, veterans hurt more. As far back as the Revolutionary War, veterans needed to mobilize, and sometimes riot, in order to get paid. At the turn of the 20th century, Civil War veterans were still being found dead in Connecticut's forests and alleys. Coroners cited alcoholism or exposure, but often the real killer was society neglecting its own. By 1932 the calls for social insurance, health care, and guaranteed income were impossible to ignore.

Navy veteran Harry Bendell of Hartford was first to call for an outdoor meeting of local veterans to join the growing protest in Washington. Local supporters donated food, gas, oil and tires to help them on their way. Cash donations allowed some unemployed workers to register their cars so they could be legally driven. Vets collected money at local baseball games and set up a headquarters across from South Green.

The Bonus had broad public support. Even though the 1924 law passed by Congress stipulated that veterans could not receive their bonus payout until 1945, across the country they were demanding it immediately. The veterans' rationale was persuasive: soldiers had been paid 33 dollars a month while in the army, and the bonus was seen as the difference between their pay and what they would have earned as factory workers.

The vets contrasted their plight with the U.S. munitions industrialists who had made billions of dollars, "a despicable group of citizenry who waxed rich while America's manhood groveled in the filth and corruption of the battlefield," argued Arthur Pease, a resident of the Newington veterans hospital.

On June 12th, more than 235 vets left the city's South Green for the nation's capital. To those who opposed the massive protest and insisted on more acceptable methods of lobbying, Simon Kaplan, a tailor, replied "We tried writing." As for being disloyal (another charge thrown at the marchers), Joe Loveland of Windsor said, "I'm not ashamed to ask for something I earned. As for being disloyal, I have an honorable discharge that says different." (Steve Thornton, A Shoeleather History Project, 11/2014)

A few days earlier, at Fitch's Home for Soldiers in Darien, a dozen inmates (as they were called) quietly snuck out and were on the road to Washington. The angry director of the home warned that they were AWOL and would be discharged from their living quarters.

Connecticut Governor Wilbur Cross was worse than useless to the veterans' cause. He argued that the vets would spread disease in the Washington camps. He warned that if the Bonus was won, it could hurt the state's own veteran aid program. None of the veterans were listening. They were creating an army without guns.

Similarly, the head of the Manufacturers Association, E. Kent Hubbard, had spoken out against local initiatives to provide old age pensions for those who could no longer work. Such a plan would throw Connecticut into bankruptcy, Hubbard argued. The businessman's solution was to improve the local almshouses and boarding houses.

The state's veterans resented these tight-fisted attitudes. "The very financiers who had gigantic interests are now hooting the bewildered veteran, stifling his protests for a just hearing," wrote John Clyde Williams of Hartford. (Steve Thornton, A Shoeleather History Project, 11/20124)

Connecticut's Bonus contingent, including a large group from Bridgeport, arrived in Washington on June 14th. Their food and shelter were stuck in Baltimore due to a truck breakdown. They slept in their cars on the first night and welcomed food from the Danbury delegation. The state veterans' camp was soon up and running, however, and well integrated into the tent city being built before their eyes.

The Bonus Army paraded through the streets and packed the congressional galleries to maintain a high profile. Constant activity also helped the men keep their promise that they would drink no liquor while part of the encampment.

Harry Bendell returned to Hartford briefly, where he picked up more donations, including the proceeds from a newspaper the veterans were producing and selling. Leon Boniface, a tobacco store owner, lent Bonus supporters an empty storefront at 33 Albany Avenue for the dozen volunteer staff who canvassed Hartford's neighborhoods. Pete Haverlic from Bloomfield donated two large pigs. An unnamed woman donated a brand new cot with mattress and bedding. Bendell continued to recruit marchers and left with 36 more men.

Authorities were so frightened of this nonviolent army there were three agencies spying on the movement: the local police, the Army's Military Intelligence Division (MID), and J. Edgar Hoover's FBI. Hoover predictably said the movement was communist-dominated and that many of the demonstrators had criminal records and were not veterans. Confidential reports listed Darien, Bridgeport and Hartford as "centers of subversive unrest."

The House passed the Bonus bill on June 16th but the Senate quickly voted it down the next day. President Herbert Hoover had already stated he would veto any bonus payments. Despite the serious blow, most of the men stayed at the camps.

Without warning, on July 28th General Douglas MacArthur led hundreds of U.S. troops on horseback to destroy the Bonus camps. With tear gas and guns they evicted the veterans and their families and set fire to their makeshift homes. Two vets were killed and many were injured.

Undaunted, the Bonus veterans came back to Washington again and again each year to win approval for the cash payments. In 1936, Congress finally overrode Franklin D. Roosevelt's veto and passed the bill.

The effect of the Bonus campaign was even more far reaching than the weary Hartford veterans could have imagined. In 1944 Congress passed the GI Bill of Rights, which provided college funds, mortgages and job training to almost 8 million vets. It was not a panacea however: African American veterans suffered widespread discrimination in employment, housing, and education from the moment they returned to these shores.

5. Strikes

It is a Subterranean Fire

"The police wagon, pulled by two large, galloping horses, thundered toward the rioting protesters. Its target was a group of socialists and anarchists – "red ruffians" who railed against big business and government-sanctioned violence. A number of them were dragged into the coach and taken to jail." (Steve Thornton, The Shoeleather History Project Online, 1/2018)

It was Wednesday, December 6, 1893. For twenty-five cents, Hartford residents could watch the whole spectacle on the stage of Proctor's Opera House. "The Police Patrol" was actually a live action theater performance that purported to be a "realistic" recreation of Chicago's infamous Haymarket Square riot on May 4, 1886 – a pivotal labor incident that riveted the nation's attention for years to come. The police wagon featured in the Hartford production was even said to be the same one on duty at the Haymarket Square on the night of May 4th.

The Haymarket Affair

Beginning May 1, 1886, striking workers at the McCormick Harvesting Company of Chicago faced an onslaught of violence from police and Pinkertons. The McCormick strikers were demanding the eight-hour day with no pay cut. Similar "eight-hour" strikes were taking place in manufacturing centers around the country.

Haymarket Square was chosen as the site for a mass protest against the assaults on the McCormick farm implement workers. On May 4th, the square filled with men, women, and children protesting the police violence

A homemade bomb exploded toward the end of the rally, which up until then had been angry but peaceful. Many participants and police were killed or wounded by the blast and by random police gunfire.

Eight men were charged with conspiring to set off the bomb. After a sensational and highly prejudicial trial, four of them were sentenced to death by hanging. One committed suicide in jail; three others were given life imprisonment.

Albert and Lucy

Albert Parsons was one of those who met the hangman's noose on November 11, 1887. His wife Lucy Parsons spent months traveling, speaking, and building public support to stop the judicial murders. Parsons was a feminist and labor organizer in her own right, who would later help found the Industrial Workers of the World (IWW or Wobblies) in 1905.

In New Haven, Parsons spoke to an enthusiastic working class crowd on October 30, 1886. Several hundred admirers came to see her; so did undercover police. To her detractors, Lucy Parsons declared: "You may have expected me to belch forth great flames of dynamite and stand before you with bombs in my hands. If you are disappointed, you have only the capitalist press to thank for it."

On that same tour Parsons spoke to an even bigger crowd in Bridgeport. According to historian Carolyn Ashbaugh's biography, *Lucy Parsons, American Revolutionary,* she was thrilled by the eagerness of the audience to learn about anarchism. "My trip is having its effect," she wrote Albert. "The powers that be don't know what to do with me." One New York newspaper suggested that Albert Parsons "be let out as a compromise to get Mrs. Parsons to stop talking.'"

During her speaking tour, Lucy Parsons sold literature to help defray her living expenses. A few months after her New Haven appearance, Parsons was selling a pamphlet that contained the courtroom speech by August Spies, one of Albert Parsons' co-defendants.

A copy of the August Spies publication surfaced, with "Lucy E. Parsons" stamped on the cover, at Wesleyan University some one hundred years after its publication.

Controlling the Narrative

Across the country, politicians, newspaper editors, and clergymen used Haymarket to condemn anarchists, socialists, unions, and striking workers by labeling all such adherents as terrorists. The word became a catch-all, applied to a wide range of undesirables. It was interchangeable with "scoundrels," "red-flag gangs" and "un-Americanized outlaws."

After the Haymarket incident, many newspapers called for swift retribution; the *Boston Herald* wrote that anarchists should be met with "hot lead and cold steel." Others suggested "Gatling guns and the hangman's noose."

The *Meriden Republican* published an interview with a local anarchist who claimed a community of sixty others. They met in New Haven where the *New England Anzeiger,* a German-language weekly, was published. In fact, there were a number of self-identified anarchist communities in Hartford, New Britain and other Connecticut cities.

Professor Graham Taylor was pastor of the Fourth Congregational Church (later known as the Horace Bushnell Church and today as Liberty Congregational) and then as head of the Hartford Seminary. Taylor saw himself as a "pastoral sociologist," more enlightened than many of his brethren.

Professor Taylor blamed the spread of radical influences on the large number of "Italians and Bohemians" who lived in the big cities.

While in Chicago on another matter, Taylor said he witnessed a planning meeting for the annual Haymarket memorial. He contrasted it to the "staunch common sense and conservation" of traditional trade unions.

Taylor urged assimilation and patriotism to cure the "dangerous" communities of immigrants. He also boosted the National Civic Federation, a big-business front for labor/management cooperation.

May Day

Pessimists pronounced Haymarket a major setback for the labor movement. They proclaimed that the eight-hour movement was lost. Hartford workers didn't see it that way.

For the next decade, May 1st was the day local carpenters, painters, sheet metal workers and carriage makers organized, struck, and frequently won their demand for eight hours.

One of the most persistent and creative groups who took May Day as their own were the Jewish bakers from Hartford's east side. May 1st was their deadline for shorter hours and a wide range of other changes, including a demand to provide part-time work for their unemployed members.

During one of their many strikes, they purchased supplies in New Britain, baked bread on their own, and sold it from pushcarts on Front and Windsor Streets. It was a popular item; they won their demands.

Although Hartford's skilled building tradesmen were the most organized and often led the way with the eight-hour demand, other workers were inspired by May Day as well.

Local cigar makers, hod carriers and vaudeville theater stagehands began or ended their strikes on May 1st. In 1909, over 200 newsboys with their own drum corps marched through Hartford streets carrying signs and waving flags. They were protesting the refusal of newspaper distributors to accept their unsold copies of two New York dailies. The boys urged customers to support their cause by only buying Hartford papers.

The "Terrific Struggle" on Stage

In June 1893, Illinois Governor John Peter Altgeld pardoned the three remaining Haymarket prisoners who had been given life sentences. Altgeld was a Civil War veteran whose political career included passing laws against child labor and dangerous workplaces.

His justification for the pardons skillfully dismantled the legal travesty that had convicted the men: an incompetent jury, a biased judge, and a lack of credible evidence.

Just five months after Altgeld's pardons, the police wagon took to the Hartford stage, reinforcing the myth of heroic law enforcement in a pitched battle with wild-eyed extremists. "Strong climaxes and sensational incidents mark the progress of the play," local theater-goers were assured.

Proctor's Opera House promised the play would be "positively the grandest production of the age."

The Haymarket martyrs' sacrifice became a militant and inspirational rallying cry for workers across the centuries and throughout the world. As August Spies declared before his execution:

"If you think that by hanging us, you can stamp out the labor movement… then hang us! Here you will tread upon a spark… and everywhere, flames will blaze up. It is a subterranean fire. You cannot put it out."

The Day Casco's Workers Sat Down on the Job

It was an event that lasted less than a day and involved only 50 people directly. It was organized, led and carried out by everyday workers and thus contradicted the official, mainstream narrative that only big people make history. Many of the participants were women, so their actions were further dismissed. Even ridiculed. Yet as the great historian Howard Zinn might have put it, mostly unknown and forgotten people employed at the Casco factory in Bridgeport took part in a sit-down strike on an early spring day in 1937 to deal a blow on behalf of themselves and city workers as a whole.

In the long history of class conflict in the United States, the decade of the 1930's was a particularly boisterous period. Virtually every part of the country saw workers fight against plant closures, unemployment and poverty and organize for democratization of the workplace. Since it was one of the nation's great industrial hubs, Bridgeport workers were very active on all these fronts, and it was only natural that the sit-down strike was one of many tactics they utilized.

The Sit-Down Strike

The sit-down strike was a tactic used most effectively by the Industrial Workers of the World three decades before the action at Casco. It was revived to great fanfare and with remarkable success by autoworkers who occupied General Motors plants in Cleveland and Flint on December 30, 1936. Between the actions at GM and the one at Casco, significant sit-down strikes had taken place at many other workplaces. Many more would follow, from New York City department stores to Akron rubber plants.

While each sit-down strike has its own particulars, the general idea is the same: to collectively withhold labor and bring production to a complete standstill by occupying the workplace rather than by withdrawing from it. Leaving the workplace and striking from the outside leaves open the possibility of employers bringing in replacements (scabs). At Casco, workers were caught off guard by a sudden edict from management to close the plant. One result was that many who would otherwise have participated in the occupation had already left the premises.

Set on the West End right next to the bustling railroad tracks used to transport both travelers and cargo to, from and through Bridgeport, Casco (Connecticut

Automotive Specialty Company) opened in 1924. Workers there made a variety of products for automobiles, including pop-out cigarette lighters that were then a relatively new feature on many dashboards. Tensions between workers and Casco's owner management over wages and conditions in the factory had been escalating for some time prior to the sit-down strike, and management was actively soliciting workers to join its company union, the Casco Employees Association (CEA). Several hundred workers, meanwhile, had signed cards with the United Electrical, Radio and Machine Workers of America (UE), one of the rapidly growing affiliates of the newly-formed Congress of Industrial Organizations (CIO). Alarmed at the growth in the plant of the UE and in an apparent attempt to cripple the workers' organizing efforts, Casco President Joseph Cohen issued an order the morning of April 6, 1937 that the plant would temporarily close at noon that day for inventory.

On Strike Inside and Out

Caught off guard, 850 of the 900 workers left at noon, including many who undoubtedly would have remained had they known that 50 of their co-workers had decided to occupy the plant. The 50 sit-down strikers announced that they intended to remain until a set of demands that included management recognition of the UE as their bargaining representative were met. Supportive workers who had left formed picket lines outside the plant on Railroad and Hancock avenues, sent word of the action to the families of those inside and contacted organizers from the UE.

Cohen and other company officials responded by declaring that the factory was shut down and would not reopen until *its* demands were met. They also announced there would soon be hundreds of layoffs. While refusing to accept that reductions were necessary, the workers and the UE countered with a plan to prevent any layoffs by temporarily reducing the hours of all. Cohen unconditionally rejected the proposal, saying, as quoted in a story in the *Bridgeport Post*, "Positively no. I'll run my own plant."

Whether he knew it or not, Cohen's words cut to the heart of what was at stake. At Casco, as elsewhere, plant occupations challenge management over how work should be organized and who should decide. The next step – and workers in many places in 1937 had come to understand this – was whether owners and managers are necessary, or even desirable. Cohen's unease was the same unease that haunted all business owners whether of smallish businesses like Casco or of the massive empire of General Motors — that through collective action, and especially workplace occupations, workers would come to envision and, more importantly, act on constructing a society without bosses.

Community Support

Meetings of management, the UE and many of those who had left the plant carried into the evening. Meanwhile, on Railroad Avenue Casco workers and others gathered to support the strike. While many workers walked the picket line, others tied mattresses and food to ropes that the occupiers, in anticipation of a potentially lengthy standoff, pulled up through open windows while officers from the Bridgeport Police Department kept watch. A photographer from the *Bridgeport Post* and *Bridgeport Telegram* was allowed inside and took two photos that appeared in both papers the following day.

Victory

Early on the morning of April 7, an agreement was reached. A significant wage increase would be implemented and management agreed to recognize the UE (soon to be a major force in Bridgeport as the representative of workers at GE, Westinghouse/Bryant Electric and many other city shops). All talk of layoffs ceased, the occupiers were not disciplined and the plant remained closed only while management took stock and made way for new production lines. On virtually every count, it was a resounding victory for the workers.

As in Flint and many other instances, the Casco workers utilized collective action to make significant gains. That should be celebrated all these years later as much as the Casco workers themselves undoubtedly celebrated in the days after the occupation. Still, there are also nagging questions that began to present themselves in 1937 that plague workers to this day.

Wittingly or not, organizers from even the most radical unions like the UE helped pull workers away from the very awareness and possible action that owners like Cohen feared the most. The objectives of the UE and the CIO as a whole were state-sanctioned exclusive representation as embodied in the National Labor Relations Act (NLRA), class peace and collective bargaining agreements predicated on the corporation's right to rule. Strikers taking over plants was fine as a temporary tactic, but long term, labor's vision and its relationship with workers were ultimately not so different from that of the business class, as became more apparent over time.

Not long after the Casco strike, the UE and other CIO unions signed contracts that almost without exception forbade work stoppages that they did not authorize. Also included in the standard CIO contracts were management prerogative clauses that ceded all decisions about production, including the right to permanently close the plant, to the company.

That does not diminish what the Casco workers accomplished in 1937. On the contrary, it is in their spirit that we struggle for a way out of a framework that workers today are trapped in.

"The People Are Indestructible":
1946 UE General Strike

Pratt & Whitney Machine Tool Company President Charles W. Deeds addressed several hundred embattled scabs and supervisors in the company cafeteria. He told them of his plans to put the plant on a 45-hour week to help recoup the losses caused by the strike that had begun in March. Deeds told his listeners not to worry about the "scurrilous" leaflets being distributed in their neighborhoods by the Union that was exposing workers who had crossed the picket line. He threatened the loss of planned vacation holidays for anyone who had not already returned to work.

July 15, 1946: Outside the Pratt and Whitney gates, members of the United Electrical Workers union (UE) were planning a different kind of holiday.

Hartford celebrated Japan's surrender almost a year earlier, signaling the end of World War II. For workers in Hartford and across the country, the war against fascism had taken its toll. The United States suffered over one million casualties from 1941-45 on the battlefield, working people who served in the armed forces. But according to *Labor's Untold Story,* more than 11 million workers were killed and injured back home in industrial accidents during that same period. Wages had risen 15% since 1941 but prices rose 45%, and profits soared by 250%. With the war over, it was time for working people to catch up.

During 1945-46, four and a half million American workers went on strike. This included the members of UE at Pratt & Whitney Tool and the Hamilton Standard propeller plant. Their goal was a pay increase of 18 ½ cents an hour, similar to the pattern just set by workers at General Motors and General Electric, and eventually by 5 million steel, auto, and electrical workers. In March, 1946, the Hartford UE workers began their struggle.

Hartford labor unions had started the ball rolling back in January when hundreds of UE workers rallied at the State Capitol to demand unemployment benefits for strikers. They demanded that Governor Baldwin call a special session to pass a law protecting their income. "Industry gets relief, why not strikers?" one union newspaper asked. Baldwin passed the buck to the federal government and refused to call for action, despite the efforts of State Representative Harold Conroy, who also served as the president of UE local 270. Undaunted, the workers at Pratt voted in March to strike anyway.

The UE workers then took their case to the Hartford City Council. There, Hartford Alderman Patrick Ward, a UE member and the CIO Council president, introduced a resolution in support of the strike. The resolution was seconded by striking worker and Alderman Vincent Argento and backed by Alderman Edward Kennedy, a Teamsters official. The vote was 9 to 9, and Mayor Moylan broke the tie with his vote of support.

Strikers also looked to the broader Hartford community for solidarity and found an important ally in Reverend Edward L. Peet, the pastor of Hartford's North United Methodist Church. Rev. Peet quickly signed on to the Union's efforts to "secure a decent standard of living for all the working population."

By May, the strike was still holding strong and production had been crippled. Governor Baldwin sent 100 State Police, while West Hartford added 40 cops to push scabs through the picket line. Twenty-two striking workers were arrested.

Strikers tried a new tactic. In May they began to picket the homes of scabs and Pratt officials, distributing "Know Your Neighbor" leaflets to the surrounding neighborhoods. The Governor ordered a halt to the picketing and 13 UE members were arrested retroactively on his order. Eight of the workers received fines and suspended sentences. The State went even further when it won a court-ordered injunction against mass picketing at the plant. The UE appealed the injunction and the Connecticut Federation of Labor filed an amicus brief. Union lawyers fought Baldwin's action, calling it a "clear example of government by executive fiat."

By July, the company started a back-to-work movement among the strikers. Every other day, anonymous letters to the editor from a "striking worker" or a "worker's wife" appeared in the *Hartford Courant* complaining about Union leadership and predicting that the strike would lose. The newspaper's owners editorialized against the strike on a regular basis.

The UE was winning more union and grassroots support, however. The Oil workers and Railroad unions refused to deliver fuel or freight to the struck plant. The UE erected a tote board announcing the financial help it was receiving from the people of Hartford. And although the strike, now in its fourth month, was taking its toll, workers at Underwood Typewriter voted to join the UE on June 3rd.

Labor planned a final pitch to win the conflict with a "United Labor Day" scheduled for Tuesday, July 23rd at the old State House in the heart of downtown. The *Courant* responded by calling the rally "illogical" and "needless." One editorial said, "certainly there is no need to stage such rallies to impress the public with the strength of labor's command." The best way to solve the dispute would be to stay at work, the paper counseled. Opinion-makers had reason to be scared. Every Hartford union had endorsed the rally, and several were planning to walk out in sympathy with the UE strikers.

The *Courant's* worst fears came true: workers at Royal Typewriter, Colt

Firearms and Whitlock Manufacturing took a labor holiday and joined the strikers in the pouring rain on Main Street at noon. Early newspaper reports from the afternoon *Hartford Times* assured readers that the crowd was small, about 1,000 people, and that no traffic disruption had occurred. But by the next day, accounts estimated "several thousand" participants and the national *UE News* counted the mass rally at 10,000. According to the labor paper, "the bastion of finance surrounding the square, including Travelers Insurance and the Phoenix, echoed the applause of the crowd as the speakers lashed out at the National Association of Manufacturers," which had spent $2 million nationwide in propaganda efforts to portray workers as "strike-happy."

Buses had to be re-routed by the police for several hours as the rally built in size. Local merchants confirmed a significant loss of business. Reverend Peet was there, too, to point out that the strike affected 12,000 other Hartford residents: the strikers' families. "How easy it is to say that, but how terrible to contemplate when you reduce it to hunger, anxiety, evictions, frustrations and despair" he told the crowd.

Three weeks later, almost a year after Japan's surrender, the company settled and the strike was over. As the *UE News* reported it, the workers won the 18 ½ cents an hour they had demanded.

Labor had won its battle, but Capital was preparing for a longer war. A change in the structure of Hartford city government was being forged by the business-dominated Charter Commission. On the agenda was a switch from the aldermanic districts (which had provided the strikers with their support at City Hall) to an at-large system and a Council-Mayor form of government.

The *Hartford Courant* labeled one side in this fight as Communist sympathizers. "It is not difficult to imagine that some of [the opponents'] innovations might have descended along that familiar party line plan from Moscow," the *Courant* warned. To make its point perfectly clear, the paper's editorial cartoon showed a bearded Communist, dressed in pajamas, decorated with a hammer and sickle design, getting into bed with a local political official who opposed the big business plan. The caption read "Move over! I'm your pal!" In fact, the Hartford branch of the Communist Party did have an opinion on the matter, which was also shared by the Republican Registrar of Voters.

It would not be too long before the UE would face the same charges of communist domination and lose thousands of members in Hartford and around the nation to red-baiting attacks from manufacturers, government, and other labor unions as well.

In 1947, the General Assembly took its cue from Governor Baldwin's strike-breaking actions by passing a law that made it a crime to picket private homes. Connecticut General Statute 31-20 stated that "no person shall engage in picketing before or about the home or residence of any individual" unless they actually lived at a strike site. The law stayed on the books for forty years until it was struck down by the Connecticut Supreme Court. The legal challenge came from striking UAW workers at Colt Firearms, which had once been a UE shop. The workers were engaged in the state's longest strike, which had begun in January, 1986. They picketed Colt president Gary French's home four times, the same way UE strikers had taken on Pratt & Whitney. French sought an injunction, but the court found the state law to be a violation of the strikers' Constitutional rights.

With a clear-sighted view of the Hartford strike and the other, larger industrial battles that had just taken place, a UE leader summed up the meaning of the 1946 strikes. "The people are indestructible," the Union wrote. "UE took the initiative and demanded the right to a living wage. The conspiracy failed because in the heat of battle, rank-and-file labor was united. The CIO, AFL, and Railroad unions in many communities worked together. The conspiracy failed because labor was not alone. The townspeople were on labor's side." And in a prescient warning, the statement concluded: "Defeated in the first battle, profit-hungry big business continues its war against unions and the people. Other battles loom ahead." (UE National Newsletter, 1946).

Bridgeport's Contentious 1978 Teachers' Strike

When Bridgeport public school students arrived for the first day of school on September 6, 1978, they discovered that their teachers were on strike. The Board of Education and the Bridgeport Education Association (BEA), the collective bargaining representative of the city's 1,247 teachers, as well as about 100 other school professionals, had been at loggerheads for months. Connecticut law forbids strikes by teachers, however, and many Bridgeporters were caught off guard by the picket lines in front of schools.

Not that the city's residents were unsympathetic. On the contrary, many parents joined the picket lines, as did students. On the West Side, a neighborhood group organized its members to gather outside Longfellow school to urge students to go home and to urge parents who accompanied their children to school to support the strike.

National Teacher Strike Wave

The walk-out in Bridgeport was one of many that September as teachers in Philadelphia, Boston, Cleveland, Seattle and numerous smaller cities and towns saw schools closed because of strikes. Not far away, teachers in Norwalk also went on strike for five days. None of those strikes, however, was as contentious or bitter as the one in Bridgeport.

Bridgeport's teachers were seeking significant increases in salaries and pensions, other benefit improvements and fewer students per class. They had accepted what many observers regarded as a concessionary contract in 1975 and were dissatisfied with the city's offer three years later. The union pointed out that salaries in Bridgeport for teachers and other school staff were the lowest in Fairfield County (as they are today) and among the lowest in the state. The union also noted the regular exodus of teachers from Bridgeport to higher-salaried jobs in nearby school districts, another trend that remains true today.

From the outset, the strike was highly successful. Only 36 teachers, or less than 3%, reported for work on September 6, and that number dropped in the days that followed. The Board of Ed kept elementary and middle schools open at first by utilizing a small number of teaching aides, substitute teachers and accredited, unemployed teachers, but only 10% of students crossed picket lines to attend classes. The city's Parent Teacher Association supported the strike by rejecting a call by the Board that they assist in staffing schools and helping scab teachers.

Mass Arrests and Imprisonment

Arrests began just days into the strike, with State Superior Court Judge James Heneby levying fines of $10,000 per day against the union. As the strike continued, Heneby ordered the union's officers jailed. The first jailings of teachers occurred on September 12, when thirteen strikers were handcuffed and carted off, the men to a prison in New Haven and the women to one in Niantic some 60 miles away. Those arrested endured degradations such as strip searches and being doused with lice spray. Adding further insult, Heneby imposed individual fines of $350 per person per day on the arrestees.

Angered by the arrests and the teachers' subsequent treatment — treatment that one arrestee later called the most humiliating event of her life, the strikers turned out to the picket lines the following day in ever larger numbers and with greater determination and militancy. One result was that the city and school board were forced to abandon efforts to keep any schools open. With all 38 city schools closed, another 115 teachers were arrested in the next few days and 274 in all were arrested during the strike, 22% of the total in the city. Many of those arrested were packed onto buses and taken 70 miles to a National Guard camp in Windsor Locks that was converted into a makeshift prison.

Standing Firm to Victory

After two weeks, with all of the other strikes around the country settled, the mass arrest and imprisonment of Bridgeport's teachers were drawing international attention and causing local elites and city residents as a whole great embarrassment. Despite the arrests, jailings, fines and some tense scenes on a number of picket lines, the teachers stood firm. Finally, on September 25, after 19 days, the teachers union and Board of Ed both agreed to accept binding arbitration. All teachers, some of whom had been locked up for 13 days, were released from prison. The final terms of the agreement were largely favorable to the teachers.

New Legislation: A Setback?

In the strike's aftermath, the Connecticut legislature passed the 1979 Teacher Collective Bargaining Act that mandates binding arbitration when teachers and the municipalities they work for are stalemated in contract negotiations. While some observers saw the law as a victory for teachers, it remains illegal for teachers in Connecticut to strike. In addition, a number of changes to the law since 1979, such as one that allows municipalities but not unions to reject the decision of an arbitrator, have weakened the bargaining position of teachers.

The law's restriction against strikes is also problematic, as conditions for Bridgeport teachers, not to mention students, have in many ways worsened since 1978. In Chicago, where strikes are not illegal, teachers who struck for nine days in 2012 and for shorter durations several times since have shown that significant improvements can be won with strikes. Those actions have countered attempts by elites intent on weakening teacher unions and underfunding schools by pitting the interests of students against those of teachers. A similar alliance of the wider public and school professionals, including 274 who endured arrest and scandalous treatment, is what enabled teachers to prevail and lift all boats in their 1978 strike in Bridgeport.

Solidarity Bridgeport Style: The 1979 Handy and Harman Strike

On July 1, 1979, 400 members of United Steelworkers Local 7201 employed at the Handy and Harman precious metals factory in Fairfield went on strike. There was nothing particularly unusual or exceptional about that; workers at factories in Bridgeport and the surrounding area regularly called strikes during the region's industrial heyday. What was exceptional was the way in which a large number of people in Bridgeport responded when Handy and Harman employment representatives began actively recruiting replacement workers – scabs – in economically depressed areas of the city.

Founded in 1867, Handy and Harman opened a factory in Bridgeport in 1902. That facility eventually closed and the company centralized its local production at a plant on Grasmere Avenue in Fairfield that opened in 1915. The factory was adjacent to McKesson Labs on land where today Whole Foods, Home Depot, a Chipotle's Restaurant and several other stores make up the Kings Crossing Shopping Center.

Even after the consolidation to the Fairfield plant, Handy and Harman continued to draw most of its workers from Bridgeport. There was an especially large number of Portuguese employed in the factory, most all of whom lived in or had roots in The Hollow neighborhood of Bridgeport. They were highly skilled technicians who took great pride in their abilities working in what the company, in its official history, calls "the largest and best equipped precious metals plant of its day."

Resisting Givebacks

In what had become the norm for companies in the Bridgeport area by 1979, Handy and Harman opened negotiations for a new collective bargaining agreement by demanding substantial givebacks of its unionized workforce. The negotiations stalemated and the workers went on strike. The company soon countered with a tactic that was once common but had fallen out of favor beginning around the Second World War: the active recruitment of replacements for the strikers.

One area where Handy and Harman attempted to recruit was a stretch of State Street on Bridgeport's West Side. The neighborhood happened to be home to an office of the Spanish American Coalition (SAC), an activist organization well known to the city's Latinos. Several young Puerto Rican men from the neighborhood walked into the SAC office on Colorado Avenue and informed members about Handy and Harman's recruitment efforts. SAC members soon discovered that youths on Bridgeport's East Side had also been approached about applying for employment at the struck facility.

Led by Willie Matos, a long-time city activist who in the early 1970's had been a leader of the Young Lords Party, SAC distributed an English/Spanish flyer that explained that Handy and Harman's workers were on strike and urged people not to apply for jobs there. They also put out a call to activists throughout Bridgeport, and a meeting to address the recruitment efforts was held at the SAC office in September. The meeting was well-attended and included, in addition to Matos and other SAC members, activists from other Bridgeport community organizations, Handy and Harman strikers, officials from the striking Steelworkers local, members and officers from other area unions, and several of the young men who had encountered the Handy and Harman recruiters.

Because of the efforts of SAC and the ad hoc committee it pulled together, Handy and Harman soon curtailed its efforts to recruit scabs in Bridgeport. As the strike dragged on, the ad hoc committee decided to support the strikers in other ways. Meetings were held, press releases were issued, and people joined the Handy and Harman workers on their picket line. Committee members also reached out to members of the International Association of Machinists who were on strike against the Olin-Winchester company in New Haven and joined the Olin-Winchester workers several times on their picket line.

As the strike entered its fourth month, the committee initiated calls for a solidarity day to pressure the company to settle the strike on the workers' terms. Together with officers and members of Local 7201, as well as other union officers and members from the area, the committee organized a march and rally on November 17, 1979.

1,000 Attend March and Rally

One thousand people gathered at the Steelworkers union hall on Kings Highway Cutoff that Saturday morning and then marched past the Handy and Harman factory to Sherman Green in the center of Fairfield. One of the co-chairs of the march and rally was Americo Santiago, an electrician at the Sikorsky Aircraft factory in Bridgeport and a member of Teamsters Local 1150. Santiago later served for three terms on the Bridgeport City Council as a state representative and as Connecticut's Assistant Secretary of State. Among those who addressed the rally were Victor Matta from Bridgeport Fight Back, Arthur Pecchillo from the union representing Bridgeport's public school teachers, the Bridgeport Education Association, and Craig Goughier, who spoke on behalf of the Olin-Winchester strikers.

Within a matter of days, the company changed its tune. Realizing that its workers were not going to give in, and having long since given up on recruiting replacements because of the spirited opposition from the Bridgeport community, the company agreed to settle the strike. The terms were very similar to the union's proposal and the settlement was widely hailed as a victory for the workers.

For several months after the strike, the strike support committee continued to meet. Members sought to establish an organization that could facilitate similar solidarity efforts while also providing area workers a venue to address the growing crisis of plant closures, layoffs and concessionary bargaining. The group also was in contact with the Plant Closures Project, a short-lived statewide effort to pass legislation that would hold companies financially liable to the municipalities and workers they left behind if they closed a factory.

The effort to transform the committee and keep it going in a different form ultimately failed, and as the 1970s turned into the 1980s, one area factory after another – Bridgeport Brass, Jenkins, Bullard, Hubbell, Bryant Electric/Westinghouse, General Electric – closed up shop. The Handy and Harman factory closed in 2002.

Still, the efforts of 1979 made it possible for Handy and Harman's workers to enjoy better livings standards and more power on the job than they would have had the company gotten its way. In addition, the actions of those who came together in a small, drafty office on Colorado Avenue on Bridgeport's West Side demonstrated the solidarity that is the single most important means available to workers to ward off the depredations of corporate elites, be it in 1979 or today.

Connecticut's Longest Strike

The Colt Firearms factory has been producing guns since the 1800s, from pistols to Gatling guns and the M-16 (now the M4 carbine). The Colt name is still known worldwide. Workers at Colt had tried to establish a union since the turn of the 20th century, and finally succeed in the 1940s.

Now, in 1986, they were in a life or death struggle with a company that would do anything to break their union, United Auto Workers (UAW) Local 376. Colt intended to roll back the gains made over the years by the white, Black, and Puerto Rican workforce. "We are not claiming that we are losing money, nor were we basing our proposals on the Company's financial condition," admitted the company's top negotiator.

Colt workers had already been protesting on the inside for nearly two years against poor treatment and blatant attempts to bust their union. Led by shop chairman Lester Harding, activists were disciplined, suspended and fired for nonexistent infractions. In response, they printed the names of the fired workers on their shirts and paraded in the plant during breaks to communicate their anger.

Once the strike began on January 24, 1986, the 1,000 strikers attempted to stop scabs from entering the factory and taking their jobs. Frequent scuffles on the picket line were met with overwhelming force by the Hartford police. There were many arrests during the strike's first months. At one point UAW leader Phil Wheeler was slapped with inciting a riot, a serious felony charge.

The boss at Colt knew that public opinion was important in this fight. He thought he could sway that opinion with full-page newspaper ads. He harped on the picket line conflicts, laying the blame solely on the strikers. He explained how reasonable his negotiating demands were, and how unreasonable was the UAW's response.

Thanks to the newly formed Labor /Community Alliance, the propaganda fell flat. On May 13, 1986, forty-five community activists, elected officials, clergy members, teachers and others converged on the Colt factory on Huyshope Avenue in Hartford. They sat down, blocking the parking lot entrance and the scabs attempting to work. The group was dubbed the "Colt 45," an ironic take on the company's most famous product.

The civil disobedience was no picnic. The Hartford Police captain in charge of the cops on the line had been biased against the strikers from the beginning. Strikers were proven correct when he quit the police force during the strike and took a job as head of security for Colt.

The nonviolent Colt 45 action was only one of many community support events and marches organized during the record four-year struggle. Critical to the strikers' morale was the solidarity they got from other unions and the city and state lawmakers who supported a successful nationwide boycott of Colt products. In fact, the strike itself was the longest sustained nonviolent action in Connecticut history.

Included in the Colt 45 were a number of peace activists. Was this some mistake? No, they said. They issued a public statement signed by many of the most locally prominent anti-war figures who declared that union jobs were good for families and neighborhoods. They understood that workers had no power to choose what they produced in this society. The activists wanted to build relationships with unions and rank-and-file workers to find common ground and ultimately achieve "economic conversion," the process by which industry changes to peacetime production.

In 1990, UAW 376 won big. The company finally gave in after labor court decisions found that Colt had been a massive lawbreaker. Workers won $10 million in back pay and benefits. All could return to their jobs. A coalition of the state government, private investors, and the UAW had bought the company.

Thirty years later, union veterans and community activists held a "commemoration of courage" to celebrate the Colt strikers' victory. At first, some openly questioned the event's purpose: did they really want to remember those hard times? But still, many strikers and their spouses attended. When asked about good memories from their historic strike, they answered "the Colt 45."

Grocery Store Workers Take on Billion Dollar Multinational

At 1 p.m. on the afternoon of April 11, 2019, 31,000 workers at 253 Stop and Shop grocery stores throughout Connecticut, Rhode Island and Massachusetts walked off their jobs. The strike came after several months of failed negotiations in which Stop and Shop refused to retract an onerous set of demands for the elimination of premium pay for Sunday work, major cuts to pensions and dramatic increases in the amount workers would have to pay for health care.

Most of the strikers are members of the United Food and Commercial Workers (UFCW); the rest are members of the Teamsters. Truck drivers both union and non-union have honored the picket lines by refusing to make their deliveries, according to strikers at four picket lines in Bridgeport and Fairfield, Connecticut. The workers at those stores also report that no union members have crossed the picket line. Most stores are open as supervisors and a small number of replacement workers have been stocking shelves and working cash registers, but business has taken a big hit.

Solid Public Support

Public support has been high and sympathetic supervisors have told strikers that the take for one 16-hour day at a store in Fairfield was a meager $2,000, a fraction of a normal day's business. Some stores have cut their hours because business has been so bad. Union officials, members of other unions and community supporters have joined with strikers for rallies at stores in a number of locations, including Bridgeport and Fairfield. Local elected officials have come to union rallies, and coverage on local television stations and in the Hearst dailies that dominate the newspaper market in Connecticut has been positive. An announcement was made at a picket line on the seventh day of the strike that community sympathizers and merchants have established a food bank where strikers can get free food.

From conversations with dozens of strikers, morale of union members is high eleven days in. Worker after worker expressed special gratitude for the overwhelming public support they've received. People who know many of the strikers by name from years of shopping have joined the picket lines, with many bringing coffee, doughnuts, pizzas and other food and beverages to the strikers. Others have contributed gift cards good at other stores and local pharmacies, and there are reports of people making cash contributions to picketers, including one for $1,500. The UFCW has also set up a website for people to contribute to the strike fund.

$2 Billion Profits in 2018

Amidst the strikers' enthusiasm, however, is an undercurrent of fear and resentment. There has been no strike at Stop and Shop for 30 years, and that one was of very short duration, so the vast majority of the chain's workers are confronting the unbridled greed of their employers in such an open way for the first time. The Stop and Shop stores are among many owned by the Dutch conglomerate Ahold Delhaize that reported $2 billion in profits in 2018.

Despite such profits, and despite the fact that Stop and Shop is far and away the dominant grocery store chain in New England (S&S also owns stores in New York and New Jersey that are covered by a different contract and thus not on strike), Ahold is demanding significant givebacks. The cuts in pensions and health coverage particularly rankle the strikers; the company's current demands, for example, include a fourfold increase in the amount workers will have to pay in co-payments for doctor's visits.

Minimum Wage Pay for New Workers

Picketers expressed a mix of astonishment and anger that a massive company that is doing so well would utterly refuse to share any portion of that wealth and instead demand significant givebacks. New hires, all of whom are part-time, start at $10.10 an hour. Stop and Shop has consciously cut the number of full-time positions, and stipulations that the company forced through in previous contracts make accepting a full-time promotion far less attractive than it could be.

At the picket line outside one of the stores in Fairfield, striking worker Rafael Quiles proclaimed that it takes years before you can even think about getting a full-time position. And if you do get a full-time position, the company had the right to transfer you to any store in the state that it wants to. He and others said the company does precisely that in order to discourage others from seeking full-time positions.

Many people who accepted full-time jobs went back to part-time a short while later because they didn't want to be moved to a store far away. That was the experience of Gin Palladino, a ten-year veteran who lived just a few blocks from the store where she worked. She proclaimed she would rather work part-time at her old store than have to travel a long distance to work full-time.

Kizzy Lewis is a full-timer who has worked in 12 stores in her 25 years at Stop and Shop. "They had me working as far away as Stamford and at other stores all over Fairfield County," she said. "After all these years, I hope this is my last one." Lewis also ridiculed the gas allotment the company pays for those it transfers, pointing out that the worker is responsible for the first 15 miles both to and from work.

Workers Struggling Amidst Fabulous Wealth

For many workers, hourly wages that are equal to or just a little above the federal minimum wage do not go far. Consider that Fairfield County is one of the wealthiest and most expensive areas in the country, where the contrast between the Super Rich who live in places like New Canaan and Greenwich and workers at Stop and Shop couldn't be starker. A number of strikers live in Bridgeport, the least expensive housing market in the area, but even rents in Bridgeport can be as high as $1,000 a month for a one-bedroom apartment. For people making $10.10 per hour, that is out of reach. People spoke of co-workers well into their 20s who live with their parents or other family members because they cannot afford to live on their own.

As with so many workers in the United States today, some of the strikers have more than one job. One man on the picket line said he averages 65 hours a week between his two jobs and is still barely making ends meet. A woman striker said she's negotiating with her boss at her other job about getting more hours if the strike lasts.

It's important that the Stop and Shop strikers win, just as it was important that the tens of thousands of teachers around the country won their strikes in the last year. It's also important, though, that workers, their supporters and allies and union staffers who are so inclined take a long, harsh look at the state of things. The Stop and Shop workers' strike is essentially defensive; they are resisting the company's attempts at more takebacks, while the union, according to workers, is putting forward few demands of their own. So no noteworthy wage increases or other improvements await them even if they score a complete victory. In the short term at minimum, their lives will continue to get harder.

Winning and Seeds of Greater Possibilities

There are, however, seeds of greater possibilities and future victories in the strength and solidarity the workers are experiencing in their strike. By virtually every account, including those by sources generally hostile to workers, the Stop and Shop strike has been overwhelmingly successful. The company is losing money in a big way, for one, and the hard line it has drawn has raised the awareness of many strikers: about their relationship to their employers, about the power of collective action, about the power of an entire workforce withdrawing its labor, about how perilous life in the 21st century United States has become for the working class.

Speaking about the experience of the strike thus far, one worker said the following: "Most of us like our jobs because we have so many regular customers who make it feel like a community, and they far outnumber the customers who make our lives difficult. What really makes it hard to like your job is not the customers who give you a bad time but knowing that you're getting a bad deal from the company. The pay is too low, the benefits aren't enough, working on weekends is mandatory, all that stuff. And then to see that they want to cut our pensions even further, make us pay more if we go to the doctor, cut Sunday premium pay and give us nothing in return for all that ... it's too much. All these people you see on this picket line and all the other picket lines at all the other Stop and Shop stores, none of them is ever going to forget this." (Author inverview on the picket line)

Asked if he meant the togetherness of the strikers or the conduct of the company, he said simply, "Both."

Perhaps one big lesson that can reverberate far and wide beyond Stop and Shop is the power of the strike. After decades where the number of strikes dwindled to a pitifully small number, accompanied by a barrage of negativity from media and political elites, workers are beginning to see that a well-planned strike is one of the most effective ways to fight back. That's true of teachers, nurses and other healthcare workers, electrical workers at Wabtec in Pennsylvania and grocery store workers throughout New England. Equally large challenges will be to bring that fighting spirit and solidarity into the workplace and the union hall as well as for workers from a variety of workplaces both union and non-union to build organizations of mutual support, where they can also strategize about how to build a different kind of society.

6. People On the Job

The Sand Hogs Set the Foundation for the Bulkeley Bridge

We might drive over the Bulkeley Bridge every day, but we seldom think about the sweat and toil it took to produce the link between Hartford and East Hartford. Even those who think they know the history of the bridge's construction probably aren't aware of the story of the Black workers who risked their lives for low pay to create the first permanent stone structure over the Connecticut River.

A wooden covered bridge spanned the river at the Bulkeley site beginning in 1818. After the bridge burned down in 1895, it took eight years before an official report recommended a new overpass to take its place. In the meantime, temporary bridges and ferries linked the two towns. Bridge construction began in 1904; the span was completed three years later and dedicated in 1908. It was first called the Hartford Bridge, and later named to commemorate Morgan Bulkeley, who, in addition to serving as Hartford's mayor, Connecticut's governor, and a US senator, had been the head of the Commission that oversaw the bridge's construction.

Discrimination Factored into Job Pay and Risk

Digging the foundation of the bridge was the first order of business. This was the job of the sand hogs, as they were known. As bridges rose along the east coast, this dirty and dangerous work went first to Irish immigrants. But by the turn of the 20th century many of those sons of Erin had acquired skilled trade jobs. The work was passed on to Black workers, who occupied the lowest rung on the job ladder.

Although unions have existed for most skilled jobs almost since this country's founding, common laborers were not invited into the trade guilds. Black workers, no matter what their skill, were seldom organized into unions. A few exceptions, such as the Knights of Labor and the Industrial Workers of the World (IWW), stood out in the early years, welcoming all workers.

The bridge's foundation averaged 50 to 60 feet in depth. Enclosures, called caisson chambers, were built so that workers could dig in a dry space and adapt to the change in atmospheric pressure as they descended beneath the water's surface. Without the ability to slowly acclimate to the differences in pressure, workers would get the "bends" — a condition known as decompression sickness, caused when the body too quickly returns to the lower atmospheric pressure above water level.

Iron pipes carried forced air from engines on shore, along the bridge's footpath to the caissons. The work took place in 8-hour shifts around the clock, but even the strongest sand hog could only work a few hours at a time under the river. Considering the difficulty of the work, sand hogs were only paid $2.50 a day.

About 100 Black workers labored as sand hogs on the Bulkeley bridge. They were supposed to be paid every Monday at noon. But the contractor, McMullen, Weand and McDermott, failed to meet the paycheck deadline on a number of occasions. Non-payment for work was so common around this period that the Connecticut General Assembly passed a law requiring businesses to pay their workers on time or face penalties.

No Pay, No Work

One Monday in August, 1904, the sandhogs' pay envelopes once again failed to appear. At 4:00 pm, most of the 40 workers on second shift refused to go down the tunnels. Their spontaneous strike had begun. At midnight, they jeered the few workers who had gone down and made sure that work was halted on the third shift. They spent the night at the worksite, celebrating their new-found solidarity. That's when the police were called in and the workers were dispersed.

The strikers knew it wasn't a lack of funds causing the delay. "Those fellows in the office don't care how they do their work," said one striker, "the money is here all right, but they don't want to trouble themselves to make out the roll." At least one other striker felt that the real issue was how much they received for their labor. "We want $3 a day," a worker told the *Hartford Times.*

An alleged threat by the strikers to cut off the air supply to the scabs who crossed the picket line may have contributed to the speed with which the contractor responded to the sand hogs' pay demand. They got their money the next day, as did the white stone masons who had also been waiting.

When contacted about the uprising, one construction supervisor denied that there had been any concerted action by the Black workers at all. He told a reporter that an air engine had broken down and that's why work had been delayed. The sand hogs knew better.

The Life of a Factory: Bryant Electric

In its manufacturing heyday, Bridgeport had a number of industrial hubs. The area where Jenkins Valves, Underwood and several other factories stood in the general vicinity of Webster Bank Arena was one such hub. The section of Boston Avenue with the General Electric factory to the north and Remington Arms to the south was another, though those two factories were so large and employed so many workers that each could be considered a hub of its own. And then there was a stretch of the West Side running along both sides of the railroad viaduct from Iranistan Avenue to the point where Fairfield Avenue meets Railroad Avenue.

West Side Hub

Some of the factories that were once part of the West Side hub – United Pattern, Casco, Bassick, Dictaphone – still stand, though all are long empty. The American Bead Chain building still stands and now houses a charter school. Others like Hubbell and Bridgeport Organ have been demolished. Another that was demolished in the 1990s was Bryant Electric, long a division of the massive multinational Westinghouse Corporation and the largest of the West Side hub, both in terms of its 340,000 square feet and the number of workers it employed. In its history we can trace the trajectory of manufacturing in Bridgeport, from an apex that seemed like it would never end to decline and sometimes bitter demise.

Bryant

The Bryant Electric Company was founded on John Street in downtown Bridgeport in 1888. The company grew rapidly and moved three years later to its long-time location. With additions over the years, the factory was composed of 20 buildings bounded by State Street to the north, Hancock Avenue to the west and Railroad Avenue to the south. On the east, it stretched as far as Howard Avenue, with buildings zigzagging alongside residential homes on Organ Street.

Workers at Bryant made wiring devices, switches and electrical components – 12 devices in all in the beginning, a number that increased to over 4,000 by 1928. The company's founder, Waldo Bryant, sold a majority interest to Westinghouse in 1901, though he continued to run the company until 1927. Bryant Electric acquired several other companies in its early years and was Bridgeport's largest employer for a time: 700 people were working there in 1905 and 1,500 in 1915.

Difficulties of Factory Work

Factory work in the early 1900's was extremely difficult and often dangerous, and wages were low, even at prosperous companies like Bryant. Workers struck the plant a number of times over the years, with the first strike of note taking place in 1915. The strike was led by women assemblers not welcome in the American Federation of Labor's craft unions who demanded an eight-hour workday and overtime pay after 40 hours. After two weeks during which the plant was completely closed, the workers won their demands.

The UE

Workers gained additional strength on the job when they elected the United Electrical, Radio and Machine Workers of America (UE), one of the most radical affiliates of the Congress of Industrial Organizations (CIO), as their collective bargaining representative in the late 1930's. Significant gains in wages and benefits were won under the UE, and those gains were compounded during the boom years of the Second World War, when the company did a significant amount of production for the military.

Despite a postwar assault on the UE by business, government and top officials of the CIO that weakened it and other unions, especially after the UE was ousted from Bridgeport's massive GE plant, workers at Bryant continued to earn important improvements in working conditions and living standards. In an effort to address widespread unemployment in the Bridgeport area, the UE initiated a campaign in the mid-1950's for the 35-hour work week which it said would enable profitable companies like Bryant to hire more workers. Bryant and the rest of Bridgeport's business class ignored the campaign.

Capital Flight and Job Loss

Bryant's parent Westinghouse was among the corporations that adopted increasingly aggressive labor relations in the 1970s. That approach involved demanding givebacks in wages and benefits as well as the shift of production to low-wage areas. Despite ongoing objections by Bryant workers and the UE, objections that were eventually echoed by local elected officials, Westinghouse moved more and more Bryant jobs from Bridgeport to North Carolina, Puerto Rico and the Dominican Republic. Workers in Westinghouse factories in those locations were paid very low wages, benefits were minimal, and workers who engaged in any kind of collective action were subject to termination, with little recourse.

Bryant workers organized demonstrations against job loss as early as 1974. By 1976, when they participated in a brief nation-wide strike against Westinghouse, the factory's workforce was about 700, down from an all-time high of 1,700. The decline continued in the years that followed as capital flight and job loss spread through Bridgeport like a contagious disease. In the 1980s, Bridgeport Brass, Bullard, Jenkins, Bassick and other industrial mainstays closed their doors, while others laid off large numbers of workers who were never rehired.

Resistance

Resistance to this trend was higher among Bryant workers than at other shops. On January 13, 1986, they demonstrated at company headquarters on Sylvan Avenue demanding that Westinghouse maintain its production operations in Bridgeport. Carrying placards that read "Bryant Belongs in Bridgeport" and "Keep Bryant in Bridgeport," the workers called on the company to cease the transfer of production to low-wage, non-union plants. They also organized a march down State Street on April 12, 1986, demanding that Westinghouse commit to keeping Bryant open.

Workers from other area factories participated in these actions, as did community residents who understood the importance of good-paying jobs to the city's well-being. Owners and employees of restaurants, diners, bars and other businesses near the plant also supported these efforts, recognizing that their employment was directly linked to Bryant's. Those concerns proved entirely justified when neighborhood mainstays Junior's Restaurant, the Flyer Diner and others went out of business not long after Bryant closed.

With profits rising because of its abandonment of places like Bridgeport, Westinghouse announced in 1987 that it would close the Bryant plant the following year exactly 100 years after its founding. The UE, the 450 workers who remained and community supporters continued to rally and protest, but production ceased for good on April 22, 1988. The sprawling factory was demolished in 1996.

A Road Not Taken

One possible way the Bryant factory might have been kept open and the jobs saved that apparently was not considered in any serious way was a combined government-union-worker purchase of the plant from Westinghouse. Unlike many countries, there is little history of such efforts in the United States despite the obvious potential benefits. Government at all levels, virulently pro-business historically, had entered a particularly toxic pro-business stage by the 1980s, leaving no will at any level for such a project. In addition, American unions, including the more militant UE, had overwhelmingly ceded decision-making about production to management long before and were thus largely rudderless when creative militancy was most needed.

Whether such a government-union-worker venture would have succeeded is something we will never know. What we do know is that Bridgeport is the less for the fact that it was not at least attempted, and many of the ongoing problems the city confronts today trace in part to its loss of tens of thousands of good-paying working class jobs such as those at Bryant.

Profits Over Human Life: The L'Ambiance Catastrophe

The collapse of L'Ambiance Plaza in Bridgeport in 1987 was the worst construction accident in Connecticut history. Both the decision-making and the construction methods used were so flawed that it doesn't do justice to call what happened an "accident." Perhaps "negligent, completely avoidable disaster" is more accurate.

It happened at around 1:30 in the afternoon of a warm spring Friday, April 23. The project was a $17 million apartment building designed to rise 16 stories on Washington Avenue several blocks from downtown and just north of Route 8. Twenty-eight of the 69 workers at the site were killed and eleven others injured, four of whom were hospitalized.

L'Ambiance Plaza was a project with both state funding and private investment. As designed by T.P.M. Architects, it was to have had 218 studio, one-bedroom and two-bedroom apartment units. Half of the apartments were to have been rented at market rates and half at less-than market for low and moderate income residents. Construction on the project began in the summer of 1986 and was scheduled to be completed in December, 1987.

The developer, Delwood Development International of Florida, had hired T.P.M. International-Macombe of Darien as the project's general contractor. T.P.M was using a construction technique known as lift-slab, and it was this technique that has drawn much criticism. Lift-slab has frequently been considered the cause of the disaster. Compounding matters, some of the elementary precautions of an already risky process may have been skirted.

Fifteen Terrible Seconds
The steel framework was already in place and the work on April 23 involved putting huge concrete slabs that essentially serve as floors into place. Starting at the bottom, each slab was lifted into place by hydraulic lifts located at the top of each structural pillar of the framework. More than half of the slabs, or floors, were in place when the uppermost of them crashed down on the one below, creating a pancake effect.

Some working high up on the framework fell with the concrete as it collapsed downward. Others working on lower slabs or on the ground below were crushed by the concrete that crashed on top of them. Witnesses from nearby offices and homes and others driving in passing vehicles watched the catastrophe in disbelief. One estimated that the collapse took 15 seconds at most and likened it to pick-up sticks. Another said the edifice fell "like a deck of cards."

Frontline Workers Save Lives

Witnesses immediately joined with workers in rescue efforts. Before long, dozens of firefighters, police and EMTs were at the scene, and construction equipment of various kinds was used to move large chunks of concrete and steel rubble. Nine lifeless bodies were removed from the rubble by early evening; the other nineteen dead were unearthed in the days that followed. One survivor was found under rubble three hours after the collapse and was taken to an area hospital. Several of the other workers who were hospitalized had suffered serious injuries.

As family and friends mourned the dead, investigations began, including one by the National Bureau of Standards and another by the Occupational Safety and Health Administration. Families of those killed and some of the injured received a $41 million financial settlement in a wide-ranging agreement reached in November 1988. Various reports on the cause of the disaster mentioned failures in the lifting system and acts of omission by numerous parties, but no criminal charges were ever brought.

A memorial statue with the names of the 28 dead stands on the spot of the disaster. Families of the victims and government and union officials hold a ceremony at the site each April 23. The lift-slab technique was banned in the aftermath of the tragedy, but only in Connecticut, and only there until 1994. It remains widely used today.

7. African Americans: Abolitionists, Civil War and Reconstruction

The Eastons

In September, 1983, the vital statistics office of the City of Hartford received a letter from a researcher inquiring about Hosea Easton, a former resident who had gained worldwide acclaim as a musician and actor. Helen Armstead Johnson wanted more information on this African American musician, who was supposed to have been born in 1854 in the city.

Johnson had traveled around the world collecting history on African-American stage performers. It was on a trip to Australia that she learned about Easton and his celebrated status in that country and the Pacific Rim.

The Hartford government records office replied that it could not find any such person.

In fact, Hosea Easton was the son of a well-respected citizen and the grandson of the well-known intellectual, abolitionist and author Reverend Hosea Easton, the original pastor of Hartford's first Black Church.

Reverend Hosea Easton, Intellectual and Activist (September 1, 1798 – July 6, 1837)

The Eastons were one of New England's most notable 19th century African American families. Their lineage can be traced back to the 1690s. They took their surname from Nicholas Easton, a slaveholder and founder of Providence, Rhode Island, and were emancipated by his relatives, who had joined the Quaker faith. Caesar Easton became a landowner who fought off a series of challenges by white men attempting to claim his property as their own. His son James Easton moved the family to eastern Massachusetts and was active in the early movement for Black freedom.

After their emancipation, the Eastons migrated to North Bridgewater (now Brockton) near a Wampanoag village in Massachusetts. James and Sarah Dunbar Easton were the parents of seven children, including Hosea Easton, who was born in Middleborough on September 1, 1798.

James, a veteran of the American Revolutionary War, possessed Native American heritage. He was a blacksmith and ironworker who sold industrial iron to big Boston construction projects. He opened an academic and trade school for Black youth, which Hosea attended in 1816. Hosea married in the 1820's to Louisa Matrick, became a minister and gained a reputation as an effective abolitionist agitator.

Hosea learned about courage and activism when he was only thirteen years old. The Congregational church the Easton family attended built a "Negro

95

porch," as it was called, in the back of the church. All Black members of the congregation were required to sit there during services. James and Sarah Easton refused. The family continued to sit on the main floor of the church until they were physically removed.

At another [Baptist] church, James Easton purchased a pew for his family from a sympathetic white member. The Eastons continued to occupy the pew against the wishes of church officials and members. The family came one Sunday to find that the pew had been painted with tar. The undaunted James Easton, his wife, Sarah, and their seven children responded by returning the following Sunday with their own chairs. This conflict continued until the Eastons were completely barred from the church.

This struggle went on for 40 years. After James' death, Hosea's mother Sarah was kicked out of her church in 1832 for writing a "very unbecoming letter" to the Elders at the East Stoughton Baptist Church in protest of her family's treatment.

As a child, the Reverend Hosea Easton engaged in at least five acts of civil disobedience, until he was a teenager. He and his family were the first African Americans known to have engaged in sit-ins for racial justice.

Reverend Hosea really came to public attention in 1828 at the age of 30 with a Thanksgiving Day address in Providence attacking racism and slavery.

It was a frank, explicit and angry condemnation of the brutalities of slavery, mixed with the call for spiritual uplift of Black people. In this sermon he also criticized the African Colonization Society, which was a "diabolical pursuit … where they will steal the sons of Africa … bring them to America, keep them in bondage for centuries … then transport them back to Africa by which means America gets all her drudgery done at little expense." (Hosea Easton et. al., *To Heal the Scourge of Prejudice: The Life and Writings of Hosea Easton*)

Rev. Easton continued to write about slavery and broader questions of racism. His major work was "A treatise on the intellectual character, and civil and political condition, of the colored people of the United States and the prejudice exercised towards them," published in March, 1837.

In 1833 Easton moved from Massachusetts to Hartford with Louisa and their son Sampson. He became the first pastor of Talcott Street Congregational Church. Beginning on June 8, 1835 for a three-day period, white crowds harassed and beat African Americans on Front and Talcott Streets and destroyed a number of Black dwellings. In 1836 the Colored Methodist Episcopal Church (Hartford's second Black church) was burned down. The cause of this was apparently the Black men's suffrage meeting near Talcott, led by James Mars, a church deacon and former enslaved man born in Connecticut.

Two months later in October,1835 a broadside was printed and distributed throughout Hartford condemning abolition, blasting anti-slavery forces for all the country's woes, upholding free commerce with slaveholders, and promoting "states' rights," the coded term meant to obscure the racism of slavery and its apologists.

During the preceding years, racist violence had dramatically increased across the North. There had been deadly white riots in Cincinnati, Boston, New York, and Pittsburgh.

In 1837, shortly before his premature death, Rev. Easton described the deadly effects of slavery, which "renders whites a compound of all evil, of all the corrupt passions of the heart…a participant in all the purposes of the wicked one … the very essence of hell." Only immediate abolition could save the souls of slave apologists," Easton declared. (Hosea Easton, *To Heal the Scourge of Prejudice,* op.cit.*)*

Rev. Hosea Easton died prematurely on July 6 1837, at 38 years of age. His father died at age 76 and his mother at 73. His cause of death is not known. Yet he might have written his own terminal diagnosis in the Treatise:

"The effect of these discouragements are every where manifest among the colored people. I will venture to say, from my own experience and observation, that hundreds of them come to an untimely grave, by no other disease than … oppression." (Hosea Easton, Hosea, *To Heal the Scourge of Prejudice,* op.cit.)

Sampson Easton, A Courageous and Honorable Life (1829 – ?)

Sampson Easton, the son of Hosea and Louise, was born in 1829, and moved to Hartford with them. He was named after his maternal great-grandfather, Sampson Dunbar of Massachusetts who died in 1804 at 83 years of age.

Sampson was not a famous man, unlike his father and other relatives (or, indeed, his own son). But there are three incidents that show the same courage and anti-slavery politics that he learned from his parents.

In the 1860 Hartford census, Sampson (age 30) and his wife Louisa (31) lived with their three children: Hosea (11), Ellen (7) and Caroline (5). At the same location, five boarders, all male aged 3 to 49, also resided.

In 1858 Sam Easton attempted to save "Aunt Mary" Robinson, a longtime friend, from being killed by her husband Ben. They and others were at a small party at the Robinsons' dwelling, playing music and dancing. Ben Robinson, who was drunk and abusive toward his wife, became angered that she was dancing with Sampson. (Mary and Sampson had known each other since childhood, and had attended school at Rev. Hosea Easton's church). By all accounts, Sampson tried to peacefully de-escalate the situation, even after Ben assaulted him. Sampson and friends started to leave, when Ben Robinson stabbed Mary Robinson many times. Sampson put himself in the middle of the attack and was also wounded. Mary Robinson died; Ben Robinson was sent to prison.

Sampson Easton was an entrepreneur. He was listed as a livery driver and a hack driver in 1858 and 1859. He also owned the Easton Academy of Music on Commerce Street in 1860, where he crafted, repaired, and played banjos, fiddles, and possibly other musical instruments. This may have been where his dance hall was also located.

In April, 1861, a Mrs. Thomas Flaherty attempted to commit suicide by jumping off the railroad bridge into the Connecticut River. Sampson dove in the cold river and rescued her with some difficulty. He brought her to shore. She rewarded him with a slap in the face. There is no evidence that the two knew each other; this was likely a spur of the moment decision on Sampson's part, exemplifying his character and personal courage.

Maybe the moment for which Sam Easton should be most remembered occurred on December 2, 1859. A dance was being held on State House square, sponsored by Engine No. 5 of the Hartford Fire Department. At about 2:00 AM on Saturday morning, some of the dancers saw a light emanating from the cupola of the State House. They called on police officer Waters, who climbed to the belfry and apprehended Sampson Easton, "a colored citizen of this city" as described by the *Hartford Courant,* and his white companion from New Haven, Charles Boyle.

But Easton and Boyle had completed their objective, "draping the figure of Justice upon the cupola with sable fabric, in view of the execution that was to take place in Charlottesville, Virginia during the day." The condemned man was Connecticut-born John Brown, the white abolitionist who electrified the nation with his October raid on the government arsenal at Harpers Ferry, Virginia. Brown visited Hartford in 1857, where he asked the crowd to financially support his cause. There is no way to know for sure that Sampson heard Brown speak, but the abolitionist's words most likely influenced the 28-year old Hartford man.

The pro-slavery Democrats of the time insisted Sampson had been hired by a Republican to perform the symbolic action, but Easton denied it. He sent a note to the daily newspapers rejecting the accusation that he had been put up to the symbolic draping of Madame Justice.

Easton and Boyle spent the night in the Hartford jail while authorities tried to figure out how to charge them. It was decided that the two "could be charged with neither insurrection nor resurrection," and were released at noon, less than an hour after John Brown was hanged.

Hosea Easton, Actor, Musical Virtuoso, Prince of the Banjoists (March 6, 1849- 1899)

Arguably the most well-known of the Eastons was Sampson's son Hosea, the namesake of both Rev. Easton and Sampson's younger brother. He was born to twenty-year old Louisa Easton in 1849. At some point he must have picked up one of the banjos his father Sampson made, and he was good at it. Really good.

Minstrel shows and other variety acts frequently visited at the Roberts Opera House and Allyn Hall, both venues that were a short walk from Hosea's neighborhood. Young Hosea likely saw some of these performances. The famous Georgia Minstrels were frequent performers in Hartford. They featured, among others, "Dick Little, the greatest banjoist living."

In 1866 the Georgia Minstrels advertised "No Burnt Cork Here" in their newspaper ads, boasting that they had replaced the white performers who sang and played in blackface since the 1830s. The white blackface acts perpetuated the offensive stereotype that deliberately corrupted the public image of African Americans among the country's white citizens. Unfortunately, the troupe's owner also advertised the musicians as "the great slave troupe," although most, if not all, of the performers were freedmen and women.

By 1875, the Georgia Minstrels were endorsed by none other than the abolitionist William Lloyd Garrison, who according to an advertisement was quoted as saying: "No imputation can be brought against them of presenting anything offensive to the eye or ear." And the next year, the Georgia troupe was boasting that they were "commended by Wm. Lloyd Garrison, Oliver Wendell Holmes, PT Barnum, etc."

Minstrelsy is historically weighted with negative baggage, and rightly so. This popular form of entertainment arose in part from the fascination white people had with the African American experience. Blackface minstrel shows featured white men in grotesque makeup, singing and dancing with an exaggerated parody of Black performers. In fact, some white audiences had never even seen Black musicians or actors. The effect only enhanced white racism and widened the gulf between the races. As the distinguished African American artist Jacob Lawrence explained: "Minstrels were whites copying Blacks who copied whites copying Blacks."

Yet the musical genre fostered authentic jubilee music (spirituals), ragtime and ultimately jazz, all of which entered into the wider public culture. And while Black minstrels played into the images of white audiences, they also subverted those images. As Amiri Baraka wrote, "in one sense the colored minstrel was poking fun at himself, and in another probably more profound sense he was poking fun at the white men."

Hosea Easton in Australia

Nowhere was this paradox more apparent than the traveling minstrel shows that sought out venues beyond the United States.

By the time he was twenty-seven years old, Hosea Easton left Hartford and arrived at Hobart, Australia as a member of the Georgia Minstrels, still at the height of their popularity. They performed along the Pacific circuit, especially in Australia, New Zealand, and China. Hosea was singled out by a *Sydney Mail* reviewer who wrote that "he draws considerably on theology and temperance for his witticisms."

Hosea also performed with groups such as the Mastodon Minstrels in Hong Kong. The various American shows were popular, but for a variety of reasons (mostly the performers not getting paid, competition between troupes who took the same names, and outright racism of owners and promoters), there was little job security and frequent turnover.

He was lucky to hook up with C.B. Hicks, the African American impresario and leader of the "Original Georgia Minstrels." Hicks was described as possessing a capable management style and engaged in "combative efforts to maintain independence from the white theatrical establishment."

Quickly, Hosea became an audience favorite who entertained with "clever banjo solos riffed on popular airs" which "earned frequent encores." Crowds were huge, and special trains were scheduled to transport fans into cities from the outlying countryside.

At the beginning of every performance, Hicks addressed the audience and focused the show's narrative. He spoke about the African American fight for freedom and the troupe's history. Most of the time this context was welcomed. But occasionally a newspaper critic would complain that the public had paid admission to be entertained, not "to sympathize with their condition."

In mid-1878 Hicks teamed up with a dramatic company and performed the internationally acclaimed *Uncle Tom's Cabin*. Hosea Easton played the title role, becoming the first African American to play Tom in the Southern hemisphere. It ran for 12 weeks to sold-out audiences in Melbourne. Hosea expanded to other roles, including in a theatrical performance of *Robinson Crusoe*. He eventually formed his own ensemble, the Easton Uncle Tom Company, which toured with other racially integrated dramatic and musical acts.

Hosea Easton spent the rest of his life in Australia, an extraordinarily beloved figure, until his death in 1899. When he was hospitalized, other performers staged a benefit concert to help pay his medical costs. When he died of cancer, his large funeral became a parade of fans and other musicians who marched with his casket down the street to the cemetery.

Virtually unknown in his country today, Hosea Easton became a legend on the other side of the world.

The End of Slavery in Connecticut

In 1784, as the American Revolution drew to a close, the new government of Connecticut passed the Gradual Abolition Act to address the issue of slavery in the state. The law freed none of the approximately 3,000 slaves in Connecticut, but rather confined itself to the fate of future individuals born into servitude–the children of slaves–by stating that all such individuals born after March 1, 1784, "shall be free" upon reaching the age of 25.

Ten years after passage of the Gradual Abolition Act, the state legislature considered and rejected a bill (forthrightly entitled An Act for the Abolition of Slavery in this State, and to Provide for the Education and Maintenance of Such as Shall be Emancipated Thereby) that called for the immediate outlawing of slavery in the state. As a result, slavery continued in Connecticut until 1848.

Nancy Jackson

In 1837, when there were approximately 25 slaves in Connecticut, a woman living in Hartford named Nancy Jackson petitioned the state for her freedom, claiming she was "illegally confined" by James Bulloch, a slaveowner from Georgia who lived approximately half the year in Connecticut. Bulloch brought Jackson, a slave born on his plantation in Georgia, to Hartford in 1835. Two years later, Jackson's claim of freedom cited the Nonimportation Act, a state law passed in 1774. The law, the full name of which was the "Act for Prohibiting the Importation of Indian, Negro or Molatto Slaves," stated that no slave could be "bought or imported" to be "disposed of, left or sold" within Connecticut.

Much of Jackson's case hinged on interpretations of the simple word "left." Bulloch claimed he was only in Hartford temporarily and intended to return to Georgia with Jackson, and therefore Jackson had not been brought to Connecticut to be "left." Jackson's counsel claimed that she had indeed been "left" in that she had lived in the state for two years consecutively, with no end in sight, while Bulloch traveled back and forth between Connecticut and Georgia.

Over the course of their deliberations, the Connecticut Supreme Court ruled out two possible interpretations of the act and its wording. First, they discarded the notion that the slave must be left permanently in the state in order to meet the law's intent. That interpretation would have made it possible for a slaveowner to bring a slave to the state with no time limit whatsoever on when the owner and slave might leave to return from whence they came.

The court also rejected a scenario where a slave might claim freedom during a temporary stopover in the state. The justices viewed the granting of freedom in such cases as a possible affront to slave states and slaveowners who, the court asserted, had the right to travel through Connecticut without risk to their property, even if that property consisted of human beings.

The Court Finds For Jackson

By a 3-to-2 decision, the court eventually found for Nancy Jackson, setting her free. The two justices in the minority interpreted the law to apply only to permanent residents of the state, as opposed to temporary residents such as Bulloch. The majority, however, opined that the law did not provide for slaves to be brought to Connecticut "for any time their owners choose." To find for Bulloch, they wrote, allowed someone to "go abroad and hire slaves and bring them to labour in the state," reinvigorating slavery in Connecticut.

A year after the Jackson decision, in 1838, the Connecticut legislature increased the rights of Blacks identified as fugitives. Connecticut did not abolish slavery, however, until 1848, when approximately six slaves remained in the state, including 74-year old Nancy Toney of Windsor. Study of the matter offers only incomplete records, but Toney may have been the last slave in Connecticut when she died on December 19, 1857, at the age of 83.

Blacksmith Isaac Glasko
Challenges the State Constitution

Isaac Glasko was born in Rhode Island in 1776. Accounts about his parents, Jacob and Martha Glasko, are sketchy, but both were apparently of mixed African American and Native American heritage. Some accounts indicate they may have been slaves in colonial Rhode Island who had bought their way out of slavery by the time Isaac was born. In a society where race is highly charged, the Glaskos were considered Black, as was Isaac.

To Connecticut

When Isaac was still a boy, the Glasko family moved to North Uxbridge, Massachusetts. He went to work as a blacksmith as a young man and married a local woman, Lucy Brayton.

Isaac, his father and his brother George, a shoemaker, did well in their various trades, and in 1806 the three bought land in Griswold in southeastern Connecticut and moved there. Located near the Pachaug River, Griswold is close by the border with Rhode Island, 17 miles inland from the point where the Atlantic Ocean, Long Island Sound and Block Island Sound meet.

In 1806 it had a population of about 1,800. The plot of land that Isaac purchased from local resident Alexander Stewart included a house where he and Lucy lived for the rest of their lives. In what proved to be a very wise move, Isaac had included in the land deal access rights to water power from the Pachaug River where a dam served a mill Stewart owned.

While his brother George went into the shoemaking business with William Kinne, a relative of Stewart's, Isaac set up a forge on his property and established a blacksmithing business. In his early years in Griswold, Isaac's customers were mostly local farmers for whom he produced spades, axes, hoes and other tools.

He and Lucy had several children including Isaac, Jr., who became a blacksmith and worked for many years with his father. They also had a daughter, Eliza, who attended the school in Canterbury established by Prudence Crandall that is thought to be the first integrated school in the United States.

Business Expansion

Once he was firmly established, Glasko expanded his business by selling to people employed in and around New London in the whaling industry. He manufactured lances, mincing knives, harpoons and other metal tools used by

103

whalers, and his reputation as an expert blacksmith grew. He also did a brisk business with shipbuilders for whom he produced chains, anchors and other metal accouterments. During this period, Glasko had up to ten people working for him in his forge.

The water access rights Glasko had included in his land purchase proved important to the success of his business, as he made and used a giant trip hammer in his forge that was powered by water directed from the Pachaug River to a water wheel in the shop. This set-up enabled Glasko to make large tools he might not have been able to make otherwise, and it allowed him to do many jobs more quickly and with less physical exertion.

Challenge to the Connecticut Constitution

In 1823, Glasko and long-time friend and neighbor Pero Moody unsuccessfully petitioned the Connecticut General Assembly for an exemption from state taxation because, as Blacks, they were barred by law from voting. The petition was rejected, and it was not until 1870 that Black people in Connecticut won the right to vote. Still, Glasko's efforts resonated among Americans of all colors. His house and the grave where he's buried have become popular stops for those honoring African-American history.

Later Years

For reasons not entirely known, Glasko's blacksmithing business eventually went into decline and he ended up having to declare bankruptcy. He continued working his trade, however, and remained a well-respected resident of Griswold, so much so that the section of the town where he, his father and brother lived became known as Glasko. Because of a bureaucratic error made when a post office was opened in the hamlet some years after his death, however, the spelling of the name of the area has been known since as Glasgo. The misspelling notwithstanding, there is no question that the word traces back directly to Isaac's name.

Glasko died in 1861 and was buried in the Kinne Burying Ground there alongside his wife Lucy, who died in 1849.

Speaking Under an Open Sky: Frederick Douglass

The great abolitionist Frederick Douglass had significant ties to Connecticut. He visited Hartford many times, spoke to appreciative crowds, and dined with elected officials. Douglass had his portrait taken by a local photographer and his autobiography was published in 1882 by Hartford's Park Publishing Company. *The Life and Times of Frederick Douglass* became so popular it went through four printings. Hartford's Reverend James Pennington, himself a fugitive from "slave justice," even officiated Douglass's wedding in Philadelphia. Douglass had not always been so popular in this state, however, and today his Connecticut presence has faded.

Frederick Douglass Escapes Slavery

In 1838 Douglass escaped from slavery in Maryland after knocking down the brutal "slave breaker" Edward Covey in self-defense. Douglass fled to the relative safety of New Bedford, Massachusetts. After a series of jobs (and a life spent constantly looking over his shoulder), he began speaking publicly against slavery alongside well-known abolitionists such as William Lloyd Garrison.

During an 1845 trip to England and Ireland aboard a Cunard steamship, the ship's captain asked Douglass to speak on the promenade deck. No sooner had Douglass begun than a hostile "Connecticut Yankee," who bragged he owned many slaves, began heckling him. Southern passengers then chimed in and a fight broke out with Douglass supporters. The ship's captain ended the melee by ordering three sets of chains prepared for the instigators. The captain revealed that he, too, once owned slaves, but due to the efforts of abolitionists like Douglass, he had freed them.

Frederick Douglass did not find his first trip to Hartford very welcoming. He and his comrades "found several towns in which people closed their doors and refused to entertain the [idea of assisting them]," he wrote in *Life and Times*. "Notably among these towns were Hartford, Conn., and Grafton Mass. In the former [we] determined to hold our meetings under the open sky, which we did in a little court under the eaves of the 'sanctuary' ministered unto by the Rev. Dr. [Joel] Hawes, with much satisfaction to ourselves and I think great advantage to our cause." The site of this speech was the First Congregational Church of Hartford.

As time went on and the pro- and anti-slavery debate sharpened, Frederick

Douglass gained greater popularity. In October, 1854 he was in Chicago to rebut the pro-slavery rhetoric of Stephen A. Douglas. An anti-slavery Hartford newspaper reported on the visit, exclaiming "the Black Douglass against the White one! Who can doubt as to the result!" The senator from Illinois, nicknamed "the little giant," later debated Abraham Lincoln in 1858 and then lost the 1860 presidential election to him.

Connecticut Denies Blacks the Right to Vote

After the Union victory in the Civil War, the Black freedom struggle continued. In 1865 Connecticut voters overwhelmingly rejected giving African Americans the right to vote. Just one town, Meriden, supported voting rights for Black people in that referendum. Frederick Douglass went on to address the people of Meriden in 1868. Despite racist treatment by Steven Ives, the landlord of the Meriden House where Douglass stayed, the speech was very well received.

Connecticut's struggle with much of its pro-slavery past remains a topic of controversy to this day. Ironically, present-day Hartford has a memorial plaque commemorating a speech by Stephen Douglas at the corner of Main and Pearl Streets. A permanent memorial to Frederick Douglass was finally established in 2017, on the site of his first Hartford speech.

The Fugitive and the Hero

The steamship Hero made its way up the Connecticut River. It was October 1, 1850. Two men with different purposes were aboard the vessel. The first was a Black man who had escaped slavery and was now working on the steamer. The second was the fugitive's owner, determined to get him back. Waiting on the Hartford docks were slave catchers, ready to help the owner when the ship reached port.

Slave hunting had always been a profitable business. The U.S. Constitution specifically required states the return of escaped "persons held to service or labor." The government passed two laws to enforce this provision, first in 1793, and then the infamous Fugitive Slave Act.

This act was part of the Compromise of 1850, a desperate measure to keep the country together. Brokered by northern politicians, the "compromise" permitted slavery to exist in some new states and gave vigorous federal support to slave owners who demanded the return of their property.

Approved less than a month before the Hero was traveling up river, the Fugitive Slave Act required local officials in every state to assist in the capture of runaways and get paid for their efforts. Any citizen who didn't help out – or worse, actually aided a fugitive – could be fined and imprisoned. In addition, the alleged slave had no legal right to protest his or her capture. The word of an aggrieved owner in court was enough.

A local anti-slavery newspaper took notice of the slave hunters hanging around the Hartford docks just before the Hero was to arrive. The *Republican* was published weekly by J.D. Baldwin from his office at 20 State Street, a short walk from the river. In the pages of his paper, Baldwin taunted the men trying to profit from slavery:

"Slave hunters made their appearance in Hartford … It was noticed that they paid particular attention to the steamer Hero which had just arrived from New York. Nice boat; isn't she, Messers. Slave Hunters?" (Steve Thornton, A Shoeleather History Online, 1/22/2023). Baldwin knew that the escapee had secretly left the steamer down river at East Haddam with the help of local abolitionists.

Baldwin called the new slave law "kidnapping made easy." He wrote that the legislation "delivers every colored person to the mercy of any kidnapper who may see fit to claim him as a 'fugitive'."

The fugitive joined with four other fugitives and all five were then spirited away to Canada where, as Baldwin later wrote, "man-stealing is not lawful."

The ABC of Freedom: Reconstruction

After the American Civil War, a handful of courageous Hartford volunteers took part in a brief but critical moment that held a promise of healing the nation. One of those brave souls was Rebecca Primus, a member of the Talcott Street (now Faith) Congregational Church.

Reconstruction was a far-reaching federal project that actually became law before the war's 1865 conclusion, despite fierce political opposition and woefully inadequate funding. But it couldn't have accomplished what it did without the efforts of thousands of Northern citizens, especially teachers.

From 1865 to 1872, the Freedmen's Bureau operated as Reconstruction's imperfect instrument of liberation. The Constitution's Thirteenth Amendment outlawed slavery and the Fourteenth Amendment declared that "all persons born or naturalized in the United States" were citizens. The Bureau mission was to rebuild the South for the four million African Americans who just achieved freedom from slavery.

Initially promoted by President Abraham Lincoln, the federal Bureau had the enormous task of feeding, educating and providing medical care for those millions who were, for all intents and purposes, impoverished immigrants in their own country.

Historian Howard Zinn describes Reconstruction as the "brief period after the Civil War in which southern Negroes voted, elected blacks to state legislatures and to Congress, introduced free and racially mixed public education to the South."

Hartford Steps Up

To supplement the Bureau's effectiveness, Hartford advocates established their own volunteer Freedmen's Aid Society in the spring of 1865. "The old New England doctrine that education makes Freedom safe is as true in South Carolina as it is in Connecticut," declared the *Hartford Courant.*

"The New England Freedmen's Aid Society, the first one of its kind, [is] building school houses, providing subsistence to teachers, and buying school books," the *Courant* continued. Mehitible (Hettie) Primus, Rebecca's mother, was the only African American on the Society's board, and had been a founder of Talcott Street Church.

The Hartford Aid office was situated in the North Baptist church (which once stood at Main and Talcott Streets). Volunteers collected financial and material donations. They also repaired and sewed clothes for shipment to the South. Many of the donations came from Hartford's Black families, according to a Society report.

Racist Reaction

A furious backlash ensued against this progress. The white Southern elite engaged in widespread terror against the Black population that was struggling to establish itself after two centuries of slavery.

This reactionary attitude carried into Connecticut, supported by an entire political party: the Democrats. At their 1869 state convention, the party's leaders accused radical Republicans of "hatred and revenge," primarily because they insisted on the full franchise for freedmen of the South.

These "copperheads" criticized Black freedom fighters who wanted to "deprive the states of the Union of their right to prescribe the terms and conditions of the suffrage of their own citizens." They were attempting to "introduce a new class of voters in the country to the injury of all other voters," the Dems warned. The old "states rights" argument, it seems, has never lost its power to enable Black disenfranchisement and oppression.

In the face of such opposition, the national Freedmen's Bureau was instrumental in building thousands of schools for 90,000 Black children and adults. These were the first Southern public schools for former slaves, "where negroes could learn the ABC of freedom," as one Hartford booster put it. The Bureau services were a lifeline for poor whites as well.

Northern politicians and industrialists saw the end of the war as an opportunity to consolidate their dreams of empire. "Nothing is so profitable as Justice," one newspaper shrewdly noted. Emancipation tipped the balance of Congressional power away from the old South, and provided cheap (non-union) labor for business. This combination of money and power inevitably spawned ruthless robber barons, a rich, powerful upper class and the start of the "Gilded Age."

Hartford's Bravest

Rebecca Primus was the daughter of Holbridge and Hettie Primus, "respectable colored citizen[s] of Hartford." The local Society was required to pay $500 a year (about $7,500 today) to support Rebecca and each teacher it sent to Southern towns. By 1866, city volunteers had collected the current equivalent of $20,000. Rebecca was also required to pass a test by the New England Freedmen's Aid Society (the regional umbrella group) to determine her competence to teach.

In her report to Hartford, Rebecca noted at her assignment in Royal Oak, Maryland:

"The children behave well during school hours, are attentive to their lessons and are neatly and comfortably clad... We are led to hope, therefore that many liberal hands will open to these humble aspirants for learning, and that, another year, Hartford will send southward double its present number of teachers." (Jasmine Farrah Griffin, *Beloved Sisters and Loving Friends: Letters from Rebecca Primus and Addie Brown of Hartford, Connecticut*)

Another Hartford-sponsored teacher, Harriet Hamilton, found a very different atmosphere at her Washington, D.C. assignment:

"White children... inherit the prejudices of their enlightened parents, for they are the systematic persecutors of the studiously inclined colored students. Students at a large nearby white school keep up relentlessly the 'war of the races'." (Steve Thornton, A Shoeleather History Online, 10/29/18)

Most likely, the unrelenting harassment by white neighbors led to Hamilton's decision to leave the school after one year.

Despite Southern hostility, by 1867 Hartford was funding five teachers and providing support for freedmen to relocate in the Hartford area. Joining Harriet Hamilton in Washington were Rebecca Elwell; Carrie Loomis, who taught in Columbia, South Carolina, and James E. Lazenby, who opened a school in Virginia, his home state.

The hiring of Lazenby, a white Virginian, was unique in several ways. Originally working as a teacher of white students, he then served as a lieutenant in the Confederate army's 11th Virginia Infantry. Thousands of Southern teachers were desperate for work after the war; almost all pledged their allegiance to the republic to get a job. Yet as few as a dozen of them desired to teach Black students, according to historian Ronald E. Butchart.

According to the publication *American Freedmen* (November, 1866), James Lazenby established a school in the Emmaus Post Office of Bedford County, Virginia. There he was aided by his daughter; together they expected to teach 100 students a year.

End of an Era

By 1877, the Reconstruction experiment was over. Many Northerners suffered from "compassion fatigue." Some political leaders who had sided with anti-slavery forces (but not with radical abolitionists) questioned whether African Americans could govern themselves.

In April, 1877, President Rutherford B. Hayes removed the last federal troops from Southern states, ending crucial defense for freedom efforts. Critics deemed Reconstruction a failure.

Southern racists mounted an effective propaganda war to help them recover political power: "carpetbaggers" were Northern meddlers; "scalawags" were moderate Southerners (and usually, 'poor white trash' who had nothing to gain by the return of the wealthy hierarchy); "mongrels" were emancipated Black people not worthy of self-determination.

A racist, reactionary U.S. Supreme Court was issuing rulings that stripped civil rights protections from individuals formerly protected by the Fourteenth and Fifteenth Amendments. One of those decisions, Plessy vs. Ferguson in 1896, dealt a severe blow to racial equality, essentially approving the "separate but equal" public facilities despite laws that had originally been adopted by Black-led Southern states just after the Civil War.

A Hidden Record

"The American landscape conspires to make sure ... Reconstruction is almost invisible all across the nation," writes James W. Loewen in *Lies Across America,* his analysis of historic sites around the country. Instead, Southern monuments lionize the "white racist Democrats," wrote Loewen, the party that rolled back the interracial progress made during the first years after the Civil War.

Of the one hundred-plus Civil War memorials in Connecticut (as documented by the Connecticut Historical Society) not one celebrates the Reconstruction efforts of men and women like Rebecca Primus.

At least 12,000 students were enrolled in the Southern Freedmen's schools funded by the Hartford and New England Aid Societies. More than 83 schools were built, employing almost 200 teachers.

A physical manifestation in Connecticut that commemorates and celebrates Reconstruction is long overdue. But somewhere, hidden deep in the family histories of thousands of African Americans, resides the real memorial to the early fight for racial freedom and justice.

Malcolm X in Hartford: "Our Mission is Not Violence, But Freedom"

On a warm summer day in 1955, fifteen domestic workers – maids, cooks and chauffeurs – packed into a small apartment in a Hartford public housing project. It was a Thursday, the one day of the week they were granted off by their employers.

They came to hear a trim young man, thirty years old, dressed in a coat and tie. He was Malcolm X, formerly Malcolm Little, a small-time criminal who remade himself into a minister for the Nation of Islam (NOI). Malcolm had just established a house of worship in Springfield, Massachusetts. He was about to do the same in Atlanta, Georgia.

But he stopped in Hartford because a woman who had traveled to hear Malcolm talk in Springfield was so impressed that she invited him to speak in her city. This he did, addressing working class members of the Black community who made up the majority of the NOI around the country.

The Hartford group soon grew to forty people, and by 1956, Malcolm X had founded Temple No. 14 in the city's north end at 2118 Main Street. He spoke to new recruits about the religious tenets of the NOI, but his topics also extended to the international stage and the organic links between Black populations everywhere: "The Black man is rising up all over the world, and now countries are starting to think before starting a war," he told the mosque crowd.

Many of these uprisings had been taking place in Africa: Ethiopia, Kenya, Algeria. Malcolm wove the stories of Black struggles against white racism at home with the fight against white colonialism abroad.

He returned to Hartford at least twice in January, 1957. By this time, the FBI and its local office in New Haven was tracking and recording his every move. The bureau files that have been publicly released provide the most accurate record of Malcolm's itinerary.

Temple No. 14 was so active that on April 28, 1957, Nation of Islam members from Hartford were asked to join Malcolm in Harlem. He organized a show of force in response to the beating of a local Muslim who had witnessed police attacking another man on the street. When the witness tried to stop it, he, too, was severely beaten by the cops and hospitalized. Militant protests against police brutality were rare; this one elevated Malcolm as a national figure.

On November 16, 1958, the first child of Malcolm X and Betty Shabazz was born in New York. Three days later he was on the road again to Hartford. An informant spied on the meeting for the FBI. "There was no talk of violence," according to the report. In fact, when Malcolm read to the crowd about the treatment of Blacks during slavery, the informant reported that it "made his own blood boil."

Temple 14 moved to 1097 Main Street, where Malcolm spoke in August, 1959: "We do not advocate violence but we do not turn the other cheek either," he told his listeners. "When you kill a snake, that is not hate. You are merely protecting yourself." (*Malcolm X in Harford*, Connecticuthistory.org) The next month he narrated a home movie about his first trip to Africa for the Hartford temple members.

All during this period Malcolm was tailed by police and federal agents: Detroit, New Jersey, Florida. Malcolm spoke and the FBI followed him: Chicago, Boston, Cleveland. He knew he was being watched. In answer to a question about the Vietnam draft, Malcolm replied that he wouldn't tell anyone to become a conscientious objector because he knew the government was listening. He would, however, personally refuse to be drafted, Malcolm declared.

In June, 1961, Malcolm was back in Hartford for a week, conducting local press interviews and drumming up support for an upcoming NOI Freedom Rally in Washington, D.C. "If Pharaoh had listened to Moses when he said 'Let My People Go,' he could have saved himself and his people," Minister Malcolm told the news media. "We believe Uncle Sam is in the same position today." (Steve Thornton, A Shoeleather History Project, 2016).

Although Malcolm X spent a lot of time in Hartford, he also accepted invitations to speak at Connecticut college campuses. He addressed Wesleyan University in February, 1962. An informant reported "there was no disorder whatsoever and he was well-received by the students." He was also invited to speak at the University of Bridgeport.

The Nation of Islam's mission was to create a separate, Black-controlled community within the United States. Malcolm expounded on this theme at Wesleyan: "The masses of negroes do not want to integrate. We are just as opposed to segregation as the most staunch integrationist. Muslims are proposing separation, not segregation ... For the Muslim the solution is for the Negro to stand up for himself, to stop trying to get whites to give him things, and to build what he wants for himself." (A Shoeleather History Project)

On July 23, 1962, he visited the Hartford mosque at its new location at 38 Albany Avenue, above a luncheonette. Once again he challenged the civil rights movement's campaign for an integrated society: "Integration is just another form of hypocrisy. Negroes make chumps of themselves calling themselves

Americans… the Black man in this country doesn't have a nationality. It sounds good in principle but it doesn't work in practice. You can't say that's my house when you haven't even been let in yet. Our aim is not violence but freedom, justice, and equality for the Black man in America … neither segregation nor integration can provide this." (A Shoeleather History Project)

Listening to Malcolm X was often a transforming moment for African Americans, and sometimes for whites as well. It was on June 5, 1963 that Malcolm spoke to his largest Hartford crowd, 800 people at the Bushnell Memorial Hall. The event was sponsored by the University of Hartford. According to African American writer J.K. Obatala, the speech was the moment when he was inspired to travel to Ghana, his ancestral homeland. "It takes a trip to Africa to realize how American we are," Obatala wrote.

Journalist Les Payne, whose family had moved from Alabama to Hartford, was a UConn student at the time. At the Bushnell, Malcolm excoriated the state's de facto segregation in housing and education. The Uconn class of 1960 had graduated only three Black students. When Payne was at Uconn, there were ten thousand students, but only sixty of them were Black. He relates the Bushnell speech in an essay entitled "The Night I Stopped Being a Negro."

For this trip Malcolm stayed at the home of Thomas J. X, leader of the Hartford mosque. Newspaper reporter Don Noel spoke to Malcolm by phone at the local minister's home. Noel, who is white, later wrote that he preferred Dr. Martin Luther King's approach to end racism, "but social change is often made meaningful because firebrands insist that problems not be swept under a rug of good feelings." Noel's liberal view contrasted with a newspaper's obituary for Malcolm in 1965, which called him "the prophet of race war and violence."

Only four months later, on October 29, Malcolm X spoke to 700 at the University of Hartford. The speech was moved outside to accommodate the overflow crowd. It was a chilly autumn afternoon, which inspired Malcolm to quip "maybe what I say will make you hot." In contrast, a representative of Dr. King's Southern Christian Leadership Conference (SCLC) gave a talk that same day which attracted only thirty people.

In 1963 the freedom struggle was burning hot; racist forces in the South were carrying on a terror campaign of intimidation and violence. In June, Mississippi civil rights organizer Medgar Evers had been murdered in his front yard. (Meredith's killer was not prosecuted and convicted until 1994.) Hartford reporters, however, seemed more interested in Malcolm's disagreements with other national Black leaders. Malcolm warned of "racial bloodshed" that was coming to America.

He was assassinated in Harlem on February 21, 1965, three months before his 40th birthday. Thousands of pages of FBI files on Malcolm are still classified, so we may never know the entire extent of the forces that conspired to murder him.

Most of white America did not know what to make of Malcolm X, except to fear him. During his short life, he did his best to tell the truth despite the consequences. He challenged the racist political, economic and cultural institutions of the United States.

Maybe that's why the white community in the 1950s and 1960s was so terrified of this convict-turned-leader. Like Nat Turner before him, and the Black Panthers after his death, Malcolm defied all the stereotypes of how oppressed people should behave in the quest for their own liberation.

Selma, Not So Far Away

Father Leonard Tartaglia was sometimes called Hartford's "Hoodlum Priest." Like the 1961 film of the same name, Tartaglia ministered to the city's poor and disenfranchised. He challenged institutional racism wherever he found it, in the state and in his own church. On March, 11, 1965, at the height of violent confrontations over civil rights in the South, Tartaglia and a handful of other clergy from New Haven and Waterbury headed for Selma, Alabama.

Father Tartaglia's trip came in response to the vicious actions of Alabama authorities during their efforts to stop the 54-mile voting rights march from Selma to Montgomery by blocking the Edmund Pettus Bridge. The now infamous police response on March 7, 1965, resulted in Sheriff Jim Clark and a posse of deputies attacking 600 peaceful activists with clubs and tear gas on a day that became known as "Bloody Sunday."

Connecticut Responds to James Reeb's Death

On the same night that Tartaglia left for Selma, Unitarian minister James Reeb died from wounds received at the hands of a Selma lynch mob. Reeb had traveled from his Boston home to support voting rights marchers under attack in Alabama. The critically acclaimed motion picture *Selma* dramatizes his story.

Thousands of Connecticut people rallied and marched to mourn James Reeb's death. At New Haven's Woolsey Hall, 1,500 gathered to protest the murder. In Stamford, another 1,500 marched to the old town hall, demanding that President Lyndon Johnson take action to protect voting rights. In Norwalk, 700 people marched from the police station to city hall, challenging federal priorities that sent troops to Vietnam but none to protect civil rights workers. In Hartford, 350 gathered at the state capitol, while in Middletown, 300 demonstrators marched down Main Street singing, "We Shall Overcome."

Events in Montgomery, Alabama Hit Home

While activists in Alabama made a second attempt to cross the Edmund Pettus Bridge into Montgomery on March 9, Hartford high school students and activists held a vigil at the governor's residence to focus local attention on the Selma attacks. They brought legislative business to a standstill a short while later, simply by entering the state capitol where an unusually large number of anxious police officers assembled to meet them.

Meanwhile, in Montgomery on March 25, a victorious rally of 25,000 people celebrated the third and final attempt to cross the bridge. Among them

116

was the Reverend Richard Battles of Hartford, who led 90 Connecticut residents in joining the southern march.

That same night, along Highway 80, the Ku Klux Klan assassinated Viola Liuzzo, a volunteer from Detroit who shuttled protestors between Selma and Montgomery. Reverend Richard Albin from the Greater Hartford Campus Ministry saw Liuzzo's wrecked car as he rode a bus along the highway. Albin acted as security at the church that had been Liuzzo's base. Exactly a week earlier – to the hour – a young Black teacher from Hartford and her coworkers had been harassed and almost run off the same road, possibly by the same men.

Unsung Heroes
Most of the people who enlisted in the war against Jim Crow, like Father Tartaglia, never ended up in docudramas or history books. They were ordinary people, both Black and white, who took extraordinary risks. Some of these lesser-known heroes include:

–Reverend Arthur L. Hardge, an African American minister from New Britain who joined the Freedom Riders in Florida in 1961 to test the federal law banning segregation at interstate bus facilities. Authorities convicted him and eight other clergy for "unlawful assembly" and sentenced them to 60 days in prison. After four days of lockup, and pressure from the ACLU, officials granted all nine protestors clemency.

–Seventy Yale students who traveled to Mississippi in October 1963 to assist a young African American running for Lt. Governor. They returned after the election with stories of bogus arrests and beatings.

–Elizabeth Faith Brown, a 44-year-old Salvation Army worker and Uconn student who spent a week in a Florida jail in March 1964 on trespassing charges. Police arrested her and other Connecticut residents while they worked to desegregate a motel restaurant.

–In Voluntown, the Committee for Non Violent Action (CNVA) responded to the Selma call by sending 19-year old Peter Kellman. He worked behind the scenes, raising and lowering tents each day for the historic march from Selma to Montgomery. One of his tasks was to scour the tent site for possible bombs. Peter stayed on after the march, building the Selma Free Library, registering voters, and organizing an alternative political party with the Student Nonviolent Coordinating Committee (SNCC).

The Legacy of the Voting Rights Act
Thanks in part to the protests and demonstrations in Alabama, legislators signed the Voting Rights Act into law on August 6, 1965, outlawing discriminatory voting practices in the United States. The act was amended many times, as

several states – including Connecticut – found ways to sabotage the law's intent. It was not until 1972 that Connecticut finally eliminated literacy tests and long residency requirements for voter registration.

In 2013, however, the US Supreme Court ended oversight of states that regularly violated the Voting Rights Act. Consequently, before the November 2014 elections, voter suppression initiatives in North Carolina, Kansas, Virginia and Florida actually denied hundreds of thousands of registered voters "their basic right of citizenship," according to the Brennan Center for Justice.

The presence of such controversies highlights the modern implications of the Selma story. As Father Tartaglia told an audience in 1966, despite years of progress the challenge still remains to "reshape the community befitting the dignity of man."

The Black Panther Party in Connecticut

At a "Colored Men's Convention" in Hartford on January 26, 1899, Connecticut's first Black lawyer took to the stage with an uncompromising message. "It is the right of the colored man to fight for his rights," Walter S. Miller from New Haven told the crowd. "When a white man shows a revolver, I want the Negro to show one also. In that way only will he be granted his rights by demanding them and being ready to insist upon them."

From the 1920s to the 1960s, Connecticut's African American activists formed a number of membership groups for self-defense. The Anti-Lynching Crusaders (led by Mary Townsend Seymour), the Negro Defense Council and the Hartford League of Struggle for Negro Rights were just some of the organizations that protested police and vigilante violence on a local and national scale.

In 1961 the US Civil Rights Commission found that as the civil rights movement grew, a majority of African Americans expected racist backlash. They feared police violence and harassment as well. The commission reported that when racial violence took place, the Black community understood that "the police will side with the white mob." The same report found that "Negroes feel the brunt of brutality proportionately more than any other group in American society.

Divided by Race and Class

In Hartford, Connecticut, downtown separated the Black, poor North End from the stable, white middle class South End. The two areas reflected America's race and class divisions, particularly the wide gap between how Connecticut's Black and white residents viewed the 1960s urban rebellions.

This racial divide encompassed discrimination in jobs, housing and education. Police brutality ranked high on the Black community's grievance list as well. Authorities released a confidential analysis of Hartford police/community relations in June 1969 just as they lifted a city-wide curfew, previously triggered by clashes between police and young Black men. Respected criminal justice scholar Dr. Sol Chaneles wrote the study at the behest of the local official leaders. His "top secret report on crime in Hartford" showed that African Americans believed the Hartford police force spent more time "harassing ghetto residents" than protecting them.

Dr. Chaneles, who previously worked for the US Chamber of Commerce, reported that whites, not Blacks or Puerto Ricans, committed the overwhelming percentage of major crimes in the city. Yet according to Chaneles's report, a "disproportionate amount of time was spent protecting downtown business establishments" from petty infractions. Meanwhile a dozen organized crime rings operated freely. Hartford's police chief denied every accusation.

The Panthers Organize

In Bridgeport, Josè Rene Gonzalves of California organized the first Black Panther Party chapter in Connecticut. "We have members in thirty-seven states and we didn't get there by killing," Gonzalves explained. "We got it by organizing and telling people what the problem is. We are dealing with the needs of the Black community." He soon started chapters in New Haven, Waterbury and Hartford. After establishing local leadership, national figures like Ericka Huggins came to the state to run political education courses and organize Panther programs. "This is a revolution," Gonzalves told a Stamford crowd. "It's a revolution against the system that teaches a man to be less than a man. A revolution against ignorance, fear and hate." The Panthers' goal, he said, was to "take the strength from the few and give the power to the people."

Walter "Rap" Bailey grew up in Hartford. He described how Black youths from the projects experienced more violence and deprivation "than any child is meant to see." His motivation to join the Panthers came after marching with John Barber, leader of the Black Caucus. On September 18, 1967, Barber led protestors on an "open housing" march from the North End to south Hartford. Their target was the practice of segregated housing that made buying or renting homes in the South End practically impossible for African American families. The marchers, an integrated group that included white students from the Community for Nonviolent Action (CNVA) in Voluntown, proved militant but peaceful.

Police stopped the protestors before they reached downtown. Bottles and rocks then began flying through the air, but apparently not from the hands of marchers. Regardless, according to Bailey, police waded into the crowd, hitting and arresting people at random. Word of the arrests spread fast, and that night Hartford experienced its first full-scale riot. When the Panthers started recruiting, Rap Bailey was among the first to join.

Charles "Butch" Lewis, a well-known and respected figure in the Black community, helped organize the Black Panther Party in Hartford. Lewis grew up in the South, moved to Hartford, was drafted and served in Vietnam for 14 months. As a veteran and a respected community figure, he became Field Captain of the Panthers. Lewis understood white people's perception of their group. "I know a lot of people fear we're a gang of thugs and hoodlums," he said during an early Panther demonstration, "but we're a political party, not a gang. We're an army of people who are fighting for the people, the oppressed people."

When the Panthers took to the Hartford streets in the summer of 1969, their first priority was to "patrol the police." Panther leader Donald Mounds told a public forum: "What we were doing was patrolling the police for the simple reason that we knew, like a lot of people know, that the police make false arrests, shoot tear gas into the houses. The police came into the area like storm troopers. We were threatened to be arrested and a few of us were arrested."

Police officials saw the Black Panther presence, and the party's use of the Second Amendment to carry arms, as a direct threat to police authority. Yet even when neighborhood groups attempted to protect Black lives and property, they found their efforts blocked by local police departments. In Waterbury, the mayor made an agreement with a group of youths (who called themselves the Young Black Militants) to patrol city streets on their own block, equipped only with bullhorns. The police union vehemently objected, declaring that the mayor had "sold out the police department." On the first two nights of civilian patrol, however, one officer admitted that it was the quietest time on the streets he had ever seen.

Hartford residents faced the same resistance. The Oakland Civic Association formed an unarmed patrol of men to watch their neighborhood. This effort had some funding behind it and the men wore berets and carried whistles and walkie-talkies. The Hartford police forced the men to abandon their berets and equipment, but still, disturbances dropped significantly while they patrolled the streets.

One Connecticut event eclipsed all the work local Panthers undertook, however. In 1969, police arrested 14 New Haven members for the murder of Alex Rackley, a Panther from New York. While the prosecutor called it an "ordinary case of murder," the trial became a showdown between the federal government and the Panthers. Authorities arrested Ericka Huggins and Black Panther co-founder Bobby Seale for the crime, which many in the movement believed was part of an effort to disrupt the Panthers' organizing efforts and required the group to spend all of its time entangled in the legal system. In the end, three men faced conviction in 1971 for Rackley's murder. The remaining defendants, including Seale and Huggins, were released.

Conflicting Views of the Black Panthers
The legendary abolitionist Frederick Douglass spoke in Connecticut many times, including an 1879 talk in Hartford on John Brown, the anti-slavery activist both celebrated and damned for his armed rebellion at Harpers Ferry. Douglass

called Brown a "moral earthquake," a metaphor that conjured up destruction on a righteous scale.

Many viewed the Black Panthers in the same conflicting light. Whites often feared and loathed the Panthers, charging them with fomenting violence and being behind much of the 1960's urban riots. This was far from a universal opinion, however: "Violence was there all along in back alleys and ghetto streets," wrote one international observer. "What the Panthers did, by standing up armed, was to become lightning rods attracting those flashing bolts of violence, and the concentration of fire power coming from police guns lit up the night."

Edward Alexander Bouchet: Pioneer and Brilliant Physicist

When Edward Alexander Bouchet was born on September 15, 1852, in New Haven, there was little likelihood he would one day attend nearby Yale University (known at the time as Yale College). Though there were no policy statements excluding African Americans, and those in charge would undoubtedly have denied there was any such policy, the fact is that no person known to be Black had ever attended Yale. As with so many American institutions, there was little reason to believe that the powers-that-be would change course anytime soon.

The Abolitionist Movement challenging white supremacy had grown quite powerful by the time Bouchet was born, and it would dramatically change the country. Those changes, Bouchet's thirst for knowledge, the commitment of a dedicated teacher and the tenacity of his parents all coalesced to open doors for Bouchet. Determined to forge a professional life befitting his intellectual skills, Bouchet himself also played a significant part in kicking in those doors.

Early Life

Edward's parents, Francis and Susan Cooley Bouchet, were respected figures in New Haven's African-American community. From working at Yale, they saw firsthand the educational possibilities that "might be" for their son. Francis was a former slave who worked at Yale as a janitor, while Susan earned part of her income by doing the laundry of Yale students. Francis was also a deacon at a New Haven church.

In keeping with the segregated norms of the time, Edward began his formal education at the all-Black Artisan Street Colored School, which employed only one teacher, Sarah Wilson. Wilson was instrumental in Bouchet's life as both a teacher and in encouraging him to pursue an education commensurate with his abilities. He moved on to New Haven High School for two years before transferring to Hopkins, a prestigious private school in New Haven, where he graduated as class valedictorian in 1870. That year, he was accepted to Yale.

Yale's First Black Student?

Over the decades, many sources, including Yale itself, have referred to Bouchet as the school's first African American student. Information unearthed in 2014, however, indicates that may not be so. Not surprisingly, the confusion lies with the complicated nature of race, both how individuals self-identify and how they are perceived and identified by others. Research by several scholars and writers, including some at Yale, indicate that three men who preceded Bouchet at the school and were thought to be white – Moses Simon (Class of 1809), Randall Lee Gibson (Class of 1853) and Richard Henry Green (class of 1857) – were identified at various times in public records as Negro, Black and mulatto. That Yale listed Bouchet as its first Black student until 2014 confirms that everyone at the school who mattered believed at the time the three male students were white.

"Passing" as white was common among Blacks who were light-skinned enough to do so, and that appears to be what Simon and Green did. Gibson, however, was from Louisiana and apparently did not know until mid-life that his great-grandfather was Black and that he was thus legally considered a mulatto (though in practice in the Deep South, there was no such thing as a mulatto; anyone with any trace of Black ancestry was Black, pure and simple). In a somewhat bizarre twist, Gibson returned to Louisiana after graduating from Yale and joined the Confederate Army when the Civil War broke out. In fact, not only did he join the fight to protect slavery, he rose all the way to the rank of colonel! It was later in life when he was running for public office on a platform in which he regularly denounced Blacks that he learned from an opponent about his Black heritage.

Whether Bouchet was the first, second, third or fourth African American to attend Yale, he was a brilliant student. After graduating, he continued at Yale in the newly-created Ph.D program in physics. When he finished his dissertation ("Measuring Refractive Indices") in 1876 after just two years of graduate study, Bouchet was one of the first six people in the United States to receive a doctorate in physics and the first African-American to earn such a degree in any field.

Teaching Career

Despite his many accomplishments and his obvious abilities, Bouchet was rejected from every university and college to which he applied for employment as a teacher. Though it's highly unlikely any of them ever admitted as much (except, perhaps, within their inner circle), it's reasonable to conclude that the administrators who refused to hire Bouchet did so because of the color of his skin. As a result, one of the most brilliant physicists in the country was relegated to teaching at segregated, all-Black high schools.

Even then, Bouchet eventually ran smack up against the color line. His first job upon leaving Yale was at the Institute for Colored Youth (ICY) in Philadelphia, a school established for Blacks by the Society of Friends. He taught there for 26 years until 1902 when he was fired, along with the rest of the school's teachers, as a result of a dramatic shift by the school's all-white board of directors. In thrall of the work and philosophy of Booker T. Washington, who was at the apex of his influence at the time, the board did away with ICY's academic, college-oriented mission and turned the school into an industrial-vocational one.

Final Years

Bouchet moved frequently over the next fourteen years and worked at a number of jobs, mostly as either a high school administrator or teacher. He developed serious health problems that forced him to retire in 1916, and he returned to New Haven. He moved into the house at 94 Bradley Street that he had grown up in and died there in 1918 at the age of 66.

For all of Bouchet's many accomplishments, an examination of his life leads away from a celebration of that life, alas, and instead toward the haunting, tragic question *What might have been?* Millions of Blacks, women and others have had their dreams and aspirations crushed by entrenched power. We should celebrate Bouchet's achievements, all the more because of the obstacles he faced. But perhaps the best way we can honor his legacy is to double down in challenging illegitimate authority and in strengthening our commitment to build a world where every human being can blossom as fully as possible.

Butch Lewis, Hartford Panther

One friend of Butch Lewis called him the Pastor of Hartford's North End: "A pastor is a shepherd, and everyone came to Butch with their problems." With his friends he established a block watch, forced the city to install a stop sign at a dangerous Vine Street intersection, and started a fishing club for kids at Keney Park. He never became a politician, never used his reputation for profit or fame.

Charles 'Butch' Lewis was born in 1944 in Fredericksburg, Virginia. An early memory he sometimes shared was the slave auction block that stood in the center of town in front of Planter's Hotel. It dated back to the 1850s. A constant reminder of the lasting legacy of racism, as if he needed one.

Butch moved to Hartford and was raised by his grandmother, Margaret "Big Ma" Havlowe. She was a domestic worker who finished the fifth grade but spoke three languages fluently. He graduated from Weaver High School and was drafted into the army in 1963.

When Butch returned to Hartford from the Vietnam War, there was more violence: the brutality of racism and poverty, the oppressive police presence in his North End neighborhood. He told an audience in 2014 that he "came back to the same bowl of crap,".

He was damaged by the war, the same way his friends were. On hot summer days he had flashbacks and swore he could smell death. At night he and his buddies went to Keney Park, smoked weed and talked about the memories they couldn't get out of their heads.

Butch said Hartford was located in the Valley of Death – Springfield to New Jersey – where weapons for personal and military use were manufactured. Colt Firearms produced the M-16s that Butch and his buddies carried during his tour in Vietnam. It was Big Ma who told him not to reenlist for a second tour.

The Panthers

The Black Panther Party for Self Defense was first organized in 1966 by Huey Newton and Bobby Seale in Oakland, California. Sparked by widespread police violence against the Black community, the Panthers became known for carrying weapons in public. Their manifesto grew into a comprehensive analysis of 20th century America and included a revolutionary call for change. Their demands included full employment, exemption from military service and the "immediate end to POLICE BRUTALITY and MURDER of Black people." The Party demanded "land, bread, housing, education, clothing, justice and peace."

In 1968, just two months back from Vietnam, Butch and his friend Donny

Mounds (who had been a Marine) started their own unauthorized chapter of the Black Panthers. "We read about it in the papers," he said. By 1969 the Panthers had reached Connecticut and established chapters in Bridgeport, Waterbury, New Haven, Norwalk and Stamford. Butch and Donny led the official formation of the Hartford chapter.

"Some people at first thought we were hoodlums, a gang, too stupid to know politics," Butch said in a 2010 interview. "Sure we armed ourselves. But we didn't go out looking for trouble. We made sure no one would step on us."

Butch successfully recruited Black youth in the city, and at one point held a meeting with 60 teenagers in the Bellevue Square housing project. He talked about the Panthers' Ten-Point Program and showed *"Huey,"* a documentary made by the radical film group Newsreel. Teens as young as 14 sold the Panther newspaper on the street and were regularly harassed and busted by the cops.

He was frequently questioned by the FBI, which sent secret memos about him directly to J. Edgar Hoover. His friend, journalist Lew Brown, had the distinct memory of being out on the street with Butch during a night-time police raid. "There was a police sniper aiming at Butch. A friendly cop warned him to move away." Because of his Panther activity he expected attempts on his life, and for a while he lived in Nigeria.

There, Butch helped activist and actor Ossie Davis produce "Kongi's Harvest," a film that starred African freedom fighter Wole Soyinka, the Nigerian 1986 Nobel Literature Prize winner, who wrote the original play on which the film was based. The movie had its 1973 American premiere in Hartford.

Responding to the Community

Whenever he was needed, Butch and his comrades were there. When Weaver High School students walked out of class to protest the suspension of three students who distributed their own newspaper without permission, Butch was called on for support and advice. His presence was a counterweight to the adults who urged the students to return to school.

As long-suppressed outrage turned to street violence in the summer of 1969, Butch and the Panthers were on the street, "patrolling the police," as another Panther described it. On one of those nights, cops shot teargas and lobbed gas canisters into nearby apartment houses, endangering small children. The Panthers organized a community meeting, along with the Urban Religious Coalition, to expose the gross police overreaction.

One eyewitness described how the police targeted Butch: "There were six people on the street, mind you. [The police] walked in the middle of the six people and they said 'Butch Lewis go home!' He said 'I'm not going home, man.'"

A Black minister witnessed the incident. "I saw Butch arrested, and I don't know if he will have to go on trial for this, for no reason whatsoever ... I also saw the role that he played when he was in the [police] wagon telling the men who got arrested after him to keep it cool. The police said there was a fight around this arrest, which was an obvious lie."

He was arrested a number of times, falsely accused of rioting, on bomb-making charges, and in connection to the New Haven murder of Alex Rackley, which had been orchestrated by a police informant. Friends mortgaged their homes to bail him out of jail.

Community Survival

Through his contacts at St. Michael's Church on Clark Street, Butch and the Hartford Panthers established a highly successful free breakfast program for children. Hot meals were served each school morning for 30 to 150 kids. Butch had asked Black churches to host the program, but all refused. Father Leonard Tartaglia opened the church doors at St Michael's. He was fondly known by Butch as the "Hoodlum Priest" (from a popular movie of the same name) whose roots were deep in the community. Fr. Lenny also left the keys to the church van, according to Butch, so the Panthers could do errands and get to meetings in New Haven. The gas tank was always full the next morning, Butch recalled with a smile.

The River of Tears

Barbara Henderson was the president of Concerned Mothers from Charter Oak Terrace. The project residents had been lobbying for more than a year to have the City of Hartford lower the Park River at Flatbush Avenue. The river was supposed to run only a few inches, but the water level was dangerously high. More than one child had drowned there. The parents had been promised in 1968 that the problem would be fixed. It wasn't, and another child died. The mothers called the stream a "River of Tears."

In 1969, Barbara called on Butch. The Panthers helped the mothers form a traffic blockade on the street. The police arrived to break up the group, but the protesters vowed to return the next day. Both the governor and the Hartford mayor responded immediately to the mothers' bold action. A city crew inspected the river bridge and found serious structural damage, which they immediately addressed. An obstruction down river had artificially increased the river's depth. It was removed and the water level returned to a safe level. "The Panthers were a force to be recognized," remembered Barbara's daughter, who had joined the traffic action as a young girl.

Change and Legacy

The Black Panther Party only existed for about four years in Connecticut, in large part due to the COINTELPRO (counter intelligence program) sabotage offensive conducted by the FBI. The debilitating 1970 trial in New Haven of Panther leaders Bobby Seale and Erika Huggins drained the national group's energy and resources. Hartford's chapter didn't last all that long. Its leadership changed on a regular basis. Butch himself was at first a Panther leader and later became a representative of the Intercommunal News Service, the Black Panthers' press affiliate.

Butch described the Panthers as "an army of people who are fighting for the people, the oppressed people." Butch and the Panthers were part of the broader fight for social justice in Hartford, along with the Black Caucus, the North End Community Action Project (NECAP), religious activists (often led by Leonard Tartaglia), the Communist Party and Education/Instrucción, which targeted institutional racism in housing, among others.

Butch died in 2015, and toward the end of his life, he was often asked about whether conditions had improved for the Black community. Butch was blunt. "Is it changed? It hasn't changed that much, it's only covered up. It's hard to get rid of northern segregation. It's the most hidden segregation." In one interview he said, "Integration is only fifty years old. You can't get rid of racism in fifty years if you can't get rid of it in three hundred … We haven't progressed, we've de-gressed."

Butch was asked to sum up his life and provide an analysis of the '60s and for the "next steps" to end racial oppression. An impossible task, but Butch was always patient with the questioners. "The first step is to be a human being," he once replied.

Dr. Cornel West, a leading African American scholar and activist, credits the Panthers for "turning scared, intimidated, helpless folk into bold, brave, hopeful people willing to live and die for Black freedom."

That is the Butch Lewis legacy.

Louis Peterson, Groundbreaking African-American Playwright

Louis Peterson was born on June 17, 1922, at 138 Standish Street in Hartford. His parents, Louis Peterson, Sr., and Ruth Conover Peterson, were both employed at the Phoenix State Bank and Trust Company. Ruth Peterson was president of the Women's League and was once awarded a citation by Eleanor Roosevelt for her work in a Hartford childcare program.

The family lived in the south end of Hartford, which Peterson described as "predominantly a white community" and "horribly middle-class." He attended public schools and graduated from Bulkeley High School in 1940. A piano prodigy, he enrolled in Morehouse College in Atlanta with the intention of studying toward a degree in music.

Catching the Theater Bug

At Morehouse Peterson caught the theater bug. His first interest was acting and he appeared in a number of school productions. After graduating with a bachelor's degree in English in 1944, he returned to Connecticut and enrolled in Yale University's School of Drama. After one year in New Haven, he moved to Manhattan to continue his studies at New York University and to begin acting. He appeared in various plays beginning in 1947, including *Our Lan'*, Theodore Ward's master work about Reconstruction.

While he worked, Peterson studied with the noted acting teacher, Sanford Meisner, at the Neighborhood Playhouse. He also studied play writing with Clifford Odets, the radical author of *Awake and Sing*, *Golden Boy* and other plays of the 1930's. Peterson took his first serious stab at writing while on tour in a dramatic adaptation of Carson McCuller's *The Member of the Wedding* in 1951. The result was *Take a Giant Step*, his best-known and best play, which he finished in early 1953.

Take a Giant Step

Though in the text the setting of *Take a Giant Step* is described simply as "a New England town," in interviews Peterson talked about the play as autobiographical and the location as drawn from the neighborhood and house he grew up in. Hartford also played host to the play's first public staging for three nights in March, 1953 at the New Parsons Theater in what was described as a pre-Broadway tryout. None other than theatrical legend Helen Hayes took an active role in getting *Take a Giant Step* staged. She likened Peterson's play to *Our Town* and other dramatic classics of family life, saying it would "certainly enrich the American theater."

Broadway

Take a Giant Step opened on Broadway at the Lyceum Theater on September 24, 1953. The story is a compelling mix of drama, humor and pathos about the difficulties of adolescence. The lead, Spencer Scott, was played by 17-year old Louis Gossett, Jr., who had just started his senior year at Lincoln High School in Brooklyn.

Take a Giant Step received stellar notices, a number of which highlighted the deft way Peterson used humor to render an otherwise serious story. Lorraine Hansberry praised the play for its sophistication, while veteran drama critic George Jean Nathan, writing in *The Atlantic*, compared it favorably to one of Eugene O'Neill's best-known works, calling it "a kind of Negro *Ah, Wilderness!*, deeper in meaning." Loften Mitchell, an African American playwright who was a contemporary of Peterson's, noted that *Take a Giant Step* was particularly popular among Blacks and credited Black theater-goers with making the play a success.

Louis Kronenberger, who served as a drama critic for the left-wing New York City daily *PM* in the 1940s and edited a book of the best plays for each theater season for many years, included *Take a Giant Step* in *The Best Plays of 1953-54*. The *New York Times* also selected the play as one of the ten best of the season. *Take a Giant Step* was successfully revived in 1956 Off-Broadway with Godfrey Cambridge among those in the cast. A film version was made by United Artists in 1959 featuring Ruby Dee and 18-year old Johnny Nash, who later achieved fame with the smash hit song *I Can See Clearly Now*.

Though Peterson lived the rest of his life in New York, he drew on his Hartford upbringing in plays and television scripts he wrote throughout the rest of his career. In none was his Hartford experience so central as in *Take a Giant Step*, and, coincidentally or not, nothing else he wrote was as successful or well-received. Peterson also taught theater for many years at the State University of New York in Stony Brook. In an obituary at the time of his death in 1998, the *New York Times* wrote that Peterson was a "playwright who opened doors" for other Black dramatists and called *Take a Giant Step* "a groundbreaking Broadway play." *Take a Giant Step* has been included in a number of anthologies, including *Black Theater, U.S.A.: Forty-Five Plays by Black Americans, 1847-1974*.

Constance Baker Motley, Warrior for Justice

The cover of *Equal Justice Under Law*, Constance Baker Motley's 1998 autobiography, is graced with a photograph of Motley, James Meredith and Medgar Evers as they exit a federal courthouse in New Orleans. The year was 1962 and Motley, a staff attorney for the Legal Defense Fund of the National Association for the Advancement of Colored People (NAACP), was there to argue on behalf of Meredith's right to attend the University of Mississippi. The school had denied him that right because he was an African-American. Evers, a long-time activist, was the head of the Mississippi chapter of the NAACP.

To a very real extent, the three figures capture the unified forces of the Black freedom struggle. Evers was a leading figure in the protests then sweeping the South, Meredith had no background as an activist but was a young man who, like so many everyday Black folk of that era, was moved to challenge institutional racism to make a better life for himself, and Motley was a lawyer who fortified Meredith's efforts and Evers's organizing with brilliant work in the courtroom.

It's striking that each of the three is smiling ever so slightly in the photo. On one level, the smiles reflect a calm determination and hint at the desire for freedom that blazed so intensely within each. Given the presence outside the courtroom of protestors opposed to their efforts, the smiles of the three also reflect a noble defiance to the resistance the Black freedom movement met at every turn. Resistance that was often quite violent. Less than a year after the photo was taken, Evers, a decorated veteran of the Second World War, would meet the fate that many in the movement met when he was murdered in front of his home in Jackson, Mississippi.

New Haven Roots

Beginning in the 1950's and for many years thereafter, Constance Baker Motley was deeply immersed in the Black freedom struggle. She was born Constance Baker in New Haven in 1921 to parents who were natives of the Caribbean island nation of Nevis. She attended historically Black Fisk University in Nashville briefly, then transferred to and graduated from New York University. She was the first Black woman to attend the Columbia University School of Law and received her law degree there in 1946. Later that year, she went to work at the NAACP Legal Defense Fund, where she remained for 20

132

years. She worked with and befriended Reverend Martin Luther King, Jr., and many other leading figures of the freedom struggle.

In the years after the Second World War, any criticism of illegitimate authority in the United States was deemed by those in power as treasonous. Revolutionary African-American giants such as W.E.B DuBois, Langston Hughes and Paul Robeson were just three of thousands who were badgered, harassed and hauled before investigative committees, and the Black freedom movement as a whole hit a temporary roadblock. As the 1950's progressed, however, the movement was revitalized and the country was forced to confront as never before the second-class status of Black people. Again and again, Motley was there, supplementing the struggle in the streets with successful legal efforts.

Groundbreaking Legal Victories

In 1954, she wrote the first legal brief in the groundbreaking *Brown vs. the Board of Education* of Topeka, Kansas case. Three years later, Motley successfully won an equally significant case in Little Rock after nine Black teenagers were spat upon and physically prevented from attending what had been an all-white school. In 1962, Motley represented dozens of young people, known ever since as the Freedom Riders, who integrated public transportation by defying violent protests to ride buses deep into the former Confederacy. That was the same year she won James Meredith's case while becoming the first Black woman to argue before the Supreme Court. It was one of nine times (out of ten cases) that Motley would win a case before the Court. And as she did for Meredith at the University of Mississippi, Motley successfully represented plaintiffs who became the first Blacks to attend the University of Alabama, Clemson University and other Southern colleges.

Elected Office and a Federal Judgeship

In 1964, Motley decided to try her hand in the political arena and she became the first Black woman ever elected to the New York State Senate. A year later, she became the first woman of any color elected as Manhattan Borough President. Her career in politics ended a short while later, however, when President Lyndon Johnson appointed her a federal judge. Once again, she was the first Black woman to hold that post and she remained in the position until her death 39 years later.

Though her professional life took her far and wide, Motley always maintained her Connecticut roots. She and her husband Joel Motley, Jr., were married in New Haven and owned a home in Chester for decades. When she died in 2005, her funeral was held in the same New Haven church where she was married.

Connecticut Public Television honored Motley's life and work with *Justice is a Black Woman: The Life and Work of Constance Baker Motley*, a documentary special that aired in 2012. In 2015, *The Trials of Constance Baker Motley*, a documentary film directed by R.E. Rogers, premiered at the Tribeca Film Festival.

Isabel Blake, Welfare Warrior

Isabel Blake challenged state legislators to "meet with us and talk things over." The legislators were silent. "We don't bite," Blake said, "we don't have much to eat, but we don't eat people."

Blake raised ten children in Hartford. She had been recognized since 1968 as a top leader of the local poor people's movement, advocating for public housing residents and welfare recipients. In 1971 she led Welfare Mothers' Rights and the statewide group Welfare Recipients Are People (WRAP).

The group's target was Governor Thomas Meskill, a conservative who called the state's welfare system "a monster" and proceeded to slash critical assistance to recipients. In just one day he vetoed tax breaks for low-and moderate-income housing, funding for vocational training in the prisons and a procedure that would make it easier for welfare recipients to save for a rent deposit.

Worst of all, the legislature established the "flat grant" payment system that meant cuts to rental assistance. "Flat grants are lower rent standards in disguise," said Blake. The activists drew up written demands ending with "Stop playing God. You're no better than we are and we are all human beings."

Isabel Blake and other leaders planned an October 13th rally at Bushnell Park bordering the State Capitol. The event coincided with a demonstration against the Vietnam War. Locally, peace activists made the connections between the war's rising costs and the resulting cuts in domestic programs: $40 billion (in today's dollars) in 1968 alone. "You want us to work but you won't train us, provide us with day care, or help us get jobs. You deceive poor people," Blake declared.

Those who were rallying decided to stand, and the occupation became the state's big news. Taking advantage of the spotlight, the protestors delivered their rent payments to Henry White, Meskill's hand-picked welfare commissioner. The cutbacks planned for November 1st would make it even tougher to pay the rent. White refused the money, but the activists made their point.

The welfare moms, backed by churches and progressive groups, spent a day inside the State Capitol to lobby legislators. "Violence in State Capitol" read a panicky newspaper headline. "The violence is being done to families by totally unjust cuts in family budgets," replied a spokesperson for the local Basic Human Rights Coalition.

Constant lobbying and rallies soon developed into a tent city on the Capitol lawn. More than 100 people stayed the night and more came by day. Meskill publicly threatened to break up the protest by force. "Are you ready to go to jail?" reporters asked Blake. "I'm ready to go to hell," she replied.

Just before dawn on October 20th, Hartford police closed in and arrested Blake and Puerto Rican leader Francesca Cruz, who alerted the other occupiers with a crude public address system before she could be stopped.

Support grew for the tent city and their demands. The state chapter of Vietnam Veterans Against the War (VVAW) occupied the Capitol overnight in solidarity with the two welfare protest leaders. Nine-year-old Aida Rivera delivered a devil's food cake to the Governor's office with the words "Meskill the Blue-Eyed Devil."

On the tent city's sixteenth day, a judge granted an injunction against the November cuts. It was a temporary win in a longer fight, but as community leader Ramon Quiros told the jubilant protestors at their victory party, "This is a night of celebration."

The jury trial of Blake and Cruz finally took place a year after the arrests. They were both acquitted. "Will you go back to the Capitol?" Isabel Blake was asked. "No," she responded. "Just wait and see what I do."

Les Payne: Trailblazing Journalist

Les Payne was born in Tuscaloosa, Alabama on June 12, 1941. But he grew up in Hartford, Connecticut and attended the University of Connecticut. He became one of the best-known African-American journalists in the United States beginning in the 1970s, winning many awards over his long career. Payne did most of his work for *Newsday*, a Long Island-based newspaper that for ten years also published a New York City edition known as *New York Newsday*.

Growing Up in Hartford

Payne was 13-years-old when he moved with his mother and brothers to Hartford's North End. He ran track at Hartford Public High School and graduated in 1960. His mother pressed clothes at a neighborhood dry cleaning establishment while Payne chipped in with money he earned shining shoes and delivering the *Hartford Courant*. He also worked for a while as a tobacco picker in the fields outside of Hartford.

In interviews he did over the course of his life, Payne spoke of the disappointment he felt at finding race relations in Connecticut only nominally better than in the South. "We had rising expectations for places like Hartford and were, in fact, disappointed — if not outright thwarted in some cases," he said in one interview. "Particularly by the criminal justice system." In another interview, Payne spoke about spending many hours at the Hartford Public Library reading out-of-town newspapers and dreaming of becoming a writer.

UConn

Payne became the first member of his family to attend college when he enrolled in the University of Connecticut as an engineering major. While at school, he became involved in the burgeoning Black freedom struggle of the 1960's, doing support work for the Southern-based Student Nonviolent Coordinating Committee (SNCC). He also mobilized UConn students to volunteer as tutors in his Hartford neighborhood.

Eventually, Payne switched his major to English. He had a new goal: to become a journalist. He graduated in 1964, but initially found it extremely difficult to find work, and enlisted in the U.S. Army. *Newsday* ultimately hired Payne after being discharged.

Newsday

Payne kicked off his journalistic career covering the Black Panthers, the Attica Prison rebellion and, as an overseas correspondent, the revolutionary forces in Zimbabwe, as well as resistance to Apartheid in South Africa. Payne also went undercover at a mostly Black migrant labor camp on Long Island harvesting potatoes — perhaps recalling his experiences as a teenager working in Connecticut's tobacco fields (as well as an even earlier stint picking cotton as an eight-year old).

A Pulitzer Prize and Almost a Second

Payne was part of the *Newsday* team that won a Pulitzer Prize in 1974 for its extensive reporting on the international drug trade and the heroin being trafficked between the poppy fields of Turkey and streets of New York City. He was also, according to one account, the Pulitzer jury's choice for another Prize in 1977 for his coverage from South Africa, before the Advisory Board intervened to overturn the selection.

Payne helped lead efforts to convince *Newsday* to hire more women and people of color, and to ensure that those who were already employed got fair opportunities for promotion. "He has a perfect sense of equality," said Murray Kempton, the legendary New York journalist who worked with Payne for many years at *Newsday*. Another colleague, Anthony Marro, said Payne was second only to former editor and publisher David Laventhol in transforming *Newsday* from primarily a suburban newspaper — into a national one.

Maintaining Ties to Connecticut

Payne returned to Connecticut many times over the course of his life. His mother continued to live in Hartford for years after he launched his career. He was a featured speaker at the Hartford Chapter of the National Association for the Advancement of Colored People's annual banquet in 1986. Payne was UConn's commencement speaker in 2003, and gave the convocation speech at Conard High School in West Hartford the following year. He also received a special proclamation from the Connecticut General Assembly celebrating his outstanding career in journalism.

Payne taught at Columbia University Graduate School of Journalism for many years, and was a founding member and president of the National Association of Black Journalists. He was also a regular on WBAI-FM in New York, especially the Global Black Experience program. Payne retired from his editor's job at *Newsday* in 2006, but continued writing columns until 2009 when he retired for good. He died in Harlem on March 19, 2018 at the age of 76.

8. Latinos/Latinas

Puerto Rico, An Experiment in Colonialism

Puerto Rico has been battered by severe crises, both economic and climate-related, and Connecticut shares some of the responsibility. After all, we made the island what it is today: a colony. Not a colony in the "Thirteen Original Colonies" sense where we cursed King George, whistled "Yankee Doodle" and kicked out the Brits. In the early 20th century, the U.S. was experimenting with a new kind of imperial domination. Call it Colonialism 2.0.

In 1898, U.S. Armed Forces invaded Puerto Rico, allegedly to free its people from Spain. But then we imposed a civilian government and passed laws in Washington, D.C. that forced the indigenous people to bend to our business whims. Since American soldiers still occupied their land, this new arrangement was not exactly voluntary.

That's where Connecticut came in. U.S. Senator Orville H. Platt represented our state in Congress from 1879 until his death in 1905. He was a powerbroker who hated labor unions and preferred secrecy in lawmaking to public scrutiny. His policy objectives regarding Native Americans and the conquest of Caribbean and Pacific countries relied on crude racist ideology and tortured logic (read any of his writings).

He wrote legislation that ensured Puerto Rico's permanent political and economic dependence on Big Brother to the north. Specifically, Platt made sure Puerto Rico would not have a voting representative in the U.S. Congress.

Dr. Ramón Emeterio Betances was the leader of the *Grito de Lares* uprising in 1868. The rebellion pressured Spain to move toward Puerto Rican independence. Since 1900, the rules have largely been set for Puerto Ricans by Washington, D.C. Spain had been loosening its grip and had granted Puerto Rico seats in its parliament, the Cortes, years before the U.S. invasion. One year before our occupation, Spain granted self-governance to the island. Platt and Congress set the Puerto Rican people back decades.

The senator from Connecticut also made sure Puerto Rican coffee, tobacco and sugar would be subject to import duties. U.S. tax policy treated the island like a foreign nation, without any of the benefits of sovereignty. You can cross that "no taxation without representation" nonsense off the list.

As a result of Platt's work, the liberation of Puerto Rico did not mean independence for its people. When the Spanish-American War ended, it was like The Who song: "Meet the new boss/Same as the old boss."

141

There is a common misunderstanding about Puerto Rico's current economic status. Many assume that it is the land of generous welfare, thanks to Washington, D.C. But consider:

~Puerto Ricans on the island can be drafted, but they can't vote for President (the U.S. "granted" citizenship to Puerto Rico in 1917 just in time to draft 18,000 islanders for World War I);

~They pay federal taxes, but they don't get as much bang for their buck in federal aid compared to Alaska or Hawaii;

~Their Medicare benefits are capped at a lower rate than in the U.S., and they are excluded from the earned income tax credit, specifically designed for low-income people;

~Tax loopholes for American corporations have meant that the U.S. has lost $3.00 in tax revenue for every $1.00 paid in wages.

In 2015, the 3.5 million people of Puerto Rico suffered under a staggering $72 billion debt. Deals and defaults only masked the real problems. At the top of the list is the fact that Puerto Rico cannot declare bankruptcy, unlike U.S. cities and states. Washington, D.C. budget battles did not make any change to that colonial stranglehold.

Orville Platt was bold about his underlying intent: "We hear a great deal about … the right of all persons in territory which we acquire, to be treated precisely as we treat all citizens of our own states. I deny it constitutionally, legally, and morally," he declared.

Erasing Platt's embarrassing legacy means Puerto Ricans should be able to freely determine their own political future with independence as a legitimate option.

Yanquis or Yankees?

Are we yanquis or yankees? In Connecticut, we have been both. The Dutch word *janke* was popularized by Mark Twain in his comic novel *A Connecticut Yankee in King Arthur's Court*. It wasn't until the 1960's that we learned the slogan "Yanqui Go Home."

Are we "Still Revolutionary?" That was the slogan of our state's advertising campaign, designed to attract tourists to Connecticut. We were, after all, one of the first American colonies to break away from England. Today, the tourism plan costs $27 million.

President Barack Obama's diplomatic initiative for normal relations helped – for a while – to redefine who we are when it comes to Cuba. But first, we must remember what originally tied us to that nation in the first place. If we promote what our two lands have in common, we might build mutual respect. Connecticut has significant historical links to Cuba, for better or worse.

In fact, three Connecticut men played major roles in shaping U.S. policy toward Cuba.

First came Samuel Colt, the most famous (or infamous) gunmaker in U.S. history. A native of Connecticut, he built his firearms factory in Hartford, the state's capital city. Historians note that millionaire Colt aided Narciso Lopez, the *filibustero* who invaded Cuba in 1851 before the U.S. Civil War, in order to "liberate" it. Lopez and his plotters hoped it would become a slave state and a new market for Colt's weapons trade.

It was the Colt revolver that Theodore Roosevelt and his "Rough Riders" carried in 1898 as they charged up San Juan Hill against the Spanish. The Colt company also produced the Gatling Gun when Sam Colt's widow became owner of the business. It was the first effective weapon of mass destruction, deployed against indigenous people in the U.S. and Canada, Filipinos, and even U.S. workers on strike.

Orville H. Platt was born in the small Connecticut town of Washington. Platt was a life-long politician who served five terms as a U.S. senator. He is known as the author of the 1901 "Platt Amendment" which established Guantanamo Bay as a U.S. naval base. The law also dominated Cuba's relations with other countries, allowing the U.S. Congress to intervene in the young nation's affairs any time we felt threatened. When Cubans opposed his plan, Platt informed them that the U.S. would occupy the island until they agreed.

Mark Twain saw Cuba as an imperialist conquest. He lived in Hartford for 17 years, writing his most famous works, including *Life on the Mississippi*, *Adventures of Huckleberry Finn* and *The Prince and the Pauper*. Twain was a prominent member of the Anti-Imperialist League, which opposed U.S. domination of Cuba, the Philippines and other former Spanish colonies. His transformation from novelist to activist came with great public criticism and at a personal cost. Yet Mark Twain continued to speak out. "I am opposed to having the eagle put its talons on any other land," he wrote.

There are other connections that we in Connecticut can dust off and restore to our popular conversation when we consider our Cuban links:

Havana tobacco seeds grew well in Connecticut soil. As far back as 1884, local farmers were growing crops from the Cuban plant. The imported seeds produced what the yankee farmers called a "superior plant," which was made into high-quality cigar wrappers. Hartford steamships carried tobacco filler from the island so that our local factories could manufacture the entire cigar.

Cuban baseball stars were recruited to Connecticut by the New Britain Aviators beginning in 1908. Armando Marsans and Rafael Almeida were among the first Cuban ballplayers to break into the American major leagues. New Britain's Cuban stars visited Hartford often, playing (and beating) the Hartford Senators.

In his journal, John F. Kennedy's biographer Arthur Schlesinger Jr., wrote that Havana in 1950 was a "giant casino and brothel" for American businessmen. After the Cuban revolution, which brought in a socialist government, however, Connecticut residents visited Cuba for entirely different reasons.

In 1970, local college students spent two-month stints cutting sugar cane with the Venceremos Brigades. On one trip, President Fidel Castro worked side-by-side with six Connecticut residents. "He is someone who risked his life, was imprisoned, and gave up a career as a lawyer to fight for his people. He can speak in the open in front of one million people ... I'd like to see Richard Nixon do that," one of the students told a newspaper reporter.

In 1977, Yale University invited 16 Cuban scholars to the United States in an academic exchange. Five years later, a University of Bridgeport professor led the first visit of U.S. philosophers to meet with their Havana counterparts. A Wesleyan University student traveled to Cuba in 2002 on a medical scholarship, one of thousands of international students who have trained each year to become doctors.

One U.S. delegation of healthcare workers visited Cuba's parliament in 1999 for a wide-ranging discussion with Julio Espinosa, head of the International Relations Commission. They challenged Espinosa on what would happen to Cuba after Fidel was gone. "Someday he will die; he is a human being," Espinosa replied (Fidel died in 2016). "But almost all our country's elected leaders are under the age of 40. If Fidel dies next year and the U.S. blockade is lifted, we as a country will be the same."

Despite setbacks later imposed by the Trump administration, the United States will still have the opportunity to relate to Cuba the same way as every other nation on earth. It will be a great chance to move from revenge to reconciliation.

Pa'lante: The Young Lords in Bridgeport

Virtually every segment of society was impacted by the democratic upsurge in the United States in the 1960's — and Puerto Ricans were no exception. Puerto Ricans in a number of places came together to form organizations and participate in multiracial coalitions in order to address a number of pressing problems. Among the most popular Puerto Rican organizations was the Young Lords Party, which was formed in the winter of 1968-69 and had an active chapter in Bridgeport for a number of years.

Puerto Ricans emigrated from the island in large numbers in the years after World War II, as they began to experience ever more acutely the ravages of U.S. imperialism. Over a 20-year span beginning in the 1940's, the Puerto Rican population in the U.S increased from 70,000 to one million. As with other immigrant groups, most settled in the nation's largest cities – New York especially — but Chicago, Philadelphia and several others as well. Bridgeport was also a popular landing point. In fact, since the 1960's, Puerto Ricans have made up a larger percentage of Bridgeport's population than New York City's. Statewide, Puerto Ricans have for many years, been a larger percentage of Connecticut's population than any other state — and remain so today.

The Founding of the Young Lords

The founders of the Young Lords (which began as the Young Lords Organization, and was soon re-named the Young Lords Party) were mostly young Puerto Ricans in Chicago and New York. Some in the group in Chicago were members of street gangs who were politicized around the oppressive conditions Puerto Ricans confronted on a daily basis, particularly police brutality. They became part of the original Rainbow Coalition that eventually included the Black Panther Party, the American Indian Movement, a Chicano group called the Brown Berets, an Asian-American group called I Wor Kuen, and several groups of radical, white working class youths – the Young Patriots, White Panthers and the Patriot Party. All were inspired by the Student Nonviolent Coordinating Committee and Malcolm X, as well as independence and revolutionary movements throughout the Global South, including the rich history of resistance to outside domination in Puerto Rico itself.

In New York City, with its large concentration of Puerto Ricans, the Young Lords Party had its biggest branches and most extensive campaigns. Most

146

involved getting basic public services, either as organized by the YLP itself – a free breakfast program, free clothes and blankets during winter, mobile health clinics, a takeover of Lincoln Hospital in the Bronx – or via direct action, such as demands for better sanitation services. The group also confronted patriarchy in ways and to an extent that few of that time did, led by a corps of women who were in the forefront of virtually every struggle the YLP participated in. The Lords also published a Spanish/English newspaper *Pa'lante* as well as pamphlets on a variety of subjects, and hosted a weekly radio show on WBAI.

From its founding, the YLP opposed the U.S. wars of aggression that were then raging in Vietnam and the rest of Indochina. In their work against the illegality of those wars, the Lords underscored their opposition to the deployment of colonial subject Puerto Ricans to fight other colonial subjects in Southeast Asia. Pablo Guzman, a YLP leader and later a longtime New York television reporter, was one of a number of Young Lords who went to prison for draft resistance and for openly encouraging others to do likewise. *Pa'lante* also regularly reported on other criminal activities of U.S. imperialism, such as the overthrow of Salvador Allende's socialist government in Chile in 1973, as well as on national liberation movements around the world.

The Bridgeport YLP Branch is Formed

In 1970, a Bridgeport organization called Spanish People in Command joined with the Young Lords to form the local YLP branch, the organization's fifth. The Lords underscored the significance of the move in *Pa'lante* on the occasion of its second anniversary, noting that the establishment of the Bridgeport chapter"was important because it was the first time the Party opened in a small, working class city.

When the branch was formed, there were approximately 15,000 Puerto Ricans living in Bridgeport, roughly ten percent of the city's population. Bridgeport's manufacturing-based economy was still thriving in 1970, but Puerto Ricans found good-paying jobs difficult to come by. Many encountered hiring discrimination from employers and apathy, if not hostility, from labor unions. Landlords charged exorbitant rents for apartments that were often substandard, if not outright firetraps. Police harassment was a regular part of life and often came at the end of a nightstick or worse. Justice was in short supply in the courts, and petty crimes of poverty frequently led to incarceration. It was in this context that the branch was formed and around these issues that it organized.

Free Breakfast for Children, Rent Strikes and Other Campaigns

Among its first projects, the Bridgeport branch established a Free Breakfast for Children program at St. Mary's Roman Catholic Church on Pembroke Street.

Patterned on similar programs set up around the country by the Black Panthers (who also briefly had a Bridgeport chapter), children of all races and ethnicities were provided free breakfast every weekday before school. The Lords were also instrumental in initiating a tenants association and rent strike at 381-387-393 East Main Street in December, 1970 when residents were forced to endure five consecutive freezing days and nights without heat. It was also at that site that the branch opened its local office.

Though the tenants' demands were initially rebuffed, they persevered and secured significant improvements. In addition to the gains won, the campaign was a teaching moment for the new YLP branch, as it demonstrated to community residents that collective action could be successful, and was ultimately the only way forward. With the police, the landlords, the local media and other segments of the city's elites all arrayed against them, many residents also learned about the hostility with which entrenched power regarded their aspirations.

Like the national organization, the Bridgeport chapter throughout its history did solidarity work with Puerto Rico and educational work about U.S. domination of the island. When the YLP organized actions around the country on March 21, 1971 to mark the 34th anniversary of the 1937 Ponce Massacre in which 22 island nationalists were shot and killed by colonial forces, the Bridgeport chapter held a demonstration in Washington Park. Bridgeport members and supporters also participated in a number of national YLP actions, including the 10,000-strong demonstration at the United Nations in New York City on October 30, 1971, demanding independence for Puerto Rico.

East Main Street Rebellion
On May 20, 1971 tensions that had been growing between the Lords and the people they were organizing on the one hand, and slumlords and police on the other, boiled over. With the East Main Street rent strike still ongoing, the owners of the property attempted to evict the Young Lords from their office. Local YLP leader Willie Matos was arrested for trespassing, the office was trashed and furniture illegally removed, all in the presence of Bridgeport police officers. An enraged group of several hundred supporters soon took to the streets and began throwing rocks at the police and the agents of the landlord.

More people were arrested when protesters blockaded a section of East Main Street. The police, meanwhile, patrolled the area with police dogs and officers armed with shotguns. Articles in the *Bridgeport Post* and *Bridgeport Telegram* were full of references to "rioters," "violence" and other code words. Excluded from their stories (though it was included in the extensive coverage in *Pa'lante*) was the fact that the landlords involved were the same ones who owned a nearby property on Arctic Street where a catastrophic fire on Easter

148

Sunday in 1969 killed eleven people.

After being released from jail and returning to the site of the conflict, Matos declared that it was the beginning of community power; that he was sick and tired of police brutality.

New Projects in Bridgeport

In 1972, the Bridgeport branch held its Ponce Massacre commemorative march in Hartford with local supporters in an effort to establish a chapter there. A short time later, a branch was, indeed, established in New Haven. The Bridgeport branch, meanwhile, relocated to Crescent Place where its new office also included a bookstore.

Substandard housing remained one of the Bridgeport branch's main concerns. When another fire at one of the properties on East Main Street where the rent strike had occurred resulted in the death of a six-year old girl — the YLP and its supporters began weekly picketing at the Lafayette Shopping Center in downtown. The purpose was to pressure business and political elites to deal with tenants' demands by boycotting stores in the recently-opened mall. Five people including several Lords were arrested at the mall on May 6, 1972.

The Bridgeport branch also worked with other city organizations to address the problems of layoffs and unemployment, which by 1972 were at crisis levels. One venue was the Committee of Unemployed Workers, established in August of that year. Also that summer, the Bridgeport branch initiated a conference to establish a statewide organization of Puerto Rican migrant workers held at the Disciples of Christ Church on East Washington Avenue.

Harassment, Repression and Decline

Throughout its history, the YLP was closely monitored by the FBI and other police agencies. A Senate Subcommittee on Internal Security chaired by the notorious white supremacist James Eastland, and also included among its members Strom Thurmond, another white supremacist—investigated the Young Lords and its successor group, the Puerto Rican Revolutionary Workers Organization (PRRWO). Among those mentioned in the 48-page report is Willie Matos.

In addition, a number of Lords were indicted and imprisoned for refusing to register for the military draft, including some of the organization's national leaders. Several other members around the country were also killed by police. The state repression and harassment, along with serious internal problems, eventually took a toll, and the organization went into decline in the mid-1970's. The Bridgeport branch was one of four remaining when the group ceased to exist in 1976.

149

Former Young Lords Carry On

In the years since, many who had been members of the Young Lords have carried on its radical and revolutionary work. Some, including Denise Oliver-Perez, Mickey Melendez and Richie Perez, a long-time activist in New York until his untimely death in 2004 at age 59, went into academia. Juan Gonzalez is an award-winning journalist who for many years was a columnist for the New York *Daily News* and today co-hosts the nationally syndicated radio show *Democracy Now!* with Amy Goodman. Pablo Guzman and Felipe Luciano, among others, have also had long, distinguished careers as journalists, a fact that prompted the late longtime New York City newspaper columnist Jimmy Breslin to say that the Young Lords produced more great journalists than Columbia University's journalism school. Other Lords have worked, and continue to work, as union organizers and for a variety of social justice organizations.

Locally, Willie Matos worked for many years for the Connecticut Human Rights Commission and was instrumental, along with other former Lords, in founding the Spanish American Coalition, a long-time activist group in Bridgeport. Matos and others were also active in the Bridgeport chapter of the Vieques Support Committee, a national group formed in 1980 to oppose the use by the U.S. Navy of the Puerto Rican island of Vieques for bombing practice.

The appearance of a number of recent books, documentary films and several photo exhibits has stimulated renewed interest in the Young Lords, especially among young people. This is only fitting, as the issues the group grappled with – national and racial oppression, substandard housing, police brutality, imperialist war, the vast gulf between the Super Rich and the rest of us – are with us more than ever.

9. Radical Women

Olympia Brown, America's First Ordained Woman Minister

When the board of Bridgeport's First Universalist Church offered Olympia Brown a position as minister in 1869, not everyone in the church's congregation approved. Congregants protested, and the protests grew when Brown arrived in Bridgeport for a trial sermon at the church. Not one to shy away from a challenge, Brown met with those who objected to her hiring and asked that they listen to her sermon before arriving at judgment. After hearing her, an overwhelming majority of the congregation decided to hire Brown.

Born in Michigan in 1835, Olympia Brown attended Mount Holyoke Female Seminary in Massachusetts, transferred to Antioch College in Ohio and graduated in 1860. Desiring a life as a minister, Brown received numerous rejections from seminary schools because she was a woman before St. Lawrence University's Theological School in New York accepted her. Brown persevered in the face of continuous hostility, and in 1863, became the first woman in the history of the United States to be ordained a minister.

Brown worked in Vermont for a year, and five years at the Universalist church in Weymouth Landing, Massachusetts. She contributed greatly to a vibrant, intellectual atmosphere there by regularly inviting prominent area residents like Ralph Waldo Emerson and David Lloyd Garrison, who shared her sympathies for the abolitionist and women's suffrage movements, to lecture at the church.

The First American Woman Ordained a Minister Comes to the Park City

Though most of Bridgeport's Universalist community eventually welcomed Brown, a small vocal minority led by long-time congregant James Staples, opposed having their church led by a woman. Though Brown's opponents never grew beyond their original small numbers, they did erode church morale. The congregation diminished in size, and the church's financial situation, always problematic, worsened.

Brown remained determined, however, and she declined an offer of a higher-paying position in Pennsylvania in 1873 to remain in Bridgeport. That year, she also married John Henry Willis, who moved to Bridgeport from Weymouth Landing to woo her. She gave birth to a son the following year.

In addition to personal happiness, Brown also passionately immersed herself in the cause of women's equality during her years in Bridgeport. She worked with Susan B. Anthony, Lucy Stone, Elizabeth Cady Stanton and other leading figures of the suffrage movement, and traveled to Hartford and Washington, D.C. to testify before various legislative committees. She actively spread the suffrage word in Bridgeport through petition drives and other efforts.

For James Staples and his allies, Brown's activism only compounded their hostility to her service as their church's minister. In 1874, they expanded their efforts beyond the First Universalist congregation with meetings around Bridgeport. They also called on local ministers to speak out against women ministers generally, and Brown in particular.

Olympia Brown Leaves Bridgeport

In early 1876, the tensions within the First Universalist congregation and Bridgeport's larger religious community reached a breaking point. Though still a small minority, James and his group successfully lobbied to get an injunction placed on the church. The board of trustees, which like the congregation still supported Brown, announced that they could no longer afford to employ a minister and Brown's term at the church ended in March.

The success of the opposition group was as big a blow as Brown had yet endured, but she moved on without missing a beat. She remained active in organizations including, the National Woman Suffrage Association, and continued traveling, lecturing, and testifying on behalf of the cause she held so dear. Brown gave birth to a daughter in 1876 and remained in Bridgeport with her husband and children for nearly three years after leaving the Universalist Church. She finally accepted a ministry position in Wisconsin at the end of 1878.

Brown was still participating in suffrage activities in 1920 when legislators ratified the 19th Amendment to the Constitution. A member of Alice Paul's National Woman's Party, she and women around the country voted for the first time that November. Olympia Brown died six years later, on October 23, 1926, in Baltimore, at the age of 91.

Ida Tarbell, The Woman Who Took On Standard Oil

Muckraking journalism emerged at the end of the 19th century largely in response to the excesses of the Gilded Age, and Ida Tarbell was one of the most famous of all the muckrakers. Born in 1857 in a log cabin in Hatch Hollow, Pennsylvania, Tarbell's first dream was to be a scientist. Science was a field largely closed to women, however, and she instead pursued teaching, a profession deemed more suitable.

In 1883, she met Dr. Thomas Flood, editor of *The Chautauquan*, a magazine published in nearby Meadville, Pennsylvania. Flood was about to retire his position and he asked Tarbell to assist him for a few months while he searched for a successor. She accepted, and ended up working at *The Chautauquan* as a writer and editor for six years.

Writing became Tarbell's passion. One of her biographers, Kathleen Brady, wrote of Tarbell that "the sight of her work in type was like magic which dispelled forever dreams of botany." Keenly aware of social problems since her days as a teacher, Tarbell wrote about inequality and injustice and encouraged colleagues at *The Chautauquan* to do likewise.

In 1890, Tarbell moved to Paris. She had written a series of articles about women of the French Revolution and went to France to research a projected biography of one of those women, Madame Marie-Jeanne Roland. She supported herself by writing articles about Parisian life for *Scribner's Magazine* and other American publications, including several owned by Samuel McClure.

Tarbell Exposes the Standard Oil Company

Tarbell never wrote the biography of Roland but she did write biographies of Napoleon Bonaparte and Abraham Lincoln, both published shortly after her return to the United States in 1894. She also accepted an offer from McClure to work for his new venture, *McClure's Magazine*, where she undertook her most famous work, her expose of John D. Rockefeller's Standard Oil Company. Her study of Rockefeller's practices as he built Standard Oil into one of the world's largest business monopolies took many years to complete. *McClure's Magazine* published it in 19 installments.

Her work was a sensation and the installments became a two-volume book entitled *The History of the Standard Oil Company*, published in 1904. Tarbell meticulously documented the aggressive techniques Standard Oil employed to outmaneuver and, where necessary, roll over whoever got in its way. A short while later, President Theodore Roosevelt used the phrase "muckraker" (from John Bunyan's *The Pilgrim's Progress*) in a speech in reference to Tarbell, Upton Sinclair, Lincoln Steffens and other journalists writing critically about the tremendous power of big business. Tarbell actually objected to the term, for she felt it belittled work she believed to be of historical importance.

One result largely attributable to Tarbell's work was a Supreme Court decision in 1911 that found Standard Oil in violation of the Sherman Antitrust Act. The Court found that Standard was an illegal monopoly and ordered it broken into 34 separate companies. Bloodied, Rockefeller and Standard were hardly defeated. Rockefeller maintained huge holdings in all 34 companies and the breakup actually proved enormously profitable. He lived out the rest of his long life with his status as the world's wealthiest man unblemished.

Retiring to Easton

In 1906, not long after her rise to fame, Tarbell purchased a home in Easton, Connecticut. Easton was a farming town and she used the home and its 40-acre spread as a country getaway for the next 18 years while living primarily in New York City. She lectured widely and continued writing for important publications of the time like the *American Magazine* of which she was also co-editor. Among the events she covered were the negotiations in Versailles at the conclusion of World War One.

In 1924, Tarbell moved permanently to Easton. She was 67, but she kept writing, producing among other works, an autobiography entitled *All in the Day's Work*. She took ill with pneumonia in December 1943, and died in Bridgeport Hospital on January 6, 1944 at age 86.

The History of the Standard Oil Company remains a classic of investigative journalism, and Tarbell's legacy as someone who took seriously the credo that journalists should "afflict the comfortable and comfort the afflicted" lives on. The Easton home she lived in became a National Historic Landmark in 1993.

Matilda Rabinowitz

Harry Hardy traveled from Boston to the borough of Shelton, Connecticut with a mission: stop IWW organizer Matilda Rabinowitz. He brought with him other employees of the Sherman Detective Agency to meet town officials ready to break the strike of hundreds of weavers and mill workers at the Sidney Blumenthal & Company, organized by the Wobblies on November 12, 1913.

Hardy offered to use the same techniques his agency had developed in Massachusetts. At a Brockton shoe strike, his men had insinuated themselves into the union leadership, won posts as treasurer and strike secretary, bankrupted the union's efforts and forced the shoemakers back to work.

This time, however, Harry Hardy had an even better idea. Strike organizer Matilda Rabinowitz was a "dangerous proposition," he said. Hardy and his men would kidnap her, depriving the workers of their young charismatic leader. The scheme was never carried out; word leaked out that Matilda was the target of the planned abduction. She briefly noted it in her report to the IWW headquarters.

Matilda Rabinowitz (born Tatania Gitel Rabinowitz in 1887 in Ukrainia) emigrated to New York at the age of thirteen. Her family soon moved to Stamford and later to Bridgeport. She worked in shirtwaist and corset factories, millinery, and department stores, a private nursery, and as a nursing home aide. Other working class factory girls labored long hours for low pay in dangerous jobs without ever having the opportunity to challenge their lot in life, but Rabinowitz was different. She identified the capitalist system as the source of women workers' suffering, and she decided to take action.

By the time she was in her early twenties, Rabinowitz had joined the socialist movement. She took a job with the Connecticut Industrial Commission and moved to Hartford, interviewing factory workers about their conditions. During this time, she considered going to college, but the union movement proved to be a stronger attraction. Rabinowitz's growing desire for justice led her first to the American Federation of Labor (AFL), which she soon discovered cared little about the plight of working women. The AFL's indifference pushed her toward the IWW.

Matilda Rabinowitz's first union experience was in the 1912 Lawrence strike, where her energy and competence caught the attention of the IWW's leaders. She traveled back and forth from Massachusetts to Connecticut, raising money for the strike from Bridgeport workers. After the historic Lawrence victory, Matilda was asked by the IWW's Vincent St. John to travel to Little Falls, New York. The textile struggle there honed her strike skills. Organizing soup kitchens, speaking to supporters and raising funds did not make headlines, but her work played the critical role in keeping up the strikers' strength and morale. After strike leader Benjamin Legere went to jail, she led the strikers in a mass meeting and victory march, and ultimately to victory.

In 1913, Rabinowitz made an extraordinary journey across Michigan, Ohio and Pennsylvania, working on IWW strikes at silk mills, automobile plants, steel mills, and cigar factories. In each of these union drives, she was the only woman organizer. Despite the fact that so many female-dominated industries were ripe for organizing, Matilda and Elizabeth Gurley Flynn were the only women paid by the IWW as organizers during this period.

When the boss at Blumenthal cut wages in November 1913, it was the spark the union needed. Rabinowitz, back from her travels, met with the workers and immediately sent a telegram to *Solidarity*, the IWW's newspaper. It was brief, like all such messages, but its tone was urgent, reflecting her excitement and determination: "Four hundred weavers out in Blumenthal Company's plant, Shelton. All joined organization. More coming: expect to tie up mill."

Matilda Rabinowitz organized a strong strike committee that was "planning to give the mill owners a hard fight ... until victory is achieved," she pledged. Their demands included the ten-hour day, abolition of forced overtime and a weekly pay system. The workers also insisted on an increase in the piece rate, and a certain level of security for weavers when their looms broke down. Breakdowns were not the weaver's fault, they argued, and they shouldn't lose pay because of it. The committee demanded a daily minimum wage of $3.00.

Early in the strike, Blumenthal had taken out full-page ads to demonstrate his weavers were well-paid. Matilda Rabinowitz replied that the company's figures were deliberately misleading, since they did not include the slow months when work was scarce, and that only a select group of higher-waged men were listed.

Maintaining the day-to-day organizing was not an easy task. Rabinowitz battled not only bosses and hostile business leaders, she was forced to challenge the prejudices that some of the strikers had against immigrant workers whose religion or ethnicity differed from theirs. Perhaps this is why the young Russian Jew later adopted the Americanized surname Robbins. She made no such accommodation, however, while she organized in the Naugatuck Valley.

She threw herself into the efforts to maintain solidarity, speaking every day to the strikers in Russian, Yiddish and English. Forced to meet outside of Shelton, she hired local halls in nearby Derby and Ansonia. The organizer encouraged local grocers to increase their prices and share the profits with the strikers. No one could help notice Rabinowitz as she led marches down Main Street. "Her petite form looked odd among the stalwart men," wrote one newspaper reporter.

On January 12, 1914, the strikers rallied at the Sterling Opera House in Derby. The meeting was chaired by Michael Dumas, an IWW leader and a weaver at the Specialty Weaving Company of Shelton. Earlier in the year, Dumas had led a strike that failed to reach its objectives, but had built IWW Local 528 and maintained a strong presence in the plant. Specialty's owner tried to fire Dumas during the course of the Blumenthal strike, but his co-workers staged their own walk-out and protected their leader's job.

Arturo Giovannitti was the featured speaker at the Opera House. "You can't win anything by staying home to sleep or by reading your Bible over again," he told the crowd. "That's all very well, but it doesn't win strikes."

Rabinowitz was the big hit of the rally. The idea that a woman might actually be an effective organizer of male textile workers was unusual; she was consistently described in the press as "frail," "diminutive," and "of girlish appearance." But no one could deny that she spoke with great force and the power of her convictions:

"I apologize to the people of Shelton who came here out of curiosity. I fear the IWW speakers here tonight have disappointed you. None of them have come to the stage with a stiletto in his teeth. They carry no guns, nor do they bring with them bombs with sputtering fuses. My aim is not to speak to those who exploit but to those who are exploited. I am not concerned with what is the reputation of the IWW in these parts. It makes not a particle of difference to me whether they like me in Shelton or not. With this revolutionary movement we recognize no country and we recognize no flag. The foreigner and the American are brothers in the misery and degradation and terrible sufferings of poverty. John Brown went to the gallows. He was sent there by the same respectable mob, if you please, that says in Shelton and in Derby that the IWW organizer ought to be tarred and feathered, and run out of town. But if I am taken out of Shelton today, six or eight or ten or twelve others will come here. And if they are driven out of town, there will be a hundred to take their places." (Robin Légère Henderson, *Matilda Rabinowitz, Immigrant Girl, Radical Woman: A Memoir from the Early Twentieth*)

Rabinowitz anticipated the Blumenthal boss would use all the forces at his disposal to beat the strike. What she had not expected was the betrayal by local socialist leader Samuel Beardsley. During the first week of the Blumenthal strike, Beardsley distributed flyers threatening strikers (in five languages!) that picket line violence was a violation of state law. His action exacerbated an already tense situation.

Every move Beardsley made seemed designed to undermine the IWW's efforts while maintaining an outward appearance of support. According to Rabinowitz, he had a spy in the strike committee who would report to him every night. Then Beardsley and other Socialist Party members would contact strike leaders individually to try and convince them to return to work. Beardsley even had himself appointed to a borough-sponsored "settlement committee" made up of prominent men. The committee interviewed Blumenthal and determined that he would never deal with the IWW. Beardsley was also behind a rumor, Matilda Rabinowitz believed, that she was mismanaging the strike's finances. In a union report, the Wobbly organizer wrote that Beardsley had been "carrying on against the IWW in the dark, using true Tammany Hall methods." (Robin Légère Henderson, op. cit.)

Samuel Beardsley served as Connecticut state secretary of the Socialist Party. He had championed a change to the party's national constitution in 1912, known as Section 6, which banned any member who "advocates crime, sabotage, or other methods of violence." Beardsley and his comrades won that fight, which led to the expulsion from the Party of many Wobblies, including leader Bill Haywood. In fact, no Wobbly organizer had ever been convicted of sabotage, as confirmed in 1939 by a Johns Hopkins University investigation. Beardsley boasted to the Blumenthal strikers that he had helped pass Section 6, a clear message that he believed Shelton would be better off without the IWW.

Shelton's burgesses, the equivalent of town councilmen, paid massive overtime to keep local police on duty, spending up to $200 a day. Blumenthal hired the notorious O'Brien detective agency to patrol the factory. The O'Briens were founded by Boss Farley, described by the *New York Times* as the "king strike breaker who developed the business into a science." The O'Brien detectives earned a minimum of $25 a day. Weavers, by contrast, had been making about $7 a week when work was available.

Blumenthal also put the O'Briens inside the mill and outfitted them with beds and gas stoves. For the Blumenthal Company and Shelton's town fathers, this fight was not just about money. It was about power, and Sidney Blumenthal intended to keep control of his mill at any cost.

Although the strikers became increasingly restless, their active hostility was only sporadic toward the scabs imported from other cities and the thugs who protected them. Violence from the police and the detectives, in contrast, was constant and ferocious. The O'Briens would "insult and aggravate the strikers in many ways," according to a news report, even though the IWW strikers "desire to conduct themselves peaceably."

For her part, Rabinowitz cautioned the mill workers against anything that would distract them from proper strike conduct. "I am not a Prohibitionist," she told IWW men in one of her daily talks. "I don't insist that men must be total abstainers. But in a time like this, men with strong drink are led to do things that they ought not to do. Let the strike breakers and the guards do the drinking. We must get along without it." (Robin Légère Henderson, op. cit.)

Despite the public criticism of Matilda Rabinowitz in the press and the treacherous undercurrent fomented by Comrade Beardsley, the strikers were not about to abandon the 26-year old organizer who had stood by them every step of the way. At one point, she offered to resign if the strikers thought it would be in their best interests. Hundreds of men responded with a "rousing demonstration of confidence."

Sidney Blumenthal's assault on the strike was unrelenting, and he had help from elements of the AFL. Blumenthal not only hired scabs from Bridgeport, Providence and Philadelphia, but had striking AFL plumbers shipped in from New Haven. He even convinced the Massachusetts Employment Bureau (an official state agency) to send workers to operate the idle looms. The Bureau's head, Harry Dunderdale, was also secretary of the Boston Central Labor Union.

Official violence against the strikers intensified. Police severely beat a woman because she failed to move along when ordered. An innocent bystander was clubbed by guards, who insisted the man had fallen from an automobile. Agents entered a private house, attacked and beat up two men, and had them arrested because "their party was too loud." One mill guard falsely accused a local farm hand as the culprit who tossed a stone through a saloon window. In response, the bartender beat the elderly farmer, Alex Havrilla, with a pool cue. Havrilla died of his injuries. The bartender was arrested, but the O'Brien guard fled across the state line to avoid prosecution.

Women played a particularly assertive role as official violence increased. They faced down both the police and the O'Briens armed only with hot water or handfuls of pepper. These homemade weapons were no match for Winchester rifles and Colt revolvers. Mary Smarsh, a 38-year-old widow with four small children, was shot during a melee between strikers and police. Mary's son was injured by clubs in the same battle.

The most shameful incident of violence took place eight weeks into the strike. Police dragged a couple, Michael and Carolyn Homick, from their home during a disturbance near the mill. Their children were left alone in the freezing apartment. The couple was badly beaten before being arrested. Michael was immediately sentenced to 15 days in jail; Carolyn was released but her injuries were so severe that she could not care for her two-month old child, Mary. The infant, already malnourished, died three days later. The strikers organized a mass funeral procession with the child's coffin at the front of their ranks.

Samuel Beardsley and his settlement committee met inside the plant with Blumenthal and were given an IWW pamphlet that the boss said was sufficient reason to exclude Wobblies from employment. "We have done everything possible to bring about the settlement of this struggle," Beardsley sadly concluded.

Over the next two days, controversy erupted among the strikers. Paranoia about the IWW was growing, exacerbated by the local socialists, and there were intense debates at the strike meetings. Three votes took place on whether or not to return to work. Finally, a vote of 137 to 133 called off the strike. According to town officials, Blumenthal had agreed to a shorter work week and weekly pay envelopes, two of the strikers' original demands.

O'Brien men stayed in the plant to watch the returning workers. Blumenthal made the former strikers raise their right hands and swear they would give up their IWW cards. The machinists, all AFL members, were refused jobs because they had honored the Wobblies' picket line. Most weavers refused to return to the Blumenthal mills under the new conditions and left town to seek work elsewhere. Someone stole the union's membership book, which ended up in Blumenthal's hands.

"Let this incident in the history of labor stand out as an example of the work some of the socialist politicians are doing in the labor movement,' wrote a bitter Matilda Rabinowitz, "and the assistance they render to labor's emancipation." David Rabinowitz, Matilda's brother who had originally helped bring her into the Socialist Party, denounced Beardsley at a party meeting for betraying the Blumenthal strike. David, who for years had been an organizer for the Socialists, was expelled from the group.

Rabinowitz left Shelton, and between 1914 and 1915, she spent five months organizing textile workers in the company town of Greenville, South Carolina. On behalf of the IWW, she traveled to this southern town with the name of only one person to contact. When she arrived, Rabinowitz set up a soapbox outside the local revival tent and soon attracted her own "converts." Now 27-years-old, Rabinowitz built the first southern IWW local in the textile town.

The poverty and oppression Rabinowitz witnessed in South Carolina had a profound impact on her. In February, 1915, she published a story in the *Waterbury Herald* about the daily life of a fictional cotton mill family. The stereotyped dialect she uses did not obscure the deep empathy with which Rabinowitz sketched the hard lives she witnessed.

Sometime after her east coast organizing, Matilda Rabinowitz became Matilda Robbins. She moved on and became an organizer for the United Auto Workers, worked as a labor newspaper editor, and later as a social worker. She always remained a Wobbly, however, and wrote for the IWW newspaper until her death in 1963.

Helen Keller, Radical

Travel north from Bridgeport through Fairfield to Sport Hill Road in the small, upscale town of Easton, Connecticut and you eventually come to Helen Keller Middle School. Go west a few miles to the other side of Easton and you can see the house where Keller lived from 1939 until her death in 1968. If you don't know the location, however, you'll never find the house. Even though Keller lived there longer than anywhere else, there is no stone or plaque marking the spot.

That there's no marker at the house is a bit surprising, for there was a time when Keller was one of the most famous people in the world, better known even than presidents and kings. Circa 1920, she was perhaps the second most recognizable Westerner on the planet behind only Charlie Chaplin—also a radical who, like Keller, used his brilliance to speak for the unrepresented.

Born in Alabama in 1880 with both the ability to see and hear, Keller lost both senses at 19 months due to disease — most likely scarlet fever or meningitis. Her parents were of some means, and she was thus spared the fate that befell thousands of blind and deaf working class children of the time — institutionalization. As a young girl, Keller developed a homemade sign language that she used to communicate with those close to her. Treatment options and educational opportunities were few, however. Her quality of life was minimal. Despite the love of her devoted but heartbroken mother, Kate Adams Keller, Helen lived much like an untamed animal.

Anne Sullivan

In 1887, an extraordinary young woman named Anne Sullivan traveled to the Keller home to be her teacher. Severely visually impaired, herself, Sullivan's early life was something out of Dickens or Engels. Orphaned at a young age, she had lived for many years in a Massachusetts institution alongside mentally ill adults who often preyed on the children in their midst. Staff were abusive and apathetic, and the facility was little more than a holding cell which few left alive. Sullivan later recalled that fewer than a fifth of the children there lived to adulthood. Among the other horrors, she watched in agony as her younger brother slowly died of neglect despite her best efforts to protect him. Thereafter, she burned with a determination to ensure that other children would not share his fate.

Just twenty years old when she arrived in Alabama, Sullivan began a remarkable relationship with Keller that lasted five decades. In a few months of incredibly intense work, Sullivan drew on teaching techniques she had barely just learned and helped Keller find herself. And the self she helped Helen find consisted of one of the greatest hearts and minds ever known.

Shocked members of the scientific and teaching communities studied Keller and Sullivan's innovative techniques. Medical experts were put in the awkward position of having to explain why so many of the great minds of the day had, nevertheless, been so thoroughly upstaged by an undereducated woman possessing little more than an iron will.

Radicalization

Some sought to portray Keller's situation as an unfortunate, but ultimately, holy burden delivered from on high. Philanthropists pressed in looking to turn her story into a drawing room freak show. Had she acquiesced and remained polite, virginal and respectable, Keller could have become part of the high society scene. But Helen was having none of that. Although she live much of her life off the largesse of several capitalists (at least in part), she refused to allow herself to be run up anyone's flagpole to wave as a testament to the good intentions of the well-to-do. Instead, she spent the rest of her long life standing up for those trodden upon.

Sullivan and her lover John Macy were both radicals, and Keller learned a great deal from them. It was mostly through her own experience, however, that she came to understand that health problems such as hers were often socio-economic in nature. She indicted industrialism and capitalism as the main causes of disease — blindness and deafness included. While advocating for better treatment, Keller insisted that the greatest emphasis be placed on poverty and unsafe working and living conditions as the root of illness.

The IWW

Once in her 20s, Keller joined the Socialist Party and campaigned for Eugene V. Debs. She soon flew past the Socialists' conservative electoralism, however, sinking deeper roots into the working class when she joined the IWW—Industrial Workers of the World—then in its heyday. The IWW "points out that the trade unions as presently organized are an obstacle to unity among the masses, and that this lack of solidarity plays into the hands of their economic masters," Keller wrote after becoming a member. "They insist that there can be no peace until the workers organize as a class, take possession of the resources of the earth and the machinery of production and distribution and abolish the wage system." (Kim Nielsen, *The Radical Lives of Helen Keller*)

As a Wobbly, Keller walked picket lines, organized support for strikes and, after learning to speak, addressed rallies and forums around the country about the need for a revolutionary transformation of society. On one occasion, she insisted on marching with the unemployed in Sacramento despite threats of state violence. "They have endured countless wrongs and injuries until they are driven to rebellion," she said, rebuking the IWW's critics. "They know that the laws are for the strong, that they protect the class that owns everything. They know that in a contest with the workers, employers do not respect the laws, but quite shamelessly break them." (Kim Nelson, op. cit.)

The well-heeled who had flocked to her side to bask in the radiance of her fame were positively scandalized, but Keller was just getting warmed up. She joined the vibrant women's movement of the 1910's, allying herself with its most radical members. She became an impassioned advocate of many controversial issues, including easily accessible birth control. Echoing not the Suffragettes so much as anarchist Emma Goldman, she dared to suggest there might even be more to female sexuality than reproduction. We can imagine some of her benefactors getting into the wind as a result (the men anyway), and more leaving her side when she came out against World War One, and in support of the Russian Revolution.

Opposition to World War One

Along with millions around the world, Keller recoiled in horror at the butchery of the Great Imperialist War. She was appalled that working class boys, and primarily female non-combatants, died by the millions so a select few who already had too much, could accumulate still more. She lectured tirelessly against the carnage, and when dissent became virtually illegal after the US entered the war, she stood strong and true behind the thousands who were locked up for demanding peace.

Like all of us, Keller was capable of misjudgment. She remained enthusiastic about the Soviet Union long after the workers revolution was hijacked by the Bolsheviks. In later years, according to historian and Keller biographer Kim Nielsen, she counted J. Edgar Hoover as a close acquaintance — even as the FBI was ruining the lives of many of her friends and associates. Unbeknownst to her, Hoover had also spent decades amassing a thick dossier on her activities, which he deemed subversive. Although it would've surprised no one had Keller actually been called before a Congressional committee or two — Hoover, apparently, thought better of subjecting an internationally-acclaimed seventy-year-old woman who could neither see nor hear to a grilling about her political activities.

Whatever Keller's overly trusting nature or occasional naiveté, they are trivial points compared to her accomplishments. She wrote extensively and traveled the world in solidarity with the oppressed. Her books were translated into many languages, and she championed the rights of the deaf and blind into her 80s. She lived to see the elimination of many of the dangerous conditions she challenged, as well as the implementation of important teaching techniques that she advocated.

The Miracle Worker

Although less engaged in her later life, Keller never wavered in her commitment to radicalism. Forty-three years after her death, Keller's story still inspires. She saw things that many sighted people miss, heard things that many hearing people ignore. To say that hers was a life well-lived would be a huge understatement. We get a sense of the fire that burned within both she and Sullivan in *The Miracle Worker*, which beautifully depicts the beginning of their relationship. Both the play and the 1962 film adaptation unflinchingly present the many obstacles both faced, including the period of Sullivan's institutionalization. All these years later, the climactic scene at the water pump when Keller's life changed forever remains incredibly powerful.

But those who relegate Keller to perpetual childhood do her legacy and themselves an injustice. The day Anne Sullivan reached through the darkness was the turning point of Keller's life, not its end. The young girl bursting with life is inseparable from the adult who stood arm-in-arm with the immigrant women who led the great Bread and Roses Strike. Although she lived in relative comfort, Keller refused to turn away from the ugliness of class society, choosing instead to do what she could to eradicate it. Amidst the darkness and ugliness that surround us, perhaps the best lesson to draw from her life is that we continue to collectively attempt to do likewise.

Josephine Bennett, City Mother

The history of the early Connecticut women's movement is not complete without the story of Josephine Day Bennett (1880-1961). A militant suffragist, feminist, anti-imperialist, and labor pioneer, Bennett played a leading role in the federal passage of the Nineteenth Amendment guaranteeing voting rights for women. As an organizer, speaker, and prison inmate (in a D.C. jail), Bennett shed her family's class privilege and became a model of tireless advocacy.

Bennett's suffragist activity centered on transforming Connecticut's women's movement "from philosophical to political work." She placed special emphasis on recruiting working women and African Americans, as well as forging links with other social movements. On April 5, 1911, she shared the stage with Dr. Anna Shaw, president of the National Woman Suffrage Association (NWSA). Women's suffrage had been an issue since 1867 when the first state women's group formed. While some of her colleagues were still in their teens (like 19-year-old cigar maker Edna Purtell), Josephine did not start her political life until she was 30-years-old. Josephine Bennett and her compatriots were determined to cross the finish line this time.

In 1913, she traveled across Connecticut, organizing the first suffrage group in West Hartford and lecturing at the Killingly Grange. The next year, she helped organize the massive suffrage parade of one thousand women through Hartford's streets, speaking from an open-air car on the corner at Main and Pratt Streets.

She lectured on suffrage and feminism throughout the country and Europe, and was considered by the press to be a "brilliant orator." She lectured in Berlin, Germany on the topic of feminism in the United States.

At a 1914 congressional committee in Washington DC, Bennett spoke against the NWSA's suffrage proposal, known as the Shafroth amendment. Shafroth would require all states to reach a threshold vote before suffrage became law. Bennett argued for the original Susan B. Anthony bill, which required three-quarters of the states to ratify. Once approved, the movement could then "force the remaining one-fourth into line." This became one of the earliest strategic disagreements between the NWSA and what was to become the National Woman's Party (NWP).

Bennett was greatly affected by the 1917 arrest of Catherine Flanagan in Washington, D.C. Flanagan was a state woman angered by Wilson's inaction on promises he had made regarding suffrage. Both Bennett and Katharine Houghton Hepburn quit the Connecticut affiliate of the NWSA (they had both been elected leaders of the group), and joined the NWP because of its strategic work and militance.

In 1919, Bennett followed in Flanagan's footsteps, burning a copy of Wilson's speech and spending five days in jail on a hunger strike. Her time in lockup was a crash course in the iniquities of the prison system. Her celebrity amplified her firsthand witness against inhumane treatment.

Bennett continued to hammer on Wilson. During a suffrage meeting at her mother's Hartford home, she declared, "It is an insult to the intelligence and self-respect of American women to expect them to accept his beautiful flowers of rhetoric, when they hunger for the bread which he has in his pocket."

In November 1919, Bennett campaigned in Maryland and returned exhausted after working on behalf of state legislative candidates who would vote for ratification of the 19th Amendment. By that time, nineteen states had voted to ratify. Connecticut did not vote to ratify until September 4, 1920, after the necessary three-quarters of the states had already ratified.

Josephine Bennett understood that women needed power not only at the ballot box, but on the factory floor. She supported union organizing efforts by garment workers, telephone operators, machinists, typewriter factory str ikers and tobacco field hands.

She also involved herself with the social and economic impact of trafficking women. There were twelve brothels in the Hartford, and many more outlets for women and men to meet, including restaurants and saloons. Mayor Edward Smith was under great pressure to control prostitution and, in fact, closed all brothels in 1911 — at least for a while.

Josephine's husband Martin Toscan Bennett was on the mayor's reform committee, which investigated the illicit trade. They exposed the economic conditions that forced females into prostitution, and proposed that property owners who profited from the trade should be publicly linked to their buildings.

"No working girl can ply her honest calling for less than $6 a week," a local union organizer wrote, "and be safe from the temptation and defilement to which she is exposed in the polluting atmosphere that environs her struggle for decent living." (Connecticuthistory.org, *Hartford's Sex Trade: Prostitutes & Politics,* 3/23/23)

In February 1913, Bennett spoke to saleswomen at a "home meeting," explaining to them that in states where local suffrage had passed, the eight-hour day had also been achieved. That same month, she spoke to workers at Brown Thomson and Company on "suffrage from the viewpoint of the mother and child." Later, she addressed 300 telephone operators at their union organizing meeting on Central Row, urging women to "pull together or you will go down."

In 1914, Bennett spoke on the child labor situation in New York, citing children from 6 to 7 years of age who were working 14 hours a day (in a state which boasted the most advanced child labor laws). Politicians decided that the canneries where they worked were not factories — they were located in sheds — and so did not come under legal protections. The CWSA later called for federal child labor law reform.

After the United States entered World War One, Josephine was an outspoken critic of capitalism's role in the weapons industry. At one rally she said:

"Anyone who profits from war industries at the expense of the United States government is not a patriot but a profiteer. Those who participate in lynchings, mob violence, or petty persecutions are not patriots but ruffians. The true patriot will have interest in the welfare of workers in industries, the negro race, the foreign born, and children." (Connecticuthistory.org, *Josephine Bennett: Hartford's City Mother,* 5/27/2020)

Soon after this appearance, she was in the news again at a mass labor meeting on behalf of Tom Mooney, the California union activist and political prisoner who had been framed for a bombing incident and scheduled for execution.

Bennett's most significant labor activity may have taken place during the 1919 garment workers strike at Union Place near the train station. On the first day of the strike, police protected scabs, roughed up strikers and had the striking women and girls arrested for violence. Bennett enlisted her brother George Day to defend those arrested, and she accompanied the group to court. She later appeared at a large union support rally, where one speaker dubbed her Hartford's "City Mother."

Her first efforts at connecting the women's cause to the international scene was in 1916 when she presided over a fundraising tour for Serbian victims of the war. A short while later, on Wall Street in New York, she protested the U.S. food blockade against Russia, describing it as "a black spot on the honor of our country."

Bennett also aided the Friends of Irish Freedom and the Friends of Freedom for India, two anti-imperialist organizations struggling for independence from Great Britain. She told the local Padric Pearse branch of the Irish group: "This country has always been about the only one in the world that was safe for a political refugee. It is our duty to protest as loudly as we can to protect ourselves against this. Both India and Ireland say, England, step out and let us settle our own troubles."

The campaign in 1913 to save an abused Connecticut Pequot woman from execution also became a suffragist cause. Bessie Wakefield, 26, was on death row for conspiring to murder her husband, until a high-profile women's movement eventually assured her parole. The suffragists argued that since women did not have the franchise and could neither sit on juries nor decide capital punishment laws, it was impossible for Wakefield to be given a fair trial.

In 1920, Bennett ran for Secretary of State on the Connecticut Farmer-Labor Party slate (an affiliate of the American Labor Party). She was also endorsed by the Socialist Party, and her name appeared on both lines.

With her husband Martin in 1921, Bennett and her family established the Brookwood Labor College in Katonah, New York. There, she explained, " We teach the truth and we train workers to work in their own movements." Their two daughters Katherine and Tanya also lived, studied and performed chores at the school. In 1923, the sisters were in the first graduating class.

Among Bennett's closest co-workers were Hepburn and Mary Townsend Seymour. With the former, she led the Connecticut Birth Control League (later Planned Parenthood). With Seymour's leadership, Bennett became a founding member of the state NAACP in 1917. The initial organizing meeting was held at Seymour's Hartford home and was attended by W.E.B. DuBois, James Weldon Johnson and Mary White Ovington.

Bennett counted among her friends and associates Claude McKay, Margaret Sanger, Emmeline Pankhurst and Ernest Hemingway. With sister suffragist Annie Porritt, she helped create the Travelers Aid Society at a time when an increasing number of women were independently taking coaches and trains alone. She financially supported her friend Agnes Smedley, the radical journalist and novelist who aided Indian and Chinese insurgents during their civil wars. Josephine gave Agnes a pistol for her protection.

By linking disparate social and political movements of the period, Josephine Bennett was "intersectional" well before the term was invented.

Malcolm X in Hartford, 1964

Vietnam peace rally, 1969

Vieques arrest event

Eugene Debs whistle stop

Women of the prison brigade

Twain mural, Campfield Library, Htfd, 1938

Matilda Rabinowitz, Bridgeport IWW

ILGWU garment strikers, 1941

Hartford Federal College

The war criminal and the patriot

Stand Against the Klan, 1981

Roving Bill Aspinwall, circa 1893

10. Students Organizing On and Off Campus

Trinity College Student Ralph Allen: "He Have More than Courage"

As 3,000 people left Connecticut by car, bus, and train to join the historic March on Washington, D.C., Hartford college student Ralph Allen was spending his 20th day in a Georgia jail. It was August 28, 1963, and Allen and five others were being held without bond for "inciting insurrection," a Civil War-era law that carried a possible death penalty. Allen's real crime? Registering Black citizens of Georgia to vote.

Massachusetts native Ralph Waldo Allen, 21, was a field secretary for the Student Nonviolent Coordinating Committee (SNCC). This multi-racial group, founded by the courageous Ella Baker, was composed mostly of Northern students. It engaged in many creative direct action tactics including sit-ins and freedom rides. For those who eschewed voter drives as insufficiently militant, Mississippi's first civil rights organizer Amzie Moore declared that in the South, "voter registration *is* direct action."

Allen had been arrested several times before, once in 1962 for "vagrancy" as he and Charles Sherrod attempted to register five black residents of Terrell County, Georgia. SNCC had successfully registered 100 black people in Terrell over the preceding nine months, a relatively small number that underlined the great opposition they faced. "Terrible Terrell" had the dubious distinction of losing the first voting rights suit filed under the 1957 Civil Rights Act. The Court's finding, however, did not deter the local registrars or police from continuing to obstruct law and the Constitution.

By 1963, he decided to skip his sophomore semester at Trinity College in Hartford to continue his SNCC work. In April, after helping a woman to register and returning her home, Allen was beaten by two white men who had followed him. The stakes had raised: SNCC's opponents were moving from vagrancy charges to assault.

Hartford's reaction to Allen's insurrection arrest took a while to build, but it eventually reached its peak in October when hundreds of students marched to the State Capitol, demanding his release. Connecticut elected officials began to pressure Attorney General Robert Kennedy to intervene in the case.

A federal court struck down the 1871 insurrection law on November 1st, which finally allowed Allen and the others to be released on bond. Among the four men who had spent three months in jail awaiting trial was Sallie Mae Durham, a 14-year-old Black girl swept up in the police attack. Allen was still tried and convicted of attempted murder of a police officer by an all-white, male jury. His conviction was overturned on appeal due to the "systematic exclusion" of Black people on the jury.

On November 9th, a week after the original insurrection charge was dismissed, Ralph Allen was back in Hartford, raising funds for the families of the four Birmingham, Alabama girls killed in a church explosion.

Ralph Allen died of heart failure at the age of 63 in 2005. Once asked why he placed himself on the front line of the Black freedom movement, Allen quoted a line from *Man's Fate* by André Malraux: "It is necessary to act my ideas." As an elderly Southern Black man who worked with Allen described him to a reporter: "He have more than courage."

The Northern Student Movement

College students were an integral part of the popular upheaval of the 1960's. Beginning with the lunch counter sit-ins one month into the decade and continuing on through 1969 and beyond — college students around the country rallied to the cause of justice and freedom. The two best known student organizations of that time were Students for a Democratic Society (SDS) and the Student Nonviolent Coordinating Committee (SNCC). Another important group, though less well known, was the Northern Student Movement (NSM). It took root in a serious way on college campuses throughout Connecticut.

Tens of thousands of young Americans were inspired by the lunch counter sit-ins that began in Greensboro, North Carolina and spread throughout the South. The lie that many knew was a lie — that the United States is based on freedom, justice and equality – was exposed by the incredible bravery of young Black people. It was as though a dam had broken and a tidal wave of people, led by college students, were suddenly passionately committed to making the world a better place — and not so concerned about forging comfortable careers for themselves.

NSM's Formation

Students at Yale University were no exception, and in the Fall of 1961 some of them got together to form an NSM chapter. One of the projects they initiated was support of SNCC, which by then had branched out from the lunch counter sit-ins to spearheading the Freedom Rides, a concerted effort to end segregation and discrimination on the nation's bus and train lines. Another project the NSM undertook was challenging racial discrimination in the North. To that end, the group organized an action just one month after it was formed, along with the New Haven chapter of CORE—Congress for Racial Equality—to protest local housing discrimination.

Like SNCC, the NSM had struck a chord, and there were soon dozens of chapters on campuses throughout the Northeast. Initially, its membership was primarily white, although it worked closely with organizations like CORE whose memberships were almost exclusively Black. Within several years, NSM had recruited a large number of Black members from both college campuses and from the communities where it established programs. NSM also began publishing *Freedom North,* with articles about its work and that of the Black Freedom Movement as a whole.

Peter Countryman, a Yale undergraduate from Chicago, was elected as the group's first executive director. Only 19 at the time, Countryman had already been active in civil rights work through the New England Student Christian Movement. He was instrumental in establishing a tutoring program in which students and recent graduates from Yale and other local colleges worked with young people enrolled in New Haven's public schools. The effort proved a success, and NSM established similar programs in several dozen cities in the Northeast. By 1963, the group had enlisted over 2,000 students from a number of colleges to tutor an estimated 3,500 children. Countryman eventually left New Haven to spearhead NSM's tutoring program in Philadelphia.

Additional Connecticut Chapters are Formed

In June of 1963, NSM members primarily from Trinity College established a tutorial program in Hartford with over 200 volunteers and a staff of 25. The tutoring sessions were held in churches and other public facilities in or near the communities where the tutees lived. They were so popular that the Hartford chapter grew to be one of the NSM's largest. Soon, the group was holding classes on Black history and the arts, as well as regular forums on police brutality and civil rights activities in the South. The NSM publicized these activities and news of the Freedom Movement through a newspaper called *North End Voice*, which members distributed throughout Hartford. NSM members in Hartford, meanwhile, established the North End Community Action Project (NECAP) which organized sit-ins and other protests against discriminatory hiring practices around the city.

As the Freedom Rides continued through 1962 and into 1963, NSM members from colleges in Connecticut traveled to the South to participate. They were also actively involved in a 1963 voter registration drive that SNCC launched in Mississippi, as well as another the following year during Freedom Summer. Yale graduate student Bruce Payne participated in a voter registration and was shot in Mississippi by armed opponents of the campaign.

More students from Yale took part in these projects than from any other school. Reverend Martin Luther King, Jr. was among those who took note. King visited Yale several times during this period, including once at the invitation of Yale Chaplain William Sloane Coffin, a supporter of the NSM, who a few years later, became one of the leading figures in the movement against US aggression in Southeast Asia. After one of his visits, King wrote to Coffin saying he was heartened by the movement in the right direction I sense at Yale.

In addition to New Haven and Hartford, the NSM had vibrant chapters on many campuses and in many cities, including New York, Detroit, and Philadelphia. In 1963, the group moved its main office from New Haven to New York City. Peter Countryman was succeeded as executive director by

William Strickland, an African-American graduate of Harvard who joined the NSM in his native Boston. After Freedom Summer, the group, while continuing to steadfastly support SNCC's work in the South, shifted more of its attention to the problems of Blacks in the North.

Black Power

By 1965, many in the NSM had grown critical of what they saw as the limitations of a movement predicated on "civil rights." Blacks in the organization, like Blacks in SNCC and the soon-to-emerge Black Panther Party, heeded the call of Malcolm X for self-determination, a broader and more revolutionary demand than civil rights. They began to see themselves, in addition to being a part of a movement for Black liberation within the borders of the United States, as part of a global upsurge of primarily people of color against colonialism and imperialism. They began to call for Black Power and saw the need to transform the NSM and SNCC into all-Black groups to better achieve that goal. Advocates of Black Power recognized the accomplishments and dedication of white members, while stating that it was for Blacks to determine what their communities needed. Rather than providing services like the tutoring programs that were decided on and initiated by whites, whites were asked to leave the NSM and SNCC and challenged to organize the broader white community to support Black liberation.

Much as happened on a larger scale in SNCC, there were tensions around these changes within the NSM. Close friendships ended and there was anger and resentment in some quarters. Though understandable, the bitterness that some whites felt was in large part a reflection of a movement that was still very young and somewhat immature. Race, after all, is perhaps the most complicated question confronting those of all colors dedicated to building a just society. For whites, it is essential to understand that it *is* for Black people to decide what is best for Black people. Blacks, especially from the poorer and working classes, and not whites, must be in leadership of the Black Freedom Movement and significantly represented in the leadership of multi-racial movements.

There's nothing easy about this, either in theory or practice. It was (and is) especially difficult for young whites from schools like Yale to learn and accept. Many have, after all, been taught all their lives that it is their destiny and their right to lead. Without disregarding the pain some people experienced, the move by the NSM and SNCC to Black self-determination was a necessary one.

The NSM continued to do important work for most of the rest of the 1960's, organizing students and non-students alike. Many joined the much-larger SNCC that, by 1966, was establishing itself in the North. Others, upon leaving campus, joined the Black Panthers in one-time NSM strongholds in Hartford, New Haven and Bridgeport, as well as other places. As US aggression in Indochina escalated and the movement against it exploded, many whites who had been in the NSM immersed themselves in anti-war work. That effort was important, necessary and, in the end, successful, though in many ways that fact has been obscured from history. Although, perhaps ironically, the massive growth of the anti-war movement in the late 1960's diverted whites from taking up the challenge of their Black comrades in NSM to organize the greater white community to support Black liberation. That challenge remains.

11. Peace, not War

War Resister: The Odyssey of Ulysses

Thirty-seven million people were killed in World War One from 1914 to 1918, including 1,100 from Connecticut. The United States armed forces averaged 297 casualties a day. Here was a conflict, historian Howard Zinn wrote, where "no one since that day has been able to show that the war brought any gain for humanity that would be worth one human life."

Like many immigrants of the early 20th century, young Ulysses DeRosa came to the United States with a dream. "After reading about Carnegie and Rockefeller," he wrote, "I was ready to become a millionaire in America."

DeRosa left his hometown in Accadia, Italy for Hartford at age twelve, thanks to the money his older brother Antonio sent him. He arrived in May 1905. Soon after Ulysses arrived, his brother was injured at work and returned to his home country. Ulysses DeRosa was left on his own. For a short while, he was taken in by a local Quaker family. Their commitment to pacifism and Quaker principles left a lasting impression.

Most of the Italian immigrant community lived in the Front Street neighborhood, the east side section of the city bordering the Connecticut River. Previous to the Italians, Front Street had been home to impoverished Irish families for at least fifty years.

As poor as it was, Front Street bustled with life. The neighborhood had a spirit that can only be duplicated when families work together to overcome their hardscrabble existence, fueled by a common determination to succeed.

Although long ago bulldozed in the name of urban redevelopment, Front Street still holds a firm place in the memories of the descendants of those who succeeded despite the disdain and rejection the original immigrants faced from the dominant Hartford WASPs.

The streets were teeming with progressive political ideas that inspired DeRosa. Various radical philosophies helped form his future beliefs and prepared him for the extraordinary dangers he would face.

DeRosa soaked in the cultural and political influences of the time. He learned English quickly, despite the humiliation of being required to attend a first-grade public school class. He attended "every free lecture, to my adulthood, on history or any other subject."

Prejudice against Italians was common in Hartford, and the leading citizens of the day did not hesitate to publicly voice their objections. One such voice was the Reverend Howard V. Ross of the First Methodist Church. From his pulpit, Ross warned his congregants that immigrants were, "A sodden, sour, bitter mass of humanity that resists the best ideals of American and Christian civilization. From the lowest peasant class of Italy, with their ideas of low living and filth and poverty, from the Balkans with low instincts of society and womanhood. If you seek the anarchist, the Bolshevist, the wild-eyed turbulent radical, when you find him and look into his face, behold it is the face of a foreigner."

Writing in his unpublished memoir, DeRosa explained that he "never joined a party, as such, but I felt comfortable with any group that helped lift the poor. I associated with socialists, anarchists, religious leaders, labor leaders, and all "isms" as long as they were for the betterment of mankind."

Considering the Italian East Side contained a total of only twenty blocks, it produced more than its share of political activists and organizers, many of whose ideas and principles DeRosa absorbed.

The DeMaio family, for instance, lived on Mechanic Street. Serephine (Rucci) DeMaio was a suffragist who bridged the gap between traditional Yankees and immigrant women. Her son Ernest became one of the founders of the United Electrical Workers Union (UE), a left-wing labor group that aggressively organized the industrial sector.

Ernie's father Donato and uncle Tony were arrested in Hartford during the Palmer Raids, the notorious 1919-20 federal crackdown on immigrants and unionists. Tony had also been an organizer for the Industrial Workers of the World (IWW). Ernie's brother Anthony joined the Abraham Lincoln Brigade to fight for the republican cause against the fascists of Franco's Spain.

Radical influences

Anarchist influence was part of the mix as well. The insurrectionist anarchist Luigi Galleani visited the city at least twice, speaking at the Venetian Hall. Galleani had a significant following the United States, although apparently not in Hartford. Galleanists adopted his strategy of "propaganda of the deed," the use of individual acts of violence for revolutionary political purposes.

Carlos Tresca, who emigrated from Italy in 1904, would become a frequent visitor to Hartford, New Britain, and Waterbury. He spoke to an Italian audience at the Princess Theater on State Street, adjacent to DeRosa's neighborhood. Tresca was sponsored by Girolomo Grasso who lived on Market Street (and was identified as an anarchist in a secret FBI report). DeRosa got to know Tresca when they were both living in New York and working for similar causes.

Hartford Italians mourned the 1909 execution of Spanish educator and anarchist Francisco Ferrer. The celebrated international figure had been arrested and tried by a military tribunal acting on highly questionable evidence. Ferrer was the founder of the Modern School movement which took hold in the United States, attracting Upton Sinclair and Jack London among others. "La Escuela Moderna" had a great influence on subsequent experimental school reform efforts such as Summerhill.

The Circolo Libero Pensiero (Freethinkers Club) was a small Hartford group that enjoyed criticizing established religion and disrupting revival meetings, especially the local Italian Congregational and Baptist missions. DeRosa attended one memorable debate between a Protestant minister and an anarchist, probably Nunzio Vayana, on the question of "Religion Across History." The purpose of the event was to challenge the historical role of the Church in its persecution during the Inquisition, and specifically the injustices done to Italian scientist Galileo and theologian Giordano Bruno, both of whom were condemned — the latter burned at the stake. As far as Ulysses DeRosa was concerned, the anarchist won the debate hands down.

This particular event made a permanent impact on DeRosa: "the experience opened my mind to many forms of social injustice," he would later write.

The Status of Italian Workers in Connecticut

The employment Ulysses DeRosa could find in Hartford was strictly limited. Italian workers were largely excluded from the skilled trades and traditional unions rejected them, so they organized themselves.

In 1907, immigrants who were digging out the foundation for the new mill owned by the American Thread Company in Willimantic went on strike to demand an increase in wages from $1.75 to $2.00 a day;

Later that year, the Italian General Labor Union led a strike of 5,000 railroad track workers across Connecticut. They stayed out for three weeks before they were forced back to work by a combination of factors: lack of financial support, no real solidarity from other unions, and the inability to gain strength by spreading their action to Boston and Maine.

In January 1910, tobacco workers went on strike at the Pinney farm in Suffield, demanding a 25-cent daily wage increase. Around this time, dozens of Italians working on the Scotland Dam in Willimantic, also struck when two of their leaders were fired. Italian weavers, trolley builders, ditch diggers and paper workers around the state, meanwhile, led strikes for better wages and a nine-hour day. The existing wages for these men were "fair pay for unskilled work twenty-five years ago," union leader Joseph C. Ciccosanti said, "but now it did not feed their families." Ciccosanti also told a newspaper reporter, "We are in danger of our lives every minute we are working. It is hard work, and in every kind of weather, and we get very low pay."

Sometimes, the noble cause of labor was not always enough to motivate the state's Italian workforce (and in this way they were similar to all other ethnicities). Forty Italian laborers were imported to Willimantic in order to break the strike of workers on the New York, New Haven and Hartford Railroad.

On the other hand, Italian railroad workers also convinced stonecutters at Hartford's Union Station to join their strike and still others, shipped into a town as strikebreakers, turned around and went home when they discovered they had been hired as scabs.

The Ludlow Massacre

Ulysses DeRosa eventually moved to New York City to seek greater opportunity. In September 1913, he read about a coal miners strike in Colorado. More than 11,000 coal miners, many of them Italian, struck the Colorado Fuel & Iron Corporation owned by the Rockefeller family.

The workers had been suffering under the tyranny of the bosses and the deprivations of the so-called "company town." The "company town" was a scheme set up by the boss to squeeze more profits from the miners, who were forced to buy groceries and pay rent to their employer. The strike was finally triggered when a union organizer was murdered by the company's private police force.

The Rockefeller corporation evicted the strikers and their families from the town. The UMWA answered back by renting land and setting up a tent colony that kept the families warm, well-fed and given medical care by union doctors.

Mining production halted and the strike survived through a tough winter — despite periodic attacks from Baldwin-Felts private detectives who used Gatling Guns in raids on the tent colonies.

On April 20, 1914, Colorado Governor Elias M. Ammons ordered the National Guard to accompany scabs across the picket lines. Undaunted, the miners continued their strike. Guardsmen attacked the largest tent colony — located at Ludlow — with machine guns. The miners returned fire.

At dusk, National Guardsmen set fire to the tents. Thirteen men died from gunfire; eight children and two women were later found burned to death in the trenches that miners had dug to protect them from bullets.

The strike was 1,800 miles away from Ulysses DeRosa and his friends, but the injustice inflamed the young radicals as if they had personally witnessed the massacre. If they couldn't provide direct support for the miners, they could at least confront the corporate owner.

DeRosa and the others joined famed anarchist Alexander Berkman and celebrated writer Upton Sinclair, who organized protests at the massive estate of John D. Rockefeller in Tarrytown, New York

On May 31st, DeRosa and some friends took the train to Tarrytown.

Almost as soon as they disembarked, DeRosa was assaulted by police and then arrested. Despite a complete lack of evidence, the local magistrate sentenced him to three months in prison.

DeRosa served the sentence on Hart Island (part of the Bronx) in Long Island Sound. The island was known as a potter's field where over one million people, mostly indigent, had been buried. The infernal place had a variety of functions over the decades. By the time DeRosa arrived, it was being used as the site of a boys' reformatory.

This was DeRosa's first introduction to the criminal justice system; a system that subjected the incarcerated to bad food, poor medical treatment, and brutal treatment by guards. It was good training for what was to come a few years later.

Drafted
Ulysses DeRosa developed his skill as a milliner, working at the Georgette Hat Company on Hudson Street, located on Manhattan's Lower East Side. On July 17, 1918, he and several of his friends, as well as and a group of women (mostly mothers and sisters) who were "weeping and wailing," appeared at the local draftee induction center. DeRosa made it clear that he would not cooperate with the induction process, including refusing to be fingerprinted. He was sent to Fort Leavenworth, Kansas on July 25th, nevertheless.

DeRosa refused to wear an army uniform or cooperate with any military orders, so he was labeled an "absolutist," in contrast to other conscientious objectors who agreed to non-combat duty. He and other "C.O.s" served their time along with groups of Mennonites and Molokans (a Russian spiritual Christian sect) who resisted the war on religious principles.

Army officers and guards, according to a later investigation by Roger Baldwin and the National Civil Liberties Bureau (forerunner of the ACLU), brutalized and tortured DeRosa and 18 other war resisters for over two months.

The men all received severe physical injuries; some of them suffered mental breakdowns as well. They were punched in the face, knocked to the ground and kicked, hit with rifle butts, prodded with bayonets and smashed against walls. In addition, they were forced into ice cold showers, awakened every two hours at night and forced to stand outside, and had large amounts of laxatives surreptitiously placed in their food. Once, in order to break their hunger strike, an army officer forbid them drinking water for three days.

The conscientious objectors refused noncombatant service because, they reasoned, it would allow the military to free up other draftees who would then be sent to the battlefield. They would not march or salute, they refused direct orders to work and resisted any action that would make them part of the Army.

They were assigned to serve as waiters for the officers' mess hall, but refused. As further punishment, they were forced to camp in the nearby woods with tents but no food.

At no time during their imprisonment did the C.O.s portray themselves as victims. Their hunger strikes were strategic: their ability to act in concert helped them maintain solidarity and a measure of dignity. They received a stove and utensils by refusing to eat bad food prepared by guards. Abusive behavior by army guards slowed down or halted when it was found to be ineffective. One soldier, ordered to hit a prisoner repeatedly, stopped after a few blows and could not continue. Another time, a soldier hit DeRosa with his gun butt instead of bayoneting him as an officer had demanded.

Some of the conscientious objectors (known in the press as "slackers" or obstructionists) maintained diaries of their treatment. Here are two excerpts:

"We were ordered to take a cold shower. DaRosa [sic], feeling that cold showers are detrimental to him, and having taken a bath but one-half hour previous to the issuing of the above order, refused to undress. The Corporal of the Guards thrust him under the spray with his clothes on.

DaRosa returned to the guard room, wearing his dripping clothes. The Corporal ordered him to undress and take a thorough shower. When DaRosa again refused, the Corporal tore his clothes from his body and at the same time delivered upon him some telling and effective blows. He was then placed under the cold shower. We were compelled to take a cold shower once in the morning and once in the afternoon. A guard stood watch and checked each man."

"Ott [another prisoner] and DeRosa, both materially weakened by their hunger strike, were forcibly dressed and put on exercise in the afternoon. Ott was shoved around a while and then left unmolested. DeRosa was pushed about, then thrown to the wet ground, punched, kicked, and spat at by the guards.

He was then raised to his feet and dragged around some more. Presently he was dropped and one guard seized him by the hair and rubbed his face in and banged his head on the ground. His cheek and forehead and bruised, leaving two ugly skin wounds.

Four guards carried him to the shower room, stripped him of what little clothes remained on his person, placed him on the cold cement floor, in an exhausted condition, and turned the cold spray on him. The soldiers then scrubbed him viciously with filthy brushes and brooms... He was finally brought back to the squad room in a semi-conscious state." (Ulysses DeRosa, *The Odyssey of a conscientious objector*, unpublished autobiography)

On September 17th, DeRosa and other C.O.s were formally arrested and sent to solitary confinement for refusing an order to clean out a large pile of trash. This order triggered a predetermined plan by which the Army could ultimately court martial them.

DeRosa and his comrades were court-martialed on October 22, 1918. They were found guilty of disobeying orders and sentenced to life in prison at hard labor. The penalty was later reduced to twenty-five years, since the life sentence exceeded the maximum penalty allowed by law.

During the trial, DeRosa was questioned about his political and religious beliefs. He described himself as having become an international socialist at age 14. His primary allegiance was to the world at large, he considered all people as equal and he refused to do harm to anyone. He also provided a letter from the Clerk at the New York Quaker Meeting where he had first become a member of the Friends Society. The official confirmed that DeRosa had joined their meetings and was a member in good standing. DeRosa explained his pacifist stand this way:

"In these trying times the only authority that I obey is the inner light — the great ideal for which Christ gave his life, namely: Humanity. It is the spirit of reconciliation, not hate, non-resistance, not aggression, that should dominate us."

Throughout their imprisonment, army officials would try to argue the men out of their nonviolent principles. "If a negro entered your house and assaulted your wife, what would you do?" one officer asked DeRosa.

After their court martial, the men were transferred to the military prison at Fort Leavenworth. They were sent to "the hole" where they were chained by their wrists to their cell doors for nine hours a day. This proved to be especially painful to DeRosa due to his small stature.

During their entire ordeal the men occasionally found a recruit who secretly sympathized with them. This allowed DeRosa and his friends to have mail smuggled to family members on the outside.

When the conscientious objectors' case was publicly exposed, it became a cause célèbre. The officers who had been abusing the prisoners did so in direct opposition of policies made by Secretary of War Newton D. Baker. A board of inquiry was established in Washington to examine the evidence and the behavior of the soldiers. Four officers, including the head of military police and the provost marshal of the camp, lost their jobs as a result. Ulysses DeRosa and his comrades were released from military prison after Christmas.

Once free from imprisonment, Ulysses DeRosa and his fellow political prisoners continued to work on behalf of the C.O.s still incarcerated.

New York Strikes and Palmer Raids

DeRosa was soon back in New York City working as a hat maker. He was active in his union. The city was roiling with strike activity: cigar makers, printers, house builders, window cleaners, shipyard workers, paper box makers, clerical workers and more. The 6,000 members of the milliners' union who worked south of 23rd Street were out on the street by mid-September, 1919. By October 1st, the other 12,000 hat makers were set to go when their contract expired, adding to the 100,000 workers of various trades who were already on strike in the city.

Their demands were similar to the other hat maker union also on strike: wage increases, union recognition (requiring employers to acknowledge their duty to bargain), holiday pay, and union consent before any workers could be fired. The United Cloth and Cap Makers Union also demanded the abolition of piecework and that women be recognized as union representatives in the various factories.

Ultimately the strike failed. DeRosa was bitter toward factory operators and the union leadership as well.

In 1919 and 1920, U.S. Attorney A. Mitchell Palmer orchestrated a nationwide roundup of thousands of trade unionists, immigrants (especially Russians), and anybody he considered too left on the political spectrum. According to DeRosa, a friend alerted him just in time that two characters were waiting at his apartment building. DeRosa avoided the agents and very likely missed another incarceration. He moved to Baltimore, Maryland, and for ten years engaged in the manufacture of men's clothes.

Justice Delayed

By 1960, Ulysses DeRosa had settled in Massachusetts and raised his family. He continued to work in the garment business, but as an owner, refused to interfere with attempts by his employees to organize.

His son Dean registered as a conscientious objector and worked as a medic during World War II. Around this time, Ulysses requested a copy of his discharge papers, which he had lost. DeRosa discovered that the Army records wrongly indicated he had received a dishonorable discharge. He worked for years with the support of the Quakers to successfully correct the record.

Ulysses DeRosa wrote about the ordeal and other parts of his life in an unpublished manuscript entitled, "The Odyssey of a Conscientious Objector." The document included a letter from the United States Disciplinary Barracks at Fort Leavenworth prison confirming the Secretary of War had released DeRosa, et. al. — and they were restored to "status of honorable discharge" as of January, 27, 1919.

190

Thirty-five-thousand young men sought C.O. status in 1971 — more than the 23,000 who were actually drafted for the Vietnam War that year. The United States Supreme Court also ruled that same year in favor of a broader definition of who qualifies as a conscientious objector.

Ulysses DeRosa died on March 1, 1989 at the age of ninety-seven.

How Should We Remember World War I?

How should World War One be remembered? The United States entered the "Great War" on April 6, 1917. Each year, Connecticut libraries and historical groups gear up for the anniversary.

Thirty-seven million people were killed in the war from 1914 to 1918. What exactly should be commemorated?

Pulitzer Prize winner Richard Hofstadter noted that "peace" president Woodrow Wilson committed the U.S. to the European bloodbath based on a "rationalization of the flimsiest sort." Congresswoman Jeanette Rankin declared, "I want to stand by my country, but I cannot vote for war." W.E.B. Du Bois warned that it was a battle for empire, natural resources, and the colonized world. The outspoken Helen Keller told reporters, "the only fighting that saves is the one that helps the world toward liberty, justice and an abundant life for all."

Will these anti-war heroes be on the commemoration program?

When Americans protested the war, they were libeled by the press, routed by the police, and jailed by the courts. The Hartford chapter of the People's Council for Democracy was thrown out in the street when speaker Anna Riley Hale was arrested after she dared to criticize the draft. The pacifist group was then banned from every hall in the city.

This suppression was repeated many times nationwide: 2,000 citizens were prosecuted under the new Espionage Act, including Eugene V. Debs, who spent nearly three years in prison for a speech he gave condemning war.

Should we celebrate the growth of our state's defense industry, which provides jobs while arming the U.S. military? More than 90,000 industrial accidents occurred in Connecticut during 1917-18. Despite the massive speed-up in war production, Hartford employees who didn't work fast enough would be shamed by bosses who placed German Deutschmarks in their pay envelopes.

How will we remember those who criticized the industrialists and financiers who reaped millions during the war? Hartford's Josephine Bennett told a local crowd that "Anyone who profits from war industries at the expense of the United States government is not a patriot but a profiteer."

Poison gas was manufactured for the war effort in Stamford, subsidized by the federal government. The Yale & Towne and American Synthetic companies produced one million pounds a month of Chloropicrin, a Class 1 toxin. When the war ended, they were forced to find a way to destroy 3 million pounds of the stockpiled deadly gas.

Who will memorialize religious objectors to the war, like Hartford's Ulysses DeRosa? How about Anthony Crasnitzki of Bristol, who failed to register and was arrested. The judge gave him the opportunity to enlist but he refused, saying that as a member of the Industrial Workers of the World (IWW), he would rather go to jail than go to war. He did, for a six-month term.

Will we recall that our civil liberties took a beating, too? U.S. District Attorney Thomas J. Spellacy admitted his department secretly arrested, charged, and imprisoned those who might "inflame the public mind" across the state. He said the secrecy was solely "for the protection of the public."

Connecticut was well-equipped to punish unpopular ideas. The state already had a ridiculously broad law against "seditious utterances" which it strengthened in 1919. Hartford aldermen passed their own law which effectively banned any sort of public speech critical of the government.

Fortune magazine estimated that while it cost a gangster $100 to kill a man, during WWI each death cost $25,000. Why? Because "killing is the industrialist's business." *Fortune* dubbed them the "Big Business armament men." Not a conspiracy as such, but still a "handful of men whose power, in some ways, reaches above the power of the State itself."

Those who attend war observances should remember they will not be viewing neutral, objective history. What we learn will either prepare us — or blind us — for the next U.S. war.

Benjamin Spock, Peace Activist

When Dr. Benjamin Spock published his book *The Common Sense Book of Baby and Child Care* in 1946, he became the world's most famous pediatrician. His book immediately changed child-rearing and, seven decades later, remains the most influential work on the subject. Though criticized from a variety of quarters, Spock's theories on raising children are more popular than ever, and are practiced around the world.

Early Life

Benjamin Spock was born on May 2, 1903 in New Haven into a blue blood, Connecticut Yankee family. His father was a corporation attorney who worked at various times for the New Haven Railroad and the Chase Brass Company in Waterbury. Like his father, Spock attended Phillips Academy and Yale University. In addition to being an outstanding student, Spock excelled on the rowing team while at Yale. He and his Yale teammates were selected to represent the United States at the 1924 Summer Olympics in Paris, and won the gold medal in the eight-man rowing event.

Upon graduating from Yale, Spock enrolled as a medical student in Columbia University's College of Physicians and Surgeons in 1929. He graduated first in his class and began practicing pediatric medicine that year in Manhattan. While in medical school, he met and wed Jane Cheney of Manchester, Connecticut (the couple later divorced in 1976). Cheney was deeply involved in research with Columbia-based psychologists, and would assist in the research and writing of *The Common Sense Book of Baby and Child Care*.

First Political Stirrings

With the onset of the Great Depression, Spock became interested in radical politics and economic ideas. He admired Socialist Norman Thomas (who he eventually befriended and worked with in the 1960's in opposition to the Vietnam War) and regularly attended socialist lectures. Prefiguring his later activism and concern about war and international affairs, Spock opposed the rise of fascism in Europe beginning with General Francisco Franco's revolt in 1936 against the new democratic government in Spain.

Baby and Child Care

Central to Spock's theories about child-rearing was that parents should be more nurturing. In the era in which he wrote, his message was directed almost exclusively at mothers, and he encouraged women to be more responsive to

194

the needs of their children. In contrast to already established approaches, Spock urged mothers to feed their babies when they were hungry, rather than adhering to a rigid meal schedule, and to pick them up, hold them, kiss them and otherwise display affection when they cried. Much of this seems obvious now, and that is due in no small part to Spock's work. At the time he was writing, however, it was very common practice for parents to ignore and/or belittle the basic needs of their children in the name of discipline and toughening them up.

Spock also encouraged parents to believe in themselves and rely less on the established wisdom of experts — doctors included. A foundation of his work was that people, mothers of young children especially, have a natural desire to nurture the young, and that they should act on those impulses rather than looking to authority figures for guidance. Though he himself was certainly an expert of sorts, Spock saw his role as refining what parents already knew intuitively, and encouraging them to trust themselves.

The Common Sense Book of Baby and Child Care became a best-seller shortly after it was published. More copies of it were sold in the next 50 years than any book except The Bible. Spock's second wife Mary Morgan, who he wed in 1976, introduced him to yoga, massage, a macrobiotic diet and meditation. Stating that Morgan "gave me back my youth," he incorporated some of these life changes into later editions of his work. For example, recommending a vegan diet for children past the age of two.

Vietnam War Era Protests

Though Spock maintained an affinity for socialism throughout his adult life, he was largely apolitical until the early 1960's when he became an active member and officer of SANE, the National Committee for a Sane Nuclear Policy. He was an early opponent of the Vietnam War and was a featured speaker at demonstrations at a time when the anti-war movement was in its early stages. Like others of that time, his politics became increasing radical quite quickly. He soon left SANE behind, finding it too passive and too concerned about maintaining good relations with liberal politicians.

This last impacted Spock directly. In 1961, he had been heartily welcomed into the White House by President Kennedy. Mrs. Kennedy, in particular, held him in very high regard. When the reality of U.S. aggression in Indochina became obvious, however, Spock became critical of the war. He also became critical of Kennedy's successor, Lyndon Johnson, as the war escalated. In 1968, Spock and four other anti-war activists were arrested and tried on federal charges of violating the Select Service laws for conspiring to actively encourage young men to resist the draft. He and three of the other defendants were convicted and sentenced to two years in prison. The convictions were set aside after appeal.

Later Life

Spock remained a radical for the rest of his life, demonstrating a commitment to long-term activism even as the ruling class became increasing right wing in the 1980's. He regularly participated in demonstrations against nuclear energy and the nuclear arms race, including at the massive disarmament demonstration in Central Park on June 12, 1982. On more than one occasion, he was arrested for acts of civil disobedience against the ever-growing threats posed by the warfare state and imperialism.

Though Spock retired from medicine in 1968, he continued writing and lecturing on pediatrics for years thereafter. He and his second wife co-authored a memoir of his life that was published when he was 86. His last "baby" book was published when he was 91. In the 69 years since the publication of *The Common Sense Book of Baby and Child Care*, the work for which he remains best known, more than 50 million copies of the book have been sold. It's also been translated into 49 languages. Spock died on March 15, 1998 at the age of 94.

The Yale Prof Who Went to Hanoi

When the 1965-66 school year began, 35-five-year-old Yale University professor Staughton Lynd was regarded by many in academia as a historian with a bright future. Based on his research and writing, there was every reason to believe that Lynd was bound for a long and brilliant career. He certainly had the pedigree; his parents Robert and Helen Lynd were sociologists (Robert at Columbia University, Helen at Sarah Lawrence University) and authors of the groundbreaking 1929 study *Middletown*.

Lynd had other commitments, however, that superseded his interest in academia. Just prior to arriving at Yale, he had served as director of the Freedom Schools in Mississippi during the turbulent, revolutionary Freedom Summer of 1964. In 1965, he also assumed an active and leading role in the developing movement against U.S. aggression in Indochina. He was, for example, chair of one of the first national protests against U.S. policy held in April at Carnegie Hall in New York City. Later that month, he chaired the first national demonstration against the war, and served as a featured speaker. The event drew 25,000 people to Washington, DC.

Liberation Magazine

In addition to his academic writing, Lynd had also, for a number of years, been a regular contributor to a variety of radical publications. Perhaps most prominent among these was *Liberation*. By 1965, Lynd was an editorial board member. *Liberation* was a beacon for young people of the New Left. Not that those associated with *Liberation* were always in harmonious agreement; quite the contrary. Earlier in 1965, for example, Lynd had sharply criticized fellow editorial board member Bayard Rustin for his support of Lyndon Johnson and the Democratic Party as "coalition with the Marines."

Historian and Communist Party member Herbert Aptheker invited Lynd to go on a fact-finding mission to North Vietnam. Lynd agreed, and at Aptheker's request, also invited Tom Hayden, former president of Students for a Democratic Society and one of the New Left's leading figures. The primary purpose of the trip was to see the effect the war (U.S. bombing, in particular), was having on North Vietnam — and, upon returning, provide the American public with information about the North Vietnamese perspective.

To Hanoi

Lynd, Hayden and Aptheker arrived in Hanoi on December 28, 1965.

Together, they toured much of North Vietnam during their ten-day stay. Though the trio were more aware than many of the nature of the war, they were nonetheless stunned by the scale of the destruction they witnessed. Lynd and Hayden authored *The Other Side*, a book about their experience published after their return.

The trip was quite controversial and much criticism was directed at Lynd in particular.

Aptheker, after all, was a longtime Communist who could be discredited easily enough by the mainstream as a dupe of Moscow and Hanoi. Hayden, meanwhile, was young enough to be dismissed as naïve and gullible (if not traitorous). Lynd, however, was an accomplished historian at one of the nation's most prestigious universities. The corporate media and many at Yale attacked him viciously. Yale President Kingman Brewster, for example, issued a press release that denounced Lynd for providing "aid and comfort to a government engaged in hostilities with American forces."

Blacklisted From Academia

Not long after the trip, Lynd was informed that the tenure track position that drew him to Yale was no longer available. He immediately set about seeking employment at other universities — but without success. While colleagues in a number of history departments pushed hard for his hiring, administrators at each of those schools overruled them. The Board of Governors of Chicago State University went so far as to rescind a written offer of an associate professor's position *after* Lynd, his wife and three children had moved from New Haven to Chicago. A decade after the death of Joseph McCarthy, Lynd was essentially blacklisted for his radical political activities.

It was a difficult time for Lynd. He worked briefly with famed organizer Saul Alinsky. After that, he went to law school at the University of Chicago. In the early 1970's, he and his wife Alice embarked on the work that produced their breakthrough book, *Rank and File: Personal Histories by Working-Class Organizers*. The book begat the Academy Award-nominated documentary film *Union Maids*.

Though he never again worked in academia after leaving Yale, Lynd has carved out an important niche as a historian. He is a prolific writer with an emphasis on "history from the bottom-up"—history that is from the perspective of workers, slaves, soldiers, and those whose voices are generally excluded from mainstream narratives. Eight-five years young at the time of this writing, Lynd lives in Ohio, churning out books and articles one after another. He and Alice celebrated their 68th wedding anniversary this year.

Vietnam Protests in Connecticut

Connecticut opposition to the war in Vietnam paralleled that found in many other parts of the United States. When the movement against the war was in its early phase, people from the state traveled to New York City and to two national marches in Washington, DC. As the war continued, opponents formed local organizations and held local protests, particularly on college campuses.

Students for a Democratic Society (SDS) was an early antiwar catalyst. Beginning in 1965, SDS established chapters at Yale, Wesleyan, the University of Hartford, Trinity College, the University of Bridgeport and the University of Connecticut. They held protests and teach-ins on each of those campuses over a period of years. One of the more dramatic actions took place in 1968 when UConn SDS members staged a series of protests over the presence of Dow Chemical employment recruiters arriving on campus. Dow manufactured napalm, an incendiary antipersonnel weapon used extensively in Vietnam. The company was a regular target of the antiwar movement. Authorities arrested eight students and four faculty members for their participation in the protests.

1969: The Vietnam Moratorium

As the war continued, the Connecticut movement expanded beyond its campus base. There were numerous protests, including a march and rally on April 26, 1969, in Bushnell Park in Hartford. A variety of organizations came together a short time later to begin organizing the Vietnam Moratorium with a plan to meet the escalation of the war with an escalation of opposition.

To that end, activists scheduled the moratorium for October 15, 1969 as the first in a series of days when there would be "no business as usual" until the war ended. People in Connecticut's towns and largest cities heeded the call. Events took place in 35 communities. All told, close to 100,000 people participated statewide.

The largest gathering of antiwar demonstrators was a march and rally in Bushnell Park where 10,000 people turned out. Of particular significance was the presence of a contingent of Vietnam veterans who increasingly joined the antiwar movement through organizations such as Vietnam Veterans Against the War, which had several chapters in Connecticut.

The Hartford action also proved noteworthy for the number of Black people who participated. Planners scheduled the march to go through a predominantly Black neighborhood with that goal in mind. Wilber Smith, a Black activist from Hartford, was one of the speakers who addressed the rally.

Protests Shutdown College Campuses

Though there were no antiwar protests in the state after the moratorium that matched the size of the October 15, rally in Bushnell Park, actions continued as people found new venues and creative ways to oppose the war. Activists in New Haven, for example, organized events at the Ingalls Skating Rink protesting the ROTC—Reserve Officers Training Corps—program on the Yale campus.

New Haven was also the site of events in the spring of 1970 that culminated in a massive rally on May 1. Activists organized the action in support of national Black Panther leaders who were on trial for murder in the Elm City. Antiwar issues became a significant additional theme after President Nixon ordered U.S. troops to invade Cambodia earlier that week.

The invasion prompted calls for a national student strike. Classes at colleges around Connecticut were either canceled or effectively boycotted. When the Ohio National Guard shot and killed four protestors at Kent State University, and Mississippi police shot and killed two students at Jackson State College, protests and strikes grew so large many schools around the country, including Yale and others in Connecticut, canceled classes for the remainder of the school year.

By 1972, with a substantial number of American troops withdrawn from Vietnam, and SDS having fallen apart, Connecticut activity against the war decreased. State residents attended several more large marches in Washington, D.C., while local protests continued — but none on the scale of those in 1969 and 1970. When the last regular American forces left Vietnam in 1973, the antiwar movement in Connecticut was about at an end. Local forces, like those throughout the country, could say they played a role in ending the worst crime against humanity since those committed by the Nazis in the Second World War.

No Business as Usual: The Vietnam War

On a cool and sunny fall day in Hartford, ten thousand people jammed into Bushnell Park with one goal: stop the war in Vietnam. As the single largest protest of its kind in the city's history, October 15, 1969 was historic. The thousands who marched to downtown Hartford were only part of the 90,000 Connecticut residents taking part in peace actions in dozens of cities, towns, schools and churches against a war that had already taken a deadly toll on two continents.

It was called Moratorium Day — a nationwide suspension of normal activity by two million people to focus on the war — and it was the result of thousands of small courageous actions by ordinary people, many of whom decided to challenge their government for the first time.

Moratorium Day was the brainchild of former staffers for the 1968 Eugene McCarthy Democratic presidential campaign (McCarthy lost to Hubert Humphrey, who lost to Republican Richard Nixon, who claimed to have a "secret plan" to end the Vietnam War). The organizers' plan was to suspend business as usual in order to discuss, debate and protest the increasingly unpopular war. It was to start with one day in October and then multiply: two days in November, three in December and so on, until the entire country focused only on the war. In the end, the Moratorium made history even if it did not succeed as a longterm national strategy.

Building Toward Critical Mass

Protests against the Vietnam War had been organized as early as 1963, but these were largely confined to a few college campuses and traditional Hiroshima remembrance activities led by Quakers. By 1965, a national demonstration called by Students for a Democratic Society (SDS) drew 25,000 to Washington, D.C. The turnout was small by today's standards, but it was the largest protest ever held at the time against an American war. Over the next few years, hundreds of college campuses exploded with teach-ins, draft resistance and administration building occupations. The growing antiwar agitation had convinced a sitting president, Lyndon Johnson, that he had no future in politics. Malcolm X and Martin Luther King, Jr. had connected the dots between racism at home and militarism abroad. The antiwar movement derailed the 1968 Democratic National Convention in Chicago. America's working class, Black and white, was painfully aware of the ever-increasing costs of war and, in fact, one famous survey found that workers' opposition to the war was greater than that of the middle class.

But beyond campus and big city demonstrations, opposition to the war had not made its presence felt in middle America, the constituency President Nixon considered his base. In November 1967, a national poll found only 10% of Americans thought the U.S. military should be pulled out of Vietnam. A Connecticut poll in April 1969 did not even ask about the war. Instead, results purported to show the public was most concerned about the "lack of respect for authority by young people."

An April 26, 1969 anti-war rally in Bushnell Park drew barely a mention in the local press. But the anticipation created by the Moratorium inspired a Hartford newspaper to rent an airplane, so it could capture images of the thousands of marchers who snaked down Albany Avenue towards Bushnell Park.

Digging in at the grassroots
Local organizing for Moratorium Day was a massive undertaking. Volunteers leafleted hundreds of neighborhoods, businesses and schools. Churches and synagogues announced the event during services. Veteran folk singer Pete Seeger and farmworkers union leader Cesar Chavez were both in town for their causes and urged supporters to join upcoming peace events (Chavez noted that the Defense Department's spending on grapes had jumped 800% since his union's boycott of the fruit had begun). Trinity College students urged the administration to shut down the school for the 15th. The president refused, but most classes were canceled anyway.

In Hartford, West Hartford and Meriden, organizers worked with local businesses to close their shops during the middle of the day. At least 60 businesses expressed their support.

Momentum around the state grew and in many places support for the Moratorium was surprisingly deep. Two-thirds of Hartford's Bulkeley High School students skipped school to attend the Bushnell Park demonstration. In Stamford, Norwalk, Waterbury, Windsor and East Hartford, students and their teachers planned assemblies during school hours to discuss the war and its impact on their lives. Town greens were rally sites in Wethersfield, Bridgeport, Simsbury and Farmington. Anti-war sentiment found its way into the streets with marches through the town centers of West Hartford, New London, Bristol, New Britain, Windsor Locks and Greenwich. In many places, activists held multiple events, combining their tactics and thinking up new ways to focus attention on the deadly impact of U.S. policy in Vietnam.

In Willimantic, protestors marched through downtown and stopped at the local IRS office to highlight the fact that "billions of dollars are spent on Vietnam each month, while national housing, medical and educational programs remain unresolved."

In Goshen, authorities refused Moratorium backers' request to plant a "peace tree" on public property, so they found willing landowners who hosted the event instead.

A number of town councils and boards of education were challenged to take a stand on the war. Most refused, as did Enfield where the vote was 5-2 against an immediate withdrawal of all U.S. troops, even as marchers paraded outside the Council chambers. But in Westport, the Representative Town Meeting backed the pullout of troops. Both the Mansfield and Manchester Democratic town committees passed resolutions against the war.

The Moratorium had its detractors, of course. Democratic U.S. Senator Thomas Dodd stated that immediate withdrawal was "immediate surrender." Republican Congressman Thomas Meskill said that he hoped October 15th would be seen as support for Nixon and his policies (the next year, Meskill was elected governor of Connecticut). New Britain's Mayor Paul Manafort, meanwhile, ordered 250 American flags to be flown in the city to protest the peace actions.

Veterans Speak Out

The local American Legion and VFW condemned the protests, arguing that dissent would only endanger U.S. combat troops. But not all soldiers agreed. Many Vietnam veterans saw the Moratorium as a time to finally speak out publicly against the war they had survived.

Dozens of Vietnam veterans joined the Hartford rally. One young vet who had been wounded in both legs and chest, told a reporter he marched because "you find you're not fighting for anything, you're just fighting to save your life." Vietnam, he continued, was a suicide mission.

Forty vets at Mattatuck Community College in Waterbury made their anti-war sentiments known during a school event. In Enfield, Navy veteran Richard Howland and WWII veteran Eugene Sweeney addressed the local peace rally. Veteran George Smith and former Marine Captain Newbold Morris addressed the West Hartford crowd. Dean Erickson told protestors in New Britain "over there I was shown that the Vietnamese do not want foreign domination, and that's why I'm here now."

For some of those who enlisted or were drafted, the Moratorium came too late. Bloomfield's Barry Jackson was one of the many killed in the war. His father, Allen, attended the massive Hartford rally with a handmade sign that read, "My Son Was Killed in Vietnam — For What?" Mr. Jackson's son had won a number of medals, but he said, "these medals don't make up for his life." Barry, he added, should not have gone to Vietnam "because it's an illegal war." Although his protest was too late for Barry, Allen Jackson thought his own presence might help others.

Ten thousand American troops were killed in 1969. Hundreds of them came from Connecticut. During the week of the Moratorium, the fatalities grew: Marine Pvt. Richard Stolarun, 19, of New Britain, died of his wounds on October 12th. Lt. Thomas Frazier, Jr., 20, of Granby, and Army Pfc Charles Bachman of Norwalk, were both killed in action the next day. Mr. and Mrs. Norman Manning received their son James' Silver Star that week. He had been killed in July after having won the Purple Heart and Bronze Star. On October 16th, Pfc James Dufault of Moosup, was killed in combat. Dufault became the 466th Connecticut resident to be killed in Vietnam.

The Consequences of Standing Up

Joining the Moratorium was a big deal for thousands of state residents young and old who had never before attended an anti-war protest. One inhibitor for these first-timers was fear — fear of looking foolish, of being labeled unpatriotic, and of the unknown. In a few cases, there were consequences for speaking out. In Farmington, 13 students faced suspension for leaving school without proper parental permission. Teenagers Gary Marone and George Cavanna were arrested by Glastonbury police for wearing the American flag as headbands. Hartford college and high school students were busted for plastering Moratorium leaflets on buildings, or for spray-painting "WAR" on Stop signs.

Eight Bloomfield elementary school teachers were reprimanded for taking their kids off school grounds for an impromptu march of their own. The brief event was a civic lesson, the teachers explained, but some parents were outraged. Robert Bligh complained that his two daughters, aged 8 and 10, should not have been part of the protest. According to their mother, the girls challenged Bligh when they got home. "What's the matter? Don't you believe in peace?" they asked their father.

Sixty Naugatuck High School students skipped school and gathered at the American Legion field on their way to the New Haven rally. They scattered when spotted by the police. The cops gave chase, but only a few of the runaway activists were caught.

Many around the state joined the protests, however, with no negative results. At East Windsor High School, about 60 students decided that the officially-sanctioned assembly was too tame, so they walked out of classes. Several teachers and the principal tried to persuade them to return without success. A local state trooper was summoned, but he had no luck either. Students told him that it was their generation fighting the war, not his. One high school girl said that the sanctioned in-school Moratorium activities were not strong enough to show how they felt about "this terrible war."

War, Race, and Gender

The Moratorium's focus was Vietnam, but Connecticut cities were still seething with unrest and rebellion. Hartford experienced this anger with street disturbances in July and September 1967, and again in April 1968, following the assassination of Dr. King. Student organizers determined that the economic and political oppression experienced by the African-American community could not be ignored. On October 15th, the march toward Bushnell Park began in West Hartford, on the University of Hartford campus. The route could have easily avoided Black communities by traveling down Prospect Avenue, passing by the governor's mansion and through the comfortable West End. But instead, 6,000 students marched down Albany Avenue through Hartford's poorest neighborhoods, picking up support as they went.

Wilber Smith was there to greet the students when they arrived. Smith was a militant African-American leader who had called for a civilian police review board after incidents of police brutality in 1968. This year, he was running for mayor on the newly-formed Liberal Party ticket. He called the Vietnam War "insane," and told the cheering crowd in Bushnell Park, "We must not lower the sound of our protest until the administration's deeds match their empty rhetoric."

Larry Babatunji told Central Connecticut State College students that it was wrong for Black men to fight in a war for "a decrepit, racist country." In Middletown, Ed Saunders of the African-American Society marched with the sign "No Vietnamese Ever Called Me Nigger"—a phrase attributed to boxing superstar and draft resister Muhammad Ali. Black Panther Doug Miranda told 2,500 UConn students and faculty, "I don't fight white racism with black racism. I fight racism with people's solidarity. I fight racism the same way the Vietnamese people fight racism."

In New Haven, the rally stage was dominated by white establishment politicians. Yale junior Glenn deChabert fought his way to the microphone to make the connections between racism and war. The rally organizers did their best to stop him, even shutting off the sound system when deChabert began to talk. But people in the crowd chanted "let him speak!" And he did. The Black Student Alliance leader addressed the crisis in New Haven's neighborhoods, including "brutal and murderous police policies." DeChabert challenged Yale and the mayor to solve the city's economic problems. "Peace is the attainment of justice for Blacks," he told the New Haven crowd.

Women were barely represented on Moratorium stages around the state, although there were a few exceptions. Ella Grasso, then Connecticut's secretary of state, was part of the establishment roster in New Haven. Marge Swann of Voluntown's Community for Non-Violent Action (CNVA) led a civil disobedience workshop in Storrs. Women played critical roles in the hard organizing work that made the day a huge success. Shirley Epstein was statewide coordinator for the Moratorium. Mary Lou Mayo and Naomi Golden pulled Wethersfield's peace activities together. West Hartford women made sure local businesses closed their doors on October 15th.

The Anti-Warriors

Local activists who were part of the Moratorium in 1969 have clear memories of that day. Mims Butterworth, 97 at the time of this writing, read the names of the Vietnam War dead with her husband Oliver in front of 2,500 West Hartford residents. She remembers being most proud of the Conard High School students who marched with her, despite being harassed by student athletes and their coach. Mims had been an anti-war McCarthy delegate at the 1968 Democratic Party Convention, and would go on to join the 1971 peace delegation to the Paris Peace talks.

John Murphy was a junior at East Catholic High School in Manchester. Unlike other schools, there was "no getting permission slips" in order to join the Moratorium activities. John and about eight other students skipped school and traveled by bus to the Hartford rally. Today, he is a leader of the Connecticut Opposes the War coalition.

Hartford's Dave Ionno, who is currently a leader of Veterans for Peace, was a young "army brat" in Washington State during the Moratorium. He watched anti-war marches with his family on television that fall. He enlisted in November. Dave served a year in Vietnam. When he returned, changed forever by the experience, Dave's first Veterans Day march was with Vietnam Veterans Against the War.

Jeremy Brecher was a regional SDS organizer in the Northwest, and is now a Connecticut-based activist and historian. He critiqued the limitations of the Moratorium in a widely distributed essay in *Liberation* magazine in December 1969. Jeremy saw some anti-war activists' turn toward electoral politics or street violence as distractions from the real work of building a movement powerful enough to stop the war. He called for future activities to be shaped more like a general strike against the war, based in workplace organizations.

The Draft Resister and the Antiwar Prosecutor

Forty years after the historic October 15th Hartford protest in Bushnell Park, David Mitchell was shocked to learn that the rally's moderator was Jon O. Newman, a U.S. District Attorney. Newman was the man who helped send Mitchell to prison for resisting the draft.

Mitchell had lived in New Canaan and attended Brown University before dropping out. In 1961, he joined Polaris Action, a campaign that used nonviolent direct action against nuclear submarines built in New London. Mitchell and others variously swam, sailed and rowed out to the subs to interfere with their launching. By the time he was 18, Mitchell had decided to refuse induction when called up by his Connecticut draft board. He based his opposition on the Nuremberg principles, arguing that America's Vietnam policy violated international law and treaties the United States had signed. Therefore, Mitchell reasoned, joining the Army only contributed to the war crimes taking place in Southeast Asia.

Mitchell was arrested for failing to show up to his draft board and for refusing to register as a conscientious objector. His first trial took place in New Haven in September 1965. The trial was a disaster: his attorney refused to follow Mitchell's carefully-planned defense strategy. The presiding judge was extremely hostile and set bail outrageously high. The U.S. Supreme Court reversed Mitchell's conviction, leading to a second trial in 1966, in which he was prosecuted by federal prosecutor Jon Newman. David Mitchell received a five-year prison sentence; he served two years at the Lewisburg federal penitentiary from February 1967 to February 1969.

Newman was known in Connecticut circles as something of a liberal. He debated William F. Buckley on the issues of the day, and later distinguished himself as a judge when he struck down the state's anti-abortion law. By 1969, his opposition to the Vietnam War led him to publicly join the Moratorium. The next year, he helped organize a group of professionals and businessmen against the war, and briefly ran for Congress on a peace platform.

When confronted by a reporter about the key role he played in sending David Mitchell to jail, Newman replied that he saw no contradiction between that and his emcee role at the Hartford Moratorium. If he had to do it all over again, Newman said, he would still prosecute Mitchell. "He felt you can call upon the courts to rule upon the validity of our foreign policy and I don't think you can," Newman stated. He admitted that even during Mitchell's 1966 trial, he harbored doubts about the war.

David Mitchell remembers Newman as "a decent sort of guy" who, after the guilty verdict, asked the defense attorney if he might shake Mitchell's hand. Still, the draft resister contrasted Newman to the Yale legal scholar and civil libertarian Thomas Emerson who "walked into the New Haven courthouse and put up his home as collateral" in order to help Mitchell make bail. "I had never even met him and he did this for me," Mitchell recalls.

Today, Newman serves on the U.S. Court of Appeals for the Second Circuit. David Mitchell (despite his felony conviction) is an attorney in New York and still an anti-war activist. He has most recently assisted Lt. Ehren Watada, an infantry officer who in 2006 refused to deploy to Iraq. Like Mitchell, Lt. Watada refused deployment on the grounds that the Iraq war was immoral and illegal and that to participate in it would make him complicit in war crimes. Watada's prosecution ended in a mistrial and his request to leave the Army was refused until he was finally discharged on October 2, 2009.

Lessons for Today's Antiwar Movement?

It's tricky to draw direct parallels between events separated by decades and circumstances. The wars in Iraq and Afghanistan sent millions of people to the streets in a much shorter time period than it took to mobilize against the Vietnam War. All protests, even massive ones, are dogged by impossible expectations: if they don't immediately achieve their objective, they are seen as having failed. In fact, the Trinity College student newspaper editorialized in 1969 that the Moratorium was a failure because President Nixon seemed to ignore the millions who marched.

In hindsight, we now know that anti-war activity, in particular the October Moratorium (and its D.C. counterpart of 750,000 protestors in November), played an important role in curbing Nixon's Vietnam policy. Seymour Hersh confirms this in *The Price of Power: Kissinger in the Nixon White House.* The investigative reporter and Pulitzer Prize-winner asserts that the administration's intention to escalate the war was thwarted in large part by the massive numbers generated by Moratorium activities. "Operation Duck Hook," as the unsuccessful secret plan was called, was designed as a "savage" and "brutal" response (Kissinger's words) that included the use of nuclear weapons, land invasions of North Vietnam and renewed saturation bombings in the South.

Although the Moratorium campaign could not be sustained as its founders had envisioned, anti-war organizing continued and grew. The 1970 invasion of Cambodia and the murders of students at Kent State and Jackson State ignited a nationwide student strike in May with four million students participating. In 1971, 13,500 were arrested while attempting to stop business as usual in Washington, D.C. A majority of the American people turned their backs on Nixon and his war policy.

On October 15, 1969, a small group of church people led by the Reverend Herbert Ackerly and Mrs. Laurence Morrison stood quietly in front of Hartford's Old State House. They had been there faithfully each Wednesday for three years. The group called it their "vigil of conscience." On Moratorium Day, their patience was rewarded: six thousand marchers on their way to Bushnell Park paraded past the silent vigil and cheered.

12. Environmental Activism

Morton Biskind Warned About DDT

Following the Second World War, the American empire was reaching its absolute apex. American businesses were enjoying previously unheard of profits and acting with previously unheard of hubris. More than ever, the natural world was seen as something to be conquered and exploited for what was generally perceived as the betterment of human life, but was really for the greater prosperity of the few. There seemed no limits on production or consumption. It was in this climate that Monsanto, Ciba, and other chemical companies began the mass scale production of Dichlorodiphenyltrichloroethane for use as an agricultural insecticide — otherwise known as DDT.

Dr. Morton Biskind

In the late 1940's, a Westport, Connecticut physician by the name of Morton Biskind began noticing new ailments, as well as new variations of old ailments in the humans he was treating. He noted the same thing in the domestic and wild animals in the area, too. The maladies he observed were initially most pronounced in dogs, cats, sheep and cattle. They included degenerative problems in their brains, internal organs and muscles. When Biskind noticed a dramatic increase in similar symptoms in humans, he began doing research and consulting other doctors about their observations.

In 1949, Biskind and Dr. Irving Bieber published "DDT Poisoning–A New Symptom With Neuropsychiatric Manifestations" in the *American Journal of Psychotherapy.* Much of the article focused on what Biskind and Bieber saw as a link between DDT exposure and the occurrence of polio. "Facts are stubborn," the authors wrote, "and refusal to accept them does not avoid their inexorable effects — the tragic consequences are now upon us."

Resistance From the Scientific and Business Establishment

Biskind, Bieber and others alarmed by the effects of DDT were bucking the status quo. Just a year before their article was published, Swiss chemist Paul Hermann Muller was awarded the 1948 Nobel Prize in Physiology and Medicine for discovering the effectiveness of DDT against yellow fever and malaria. Chemical giants such as duPont and Geigy manufactured large quantities of the insecticide for use during World War II. Government regulators such as those at the Food and Drug Administration dismissed Biskind's claims.

211

In reality, it was already well known among scientists that DDT had a devastating impact on life forms beyond the insects it was intended to kill. In addition to the humans and other mammals Biskind had observed, virtually every kind of fish, bird, mammal and insect exposed to even small doses of DDT suffered adverse health consequences. Compounding DDT's impact was that it was stored in the body fat and milk of both humans and animals alike – essentially, a toxic poison embedded in the organism for as long as that organism lived.

Biskind's Continued Efforts

Though he was largely ignored and often reviled, Biskind continued to spread his message of warning. In 1950, he testified before Congress about the harmful effects of DDT. In 1953, he published another important article, "Public Health Aspects of the New Insecticides," in the *American Journal of Digestive Diseases*. Though resistance from powerful quarters continued, the message began to get through. More and more studies showed the destructive impact DDT spraying had on all forms of wildlife as well as direct links to cancer and other diseases in humans.

Silent Spring

By the 1960's Biskind's work had begun to bore fruit as others, including the eminent biologist Paul Shepard, carried his efforts forward. Most famous among those inspired by Biskind, however, was Rachel Carson, a marine biologist who, in 1962 authored *Silent Spring*, perhaps the most important environmental book ever written. In 1967, a group of scientists and lawyers formed the Environmental Defense Fund for the express purpose of getting the production and use of DDT banned.

Hungary became the first nation to ban DDT for agricultural use in 1968. Other countries soon followed suit — including the United States in 1972. DDT manufacturers sued the Environmental Protection Agency in response, but the ban was ultimately upheld. In the years since, DDT has only every been authorized for use in extreme cases, such as possible threats of bubonic plague being spread by fleas or yellow fever spread by mosquitoes.

Biskind died in Westport in 1981 at the age of 74. His celebrated work lives on, however. Environmentalists and writers everywhere have carried it forward. Biskind's efforts underscore the clash of interests between money and power on the one hand — and the public's welfare on the other. His work also serves as a warning about mainstream notions of progress and the obsession with consumption that is central to such notions.

Godzilla is Really Hard to Kill

It's hard to believe after the atomic attacks on Hiroshima and Nagasaki—but proponents of nuclear power once pushed the spurious notion of the "peaceful atom" with little public opposition. Nuclear energy, the pro-nuke crowd said, was "too cheap to meter."

Dominion Energy, owner of the Millstone multi-unit nuclear plant in Groton, Connecticut, however, has failed to convince the public that it needs a new deal to ensure longterm profits. It's another corporate myth that should be debunked, once and for all.

So, what's all the fuss about Millstone? The way it works is deceptively simple. Dominion's plant — our fourth and final nuclear plant — creates the extremely dangerous process of nuclear fission to boil water. The resulting steam, in turn, runs a generator to make electricity. This whole process has been compared to using a buzz saw to cut butter.

In the 1950s, Madison Avenue cooked up the "Atoms for Peace" conceit designed to convince the public that uranium wasn't just for atomic explosions. The radioactive process could be harnessed as a "giant of limitless power," General Electric boasted.

Then came the Clamshell Alliance in the 1970s, the first of many grassroots organizations that would spring up around the country to oppose nukes. The Clamshell Alliance used nonviolent direct action and popular education to expose and prevent the imminent dangers posed by commercial nuclear power.

The group also stressed that nuclear power plants and nuclear weapons are inextricably linked, since they both employ the same radioactive element that can cause potential disasters. Chernobyl, Three Mile Island and Fukushima later proved the point.

The Clamshell Alliance was born on the New Hampshire sea coast, organized by local residents who figured they should have a say in whether or not two Seabrook nuclear units should be built near popular Hampton Beach. The people-powered group quickly grew into a New England-wide network that included a dozen Connecticut affiliates.

On May 1, 1977, more than 1,400 people, including at least 200 from our state, were arrested after occupying the Seabrook construction site. They were trained in civil disobedience and prepared to take up permanent residence to prevent the nuke's operation. It remains one of the biggest nonviolent direct actions in U.S. history.

"The Clams" were packed into New Hampshire state armories and jails for two weeks, refusing bail and insisting to be released on their own recognizance. To their regret, Governor Ella Grasso provided Connecticut state police to assist the New Hampshire force.

The Alliance stood on the legal principle of "competing harms," i.e. breaking a minor law to prevent a catastrophe. Catholic nun Carolyn Jean Dupuy of Hartford, was the first protester to be prosecuted. She was sentenced to six months in jail for the simple act of trespassing.

Why such an extreme reaction by the authorities? Because the Seabrook action touched a nerve. Rather than relying on profit-driven corporations and their overpaid lobbyists to tell us nukes were a good bargain, citizen activists asked the hard questions about nuclear power's efficacy. The public has realized that the dangers of nuclear power far outweigh its benefits:

–Nukes are too expensive to build, even Wall Street won't finance them. Instead they must be massively subsidized by the federal government;

–Nukes are too expensive to insure, so the government must once again step in and provide insurance coverage for the energy corporations;

–Nuclear waste has no permanent storage facility, despite searching for one since 1982. Instead, there's a patchwork of 100 temporary sites – including in *casks on the roofs of operating plants* – that provide an easy target all across the country for terrorists;

–Nuke advocates say they produce "clean" and "carbon free" energy, but the entire chain of the nuclear process is anything but. Uranium mining, processing, extraction, and transportation, not to mention accidents and leaks, have left a legacy of contamination and cancer;

–There is no place to hide from a nuclear meltdown. Despite the official plans to evacuate southeastern Connecticut – an entire population by highway, no less — any attempt to escape radiation poisoning will be a futile and chaotic exercise. And finally,

–Nuclear power is not profitable, as Dominion has conceded. Better energy solutions are cheaper. The Virginia-based company expects Connecticut to guarantee long-term profits even if demand for their energy drops. This is just one way the nuclear pushers crave public welfare to stay in business.

In the 1950s, we were subjected to the nuclear industry's cartoon defense of atomic power. Anybody remember Reddy Kilowatt? That era also introduced us to Godzilla, however, the monster awakened by an atomic blast. The movie beast came back for 18 sequels.

Dominion Energy and its army of lobbyists will be back, too, with another scheme to cajole and threaten our state for its own private profit.

Godzilla reminds us all that a nuclear monster is really, really hard to kill.

13. LGBTQ

Lesbian Community Says, "No!"

In 1970, American students shut down hundreds of schools and universities across the nation after the illegal U.S. bombing of Cambodia, and the killings of four young people at Kent State in Ohio, and two at Jackson State in Mississippi. The year marked a new decade of war in Vietnam, the FBI targeting of civil rights leaders, and the rise of a president who called students "bums" and drew up an "enemies list." It also marked a new phase for the growing lesbian and gay liberation movement.

That year, some wouldn't wait for a mass movement to stop the violence, repression and imperial excesses of the United States. Hartford native Susan Saxe, Katherine Power and a handful of others decided to rob a Massachusetts bank in 1970 "for the revolution." A police officer was killed by one man in the group. Saxe and Powers went underground.

The FBI organized a nationwide dragnet for the fugitives. The feds invaded women's groups and swept through lesbian communities in Hartford, New Haven and around the country with a newly sharpened tool: the grand jury.

Originally developed in old English law as a shield against arbitrary action by the king, grand juries were being used by the government against political activists in over thirty political cases across the nation.

If you were called to testify, whether or not you knew anything about fugitives, you could not refuse to answer a prosecutor's questions. This gave the government full license to collect information on all activists and movements, whether or not they had any connection to illegal activity.

William Kunstler, famed defense attorney, came to Connecticut to tell the public that grand juries were being used by prosecutors as "tools" to strip citizens of their rights. "They are running wild over this country," Kunstler warned.

In Connecticut, women activists found this out the hard way. Ellen Grusse, Terry Turgeon, Diana Perkins and Marianne Palmer were subpoenaed in March 1975 by the prosecutor, but refused to talk to a New Haven grand jury. Perkins eventually provided limited testimony; Palmer's case was dismissed. The legal action sent a chill through feminist and lesbian organizing efforts.

Radical Hartford attorney Mike Graham proclaimed that they were being sent to jail, not for failing to give information about the fugitives and not for committing any crime, but for refusing to divulge the names of their friends and the groups to which they belonged.

Ellen Grusse and Terry Turgeon initially spent 28 days in jail for refusing to cooperate with the feds.

The two women and their lawyers were pretty sure the FBI was bugging their phones. The feds insisted they were not (in 1977, a local newspaper revealed that 3,000 Connecticut residents had been wiretapped in the course of a Black Panther trial in 1970. Over one thousand of them were later awarded damages by a court).

Grusse and Turgeon were recalled to the grand jury in 1975, and once again refused to name names. Grusse said that she and her comrades did not want to go to prison, but were willing to go. They spent seven months in the Niantic State Prison, the length of the grand jury's operation. The National Council of Churches filed a friend-of-the-court brief supporting the pair's fight against abuse of the grand jury system.

After five years on the run, Susan Saxe was arrested in Philadelphia when a bank security camera photo surfaced showing her cashing a check in Torrington. Saxe eventually pled guilty, with the proviso that she would not testify about any other person. She served eight years in prison. In 1993 Katherine Powers turned herself in after 23 years underground and was incarcerated for six years.

Not one National Guardsman or police officer was convicted in the deaths of the unarmed Kent State and Jackson State students. No U.S. Army or government official was prosecuted for war crimes in Southeast Asia.

Terry Turgeon and Ellen Grusse were released from prison on December 20, 1975. Their courage and principles proved stronger than the federal government's threats and vindictive actions.

Two months later, grassroots activists and progressive lawyers in Connecticut organized the "Committee to Defend Our Democratic Liberties" which exposed grand jury abuses and the new push by President Ronald Reagan to consolidate and ratchet up the federal criminal code in order to dismantle opposition communities, repress labor rights, quash the free press, and curb the right to privacy.

Queer Power, From Stonewall to Hartford

Hartford's first gay liberation group decided that 'coming out' meant direct action — and if necessary, confrontation with the police.

On September 3,1971 eleven Kalos Society members were arrested while protesting at a local gay bar where lesbians were being harassed by the management. The owners of the Park West club wanted women customers to dress "properly." They ejected those who ignored the gender norms of the day.

Undeterred by the busts, Kalos members kept up their nightly pickets until the owner capitulated.

The Kalos Society began in 1968 as a social organization (known as Project H) with the support of Episcopal Canon Clinton Jones. One of their early public events occurred at a Goodwin Park picnic outing in September 1970, despite neighbors' protests.

The group quickly became the local "gay liberation front" inspired by the 1969 Stonewall Rebellion in New York, a response by trans militants to constant police raids. Gay advocacy, which had mostly been quiet lobbying, took on a public and assertive social justice quality.

Brother Richard Cardarelli, a Franciscan who was excommunicated for his advocacy of gay inclusion in the Catholic Church, was a Kalos member. He was a student of liberation theology (the radical grassroots Latin American Catholic movement) and developed his own concept of "gay liberation theology."

Kalos published a regular newsletter, *The Griffin,* which was available at gay bars and in the stores at Hartford's Union Place (known for radical and counterculture activity). The group related to politics of the left: the *Griffin* quoted Black Panther leader Huey Newton and sponsored a bus to the 1972 Vietnam War protest in Washington, D.C.

Less than a month after the bar protests, Connecticut became the second state in the nation to decriminalize private sexual relations between consenting adults. There were many more fights to come.

14. Youth in Revolt

Rock and Roll vs. Racism

In 1955, the most racially integrated public space in Connecticut may have been the rock and roll concerts at Hartford's State Theater. Despite widespread discrimination against African Americans in jobs, housing and schools, Black and white kids came together here on common ground. Located at the intersection of Main, Morgan and Village streets, the State Theater featured a new musical genre that both revolutionized American culture and played a lesser-known, but significant role in the fight for racial justice.

The first rock and roll performers to appear in Hartford were the Penguins, a Black doo–wop quartet whose biggest hit, "Earth Angel," had just reached the Billboard charts. The song was an early "crossover" hit, its popularity breaking the barrier between Black and white radio audiences. Bo Diddley, Etta James, Fats Domino, Frankie Lyman and the Teenagers, and dozens of other performers followed at the State — all with white acts, including Bill Haley and His Comets, Jerry Lee Lewis, and Buddy Holly on the same billing.

Racial Tensions on the Rise in 1955

Racial turmoil swelled that year. In 1955, two white men lynched 14-year-old Emmett Till in Mississippi. Authorities also arrested Rosa Parks in Montgomery, Alabama, sparking the famous bus boycott that same year. On August 1, 1955, the Georgia Board of Education fired all teachers who held membership in the NAACP.

During this same period, the Connecticut state civil rights commission reported that it was "virtually impossible for a Negro to rent a home in a white neighborhood." The state's NAACP targeted banks that refused to grant housing loans to Black families. Literacy tests for voting were still part of state law. Two skilled electricians, both African Americans, struggled for five years to join an all-white union in order to work at their trade. According to one poll, only 20 percent of Connecticut's white population supported full integration of the races.

It was remarkable, then, that the local press did not identify Black rock and rollers who came to town by their race. Instead, the musicians were described by their particular styles — both in paid advertisements and in concert reviews. In almost every other case, newspapers of that time labeled African-American individuals as "colored" or "Negro," especially when reporting a crime.

That is not to say Connecticut's white majority was happy with early rock music. Racist press commentary was frequent, using not-too-subtle code words. Rock and roll was "jungle stuff" wrote one local critic. It was "cannibalistic" and "tribalistic" according to Dr. Francis Braceland, head of Hartford's exclusive Institute for Living.

The first official crackdown on rock and roll took place on March 19, 1955. Police halted a New Haven festival "when it seemed the dancers were getting out of hand." Concert goers were all over 21. Vendors legally sold beer, but it was the "uninhibited" and "touchy" dancing that really seemed to disturb the authorities. "There will be no more of that," stated Chief Francis McManus. Bridgeport then banned all rock events, three of which promoters had already scheduled for April. In contrast to these crackdowns, after Hartford's police chief suggested banning rock and roll (after eight arrests at a concert for fighting), Councilman James Kinsella strongly denounced the proposal as "censorship."

Alan Freed Helps Integrate Rock and Roll Audiences
One man more than any other proved responsible for the integration of rock and roll audiences in Connecticut. Alan Freed, a Cleveland, Ohio disc jockey, first played Rhythm & Blues (R & B or "race music") in 1951. Until that time, the music remained largely in the Black community. Freed earned national attention for a huge integrated concert in New York just a few months before the first Hartford event. He was in Hartford frequently, acting as master of ceremonies at every concert he produced. "Mr. Rock and Roll" became as popular as the groups he promoted.

Many also credited Freed for coining the term "rock and roll." While some critics called the music "noise," Freed understood the historic roots of rock. The music "began on the levees and plantations," he explained. "It took on folk songs and features blues and rhythm. It's the rhythm that gets to the kids." The controversial DJ is remembered today for his part in the payola scandal, a pay-for-play scheme with the record companies. But his legacy is really as the pioneer of rock and roll on radio, and his successful efforts to help integrate a new generation of youth.

The State Theater closed its doors in 1960 and workers demolished it two years later. Alan Freed died in 1965. He was among the first group of inductees - Black and white - to the Rock and Roll Hall of Fame in Cleveland.

Puerto Rican Youth Liberate Their Space

Just after dark, a dozen young Puerto Ricans approached 21 Kennedy Street, an abandoned building near Keney Tower. Within minutes they were inside, establishing the space as a liberated area to be used for a breakfast program, free clothing distribution, and drop-in center. Hartford Police showed up but took no action against the teenagers, who called themselves the Peoples Liberation Party (PLP).

The day of the occupation, November 23, 1970, coincided with a surge in community anger over police brutality. Abraham Rodriguez, an unarmed 19-year old, had been killed the previous spring by Officer Anthony Lombardi (subsequently fired by the department). A recent small disturbance at the Lyric Dance Hall on Park Street turned into a police riot where women and men were indiscriminately beaten.

The PLP was influenced by the Young Lords Party, the New York City group that had been engaging in militant community organizing. The Lords occupied an empty church and used it as a community center. They commandeered an unused medical testing truck to conduct the TB tests that were otherwise not available. And in their boldest move, the Young Lords took over Lincoln Hospital in the South Bronx on July 14th, in protest of the substandard care the city provided. In solidarity, most of the hospital staff stayed in the facility, too, and continued their work. Their action forced the city to build a new hospital.

As described by 17 year-old PLP leader Jose Claudio, the Kennedy Street building was owned by the Hartford Housing Authority, one of many abandoned buildings throughout the city's North End. Now, the structure will have a purpose, he said, as party members painted the walls and fixed the water pipes.

In less than a month, the group set up a second site at the South Park Methodist Church. They planned to provide political education classes and work on the desperate living conditions in their neighborhoods. The community space was called the Abraham Rodriguez Memorial Center.

15. Standing up for Free Speech

How the Wobblies Won Free Speech

Free Speech in America? For working people in the early 1900s, the right didn't exist. Until workers and their unions fought for it, in the courts and on the streets, the First Amendment was an illusion for many Connecticut citizens.

In 1791, a sufficient number of states approved the Bill of Rights, which guaranteed that Congress could not infringe on the right of free speech or assembly (our state failed to vote for it). But in practice, ordinary people could not speak on public property unless they won explicit permission from local authorities.

Laws Used to Suppress Union Movement

Hartford's Amalgamated Trades Union wanted to use Bushnell Park for a mass meeting in 1884. The Board of Aldermen approved the rally. The Mayor vetoed the Board's action. Special meetings were called to reject the veto and uphold the union's request. "The general argument was that the park belonged to the people," the *Hartford Courant* reported.

Despite that democratic sentiment, local authorities' right to limit rallies or speeches on public property was affirmed by a U.S. Supreme Court ruling (Davis v. Massachusetts) in 1897 when a pastor challenged a Boston law. The Court wrote that the Constitution "does not have the effect of creating a particular and personal right in the citizen to use public property in defiance of the Constitution and laws of the state."

For the next four decades, local Connecticut activists suffered the consequences of that decision. Enforcers frequently targeted groups, including unions, that were suspected of being aligned with socialist or communist politics. In 1904, for example, union organizers were arrested for violating Torrington's "hand-bill law" when they distributed leaflets.

In 1912, Irish socialist Cornelius Foley tried to speak in downtown Hartford but was denied permission, forcing him to a corner where hustlers hawked medical cures and novelties. In 1914, another socialist began to talk in front of Parsons Theater but was interrupted by a police officer. The soap-box orator was charged with breach of peace for speaking in public without a license.

Workers Use Civil Disobedience Tactics

The Industrial Workers of the World (IWW), popularly known as the Wobblies, devised a strategy to win the freedoms that the law denied them. The radical union mounted "free speech fights" wherever authorities banned their organizing efforts. They defied local laws and filled the jails, forcing city governments to go broke or give in. Despite the terrible hardships they faced in jail, the Wobblies compelled cities from Spokane to San Diego to rescind legal prohibitions.

In Willimantic, IWW organizer J.T. Bienowski threatened to bring in dozens of other union activists to challenge a 1912 city ban on street speaking. He didn't have to follow through on the threat; a month later, 500 workers crowded Lincoln Square to hear Wobbly Ben Legere speak for over an hour with no police interference. In Bridgeport and Waterbury, however, IWW organizers defied similar city ordinances and paid the price.

In 1919, the Connecticut General Assembly enacted laws aimed at the IWW. Long jail sentences could be imposed for speaking in a "disloyal, scurrilous or abusive manner," addressing 10 or more people in a way that could "injuriously affect"[sic] the state government, or carrying a red flag. (Steve Thornton, *A Shoeleather History of the Wobblies*)

It took the U.S. Supreme Court until 1939 to validate one of the basic concepts of free speech as we now know it. Again, a union championed the change. After the IWW was effectively disrupted by the government, the Congress of Industrial Organizations (CIO) took up the cause of America's workers. In New Jersey, the CIO challenged political boss Frank Hague who, in 1937, had banned public union meetings by invoking a city ordinance that barred the assembly of persons seeking to obstruct government by unlawful means. The Court ruled that the use of public places was "a part of the privileges, immunities, rights, and liberties of citizens."

Although the ruling did not acknowledge past abuses of workers' freedom of assembly, the First Amendment was finally becoming a reality for a greater number of citizens. And eventually, our state followed suit. In 1939, 150 years after its original passage, Connecticut finally ratified the Bill of Rights.

Waiting for Lefty: A Free Speech Fight

Rarely has an American play met with the kind of government opposition that Clifford Odets' *Waiting for Lefty* faced in 1935. Mayors and police departments forbade the staging of the play in a number of cities and stopped performances mid-play in others. Audience and cast members were arrested for protesting police actions. Locally, the Bridgeport *Sunday Herald* rallied to the cause of the play after it was banned in New Haven, and thus, played an important and honorable role in defending free speech.

Clifford Odets was 28-years-old and a member of the left-wing, New York-based Group Theatre ensemble when he wrote *Waiting for Lefty*. It was the first of his plays to be staged when it opened in a Group production at the Civic Repertory Theater on West 14th Street in Manhattan on January 5, 1935. Among those in the cast were Odets, Elia Kazan and Lee J. Cobb.

Waiting for Lefty

Waiting for Lefty is often described as a play about a group of hard-pressed New York City taxicab drivers contemplating a strike. While it is that, it's more a penetrating look at the lives of a group of people who happen to be cab drivers as they cope with crises of poverty, familial breakdown, and identity at the low-point of the Great Depression. The cabbies do discuss going on strike, but they also struggle with the risks involved — not the least of which involves their union being corrupted by racketeers violently opposed to any kind of independent labor action.

The drama in *Waiting for Lefty* resonated with audiences already familiar with the labor fights making headlines across the country. In the months leading up to the play's opening, there had been general strikes in San Francisco, Minneapolis and Toledo. Workers were organizing in great numbers and left-wing parties and organizations were stronger than they had been in many years.

Waiting for Lefty's run at the Civic was such a rousing success that it moved to Broadway in June 1935. Due to its popularity, however, and in keeping with their own philosophy of making theatre easily accessible to the poor and working classes, Odets and the Group took the unusual step of approving productions throughout the country prior to the play's Broadway premiere. In no time, labor unions and cultural organizations began staging *Waiting for Lefty* in dozens of cities and towns throughout the nation. Among them, a production by the New

Haven John Reed Club's Unity Players at Yale University's University Theatre.

Officials in at least six cities, including Philadelphia, Boston and Newark, either forced the cancellation of performances before the curtain went up, or shut them down after they'd already begun. In Newark, a performance of *Waiting for Lefty* was stopped mid-way through and a number of audience members who protested were arrested. City officials justified their actions, in some cases, by claiming the play was "Communist propaganda" and "un-American." In Boston, profanity — use of the word "God-damn" — was specifically cited as pretext.

New Haven Performances

The production in New Haven, meanwhile, went on to win the George Pierce Baker Cup at Yale's annual Drama Tournament held on April 11th. In response to the wildly enthusiastic reception, the Unity Players booked space at Commercial High School for additional performances. Several days before the first scheduled show, however, the New Haven Board of Education rescinded the agreement. Police Chief Philip Smith declared the play was not to be performed anywhere in the city on the grounds it was "blasphemous and indecent." He declared anyone attempting to do so would be arrested.

The Unity Players, along with the American Civil Liberties Union, several community organizations, Yale students and faculty, and others, then formed the New Haven Anti-Censoring Committee. They held rallies and meetings demanding the city allow *Waiting for Lefty* to be staged. Police Chief Smith, however, did not budge. Then the Bridgeport *Sunday Herald* got involved.

The Bridgeport Herald

Founded in 1805 and located at 200 Lafayette Boulevard in downtown Bridgeport, the *Herald's* motto was "No Fear, No Favor – The People's Paper." The newspaper first reported on the controversy in New Haven on the front page of its April 14th edition. In that same issue, it ran a glowing review of the New York production of *Waiting for Lefty* by Leonardo Da Bence across three pages. On April 21st, the *Herald's* editors responded to the continuing ban in New Haven by printing the play in its entirety. Also included was a lengthy introduction that included criticisms of Chief Smith. The *Herald's* intention, the editors said, was to give "readers an opportunity to judge for themselves."

Though based in Bridgeport, the *Herald* had influence well beyond the city. It published editions and special sections for areas throughout the state, including a New Haven edition that was sold at local newsstands. Among its criticisms of New Haven officials, the *Herald* editors noted that while banning *Waiting for Lefty,* space at a local public school was provided to an avowedly fascist organization to hold a meeting.

In its May 5th edition, the *Herald* reported the results of a readers poll, in which respondents in favor of staging *Waiting for Lefty* in New Haven outnumbered those supporting the ban 10 to 1. The *Herald's* "Letters to the Editor" section often extended over several pages with further support of the play. One letter from Allen Touometoftosky began as follows: "Long live the militant, truthful Bridgeport HERALD! Long live 'Waiting for Lefty!'"

The Ban is Lifted

With the groundswell of protest growing, Chief Smith and the City of New Haven finally relented. The Unity Players were allowed to reserve the Little Theatre on Lincoln Street several blocks from Yale. Performances of *Waiting for Lefty* began there on the evening of May 9th. The play was received much as it was around the rest of the country — with enthusiastic, full houses. There were no further incidents or police interference.

While *Waiting for Lefty* has never been revived on Broadway, it remains popular in local theaters and union halls. It has played any number of times in Connecticut, including a production by The Connecticut Repertory Theater that ran in Storrs. When the New Haven Theater Company most recently did the play in 2012, some newspaper commentary recalled the controversy of 1935.

The *Bridgeport Herald* published until 1974, and is remembered with a degree of fondness by older Bridgeporters. It was the subject of a panel discussion at the Fairfield Museum and History Center in 2015. It should continue to be honored for the vital role it played in an important free speech fight fought almost a century ago.

High School Students Teach Elders About Free Press

May 3rd marks World Press Freedom Day, first designated by the UN General Assembly in 1993. Across the globe, students have played a critical role in using and maintaining unrestricted media to promote democracy and justice. Witness, for example, the use of social media tools like Twitter and Facebook during the Arab Spring in 2011. Two decades before the UN declaration, however, African-American high school students in Hartford decided they needed to teach city authorities something about freedom of the press, too.

Marcus Manselle was a Weaver High senior who published the student newspaper the *People's Press*. He was first to report that faculty and students began a picketing campaign at the Hartford Chamber of Commerce on February 7, 1969, to protest a proposed $3.5 million cut to the Board of Education budget. Initially, the *Hartford Courant* relied on Manselle's reporting to learn about the source of all the commotion.

Students wrote and published the "underground" newspaper at their own expense and distribution took place on school property, without official approval. Hartford's corporation counsel ruled the paper was "hate literature" filled with "racist" and "obscene" language. In fact, the students were speaking out about student rights, irrelevant education, and their alienation from school and society.

Punishing Weaver High School Publishers

The Weaver administration informed Manselle, Clifford Hankton and Louise Billie they had to stop handing out the paper. The three publishers refused. The Board of Education suspended all three students on February 21, without bothering to engage the students in a discussion about their activity. Administrators forced Manselle into "home instruction" during his suspension. Even after the other two students received permission to return to school, Manselle's discipline continued.

The newspaper did not stop publishing, however. It surfaced again in April with more support than ever. Students, teachers, and the Ebony Businessmen's League all spoke out for Manselle and criticized the students' suspensions. The 120-member Weaver Student Senate also backed Manselle and raised many of the demands that he championed. Parents and alumni also met to support the cause. The University of Hartford's student newspaper, *UH News/Liberated Press*, followed the story, too, and published Manselle's essays. They even

234

listed Manselle as a staff member. A state judge refused to issue an injunction on Manselle's discipline, however, despite a 1968 US Supreme Court decision upholding the right of Iowa students to wear black armbands after Martin Luther King Jr.'s assassination.

On May 1, another issue of the *People's Press* was ready for distribution, this time on the Blue Hills Avenue sidewalk in front of Weaver High. Students also leafleted at city hall and urged Mayor Ann Uccello to support their fight. She replied that the issue was not within her jurisdiction. The Weaver Student Senate then took the controversy to the Board of Education office, calling for Manselle's reinstatement and the establishment of a student court for reviewing and overturning disciplines.

Students Strike for Free Speech

On May 27, after finding themselves stonewalled at every level of city government, 500 Weaver students went on strike for three days. Strikers urged those still inside the school to join them, and more students left class. They marched to the Board office on High Street. They tried to join a Board-faculty meeting but authorities refused to admit them. An exasperated Board President Alfred Rogers told the strikers, "I want nothing more to do with you."

The fight continued into June. Finally, with the help of local NAACP President Wilber Smith, a working group of students, parents, school officials and Board members hammered out a proposed resolution. It recommended on-campus distribution of independent publications as long as the publications did not "inflame or incite" students or interfere with normal school business. Marcus Manselle's suspension continued, however. He did not graduate with his class.

Weaver High School was renovated in 1976 and rechristened the Martin Luther King Jr. elementary school. The keynote speaker at the school's rededication was Dr. King's niece, Alberta King Neale, an Atlanta journalist. It was Dr. King, speaking at the 1963 March on Washington, who told the crowd, "Somewhere I read of the freedom of press. Somewhere I read that the greatness of America is the right to protest for right."

16. Taking on the Terrorists

Hartford's Challenge to *Birth of a Nation*

Can a movie change history? *The Birth of a Nation* did. The original 1915 film fomented racial bigotry and consciously distorted the history of the post-Civil War era.

D.W. Griffith's silent movie extravaganza was a technical marvel and a historical travesty. The entire second act portrays its African-American characters as boorish fools or scheming sex fiends. After its initial release, hundreds of thousands of people flocked to movie houses to pay as much as $45.00 a ticket (in today's dollars) for the three-hour spectacle.

It did more than any other medium to convince the white public that Reconstruction was a swindle and a crime against white Southerners. Only months after the movie's nationwide premiere, the Ku Klux Klan — defunct since the 19th century — reorganized in the state of Georgia.

Birth of a Nation Comes to Hartford

It all started with *The Clansman: A Historical Romance of the Ku Klux Klan,* a novel by Thomas F. Dixon Jr. published in 1905. No sooner was the book obtained by the Hartford Public Library than anonymous readers wrote "slurs upon the Negro" in the page margins, reported Reverend W. A. Harrod of the Shiloh Baptist Church. Worse yet, an effigy had been set ablaze and thrown on Rev. Harrod's porch while the offenders yelled "Lynch him!"

Harrod was one of four African-American clergymen who met with Hartford Mayor William F. Henney to express their concern when *The Clansman* became a hit stage play bound for Hartford. The production was due to open at the Parsons Theater in December of 1906.

After Henney proved reluctant to take action, physician and reformer Dr. Patrick Henry Clay Arms pointed out the hypocrisy of his decision. Arms argued that if a play like George Bernard Shaw's "scandalous" *Mrs. Warren's Profession* (which met with controversy in New York and London) could be excluded on moral grounds, the same standard should apply to *The Clansman.*

After a second Hartford protest by a growing number of Black and white clergy, Mayor Henney promised to travel to Manhattan and see the play for himself. He watched a performance on December 5, 1906. When he returned to Hartford, the mayor admitted there were "some uncomplimentary allusions to the negro that were liberally applauded." Ultimately, though, Henney believed there was nothing "immoral or objectionable" to the play's content. The show premiered as scheduled at the Parsons Theater.

Rebirth of The Clansman

The Clansman proved so popular with white audiences that in 1915 it became the now-infamous movie by D. W. Griffith and retitled *The Birth of a Nation.* In September, Rev. Walter Gay and a group of Hartford residents who opposed the film, called on Mayor Joseph Lawler. Rev. Richard R. Ball told the mayor that the film was "a gross injustice to the negro [that] breeds social strife."

The pastor of St. Paul's Methodist Church, John E. Zeiter, then joined the chorus of protests when he denounced the movie from his pulpit. His address was not just a critique of the film, it was an insightful analysis of Reconstruction and the rise of southern Jim Crow laws. The minister seemed to have a deep understanding of the contribution African Americans had been making to the United States despite centuries of crippling slavery. "The American negro owes this nation nothing but loyalty and citizenship—and in all other things the nation is his debtor," Zeiter proclaimed. (Steve Thornton, Connecticuthistory.org, 8/1/2022, *Hartford's Challenge to The Birth of a Nation*)

In spite of these objections, the film played to sold-out Hartford audiences. Forty thousand people reportedly saw it in Bridgeport in its first week. The movie house projected the movie twice a day, with special added holiday performances. There is little doubt that President Woodrow Wilson's hosting of a private viewing in the White House helped give the film respectability in many proponent's eyes.

Following a successful run of the film, the Parsons Theater returned to its normal vaudeville fare, which included Lasky's Darktown Revue and its twelve "ebony entertainers." *Birth of a Nation* then returned for another Hartford run in 1916.

"Patriotic Suppression"

It was not until 1919, however, that public officials took any significant action against *The Birth of a Nation.* After some 350,000 African-American soldiers returned from the battlefields of the First World War, the Black community began finding its political voice and challenging white supremacy at every level. It was around this time that authorities proposed censorship of the racist movie. In one such instance, The Hartford Americanization Committee asked Mayor Richard J. Kinsella to stop an upcoming 1919 run of the film at the Empire Theater and Kinsella agreed. "I was requested by the Americanization committee to suppress it," the mayor told a reporter. "This is a very inopportune time for showing such a picture. I don't think such a subject should be given publicity at this time." Nearly one hundred years later, however, *The Birth of Nation* reappeared in Hartford theaters, but this time in the form of a 2016 film intended to re-envision the story of Nat Turner's 1831 slave rebellion in Virginia.

The Ku Klux Klan in Connecticut

Within months of the Union's Civil War victory in 1865, a small band of soldiers from the defeated Confederate army gathered in Pulaski, Tennessee and formed an organization they dubbed the Ku Klux Klan. Very quickly, like-minded individuals — mostly professionals and former plantation owners — joined what was initially a loose network of chapters located throughout much of the South. Their primary focus was to oppose Reconstruction. To that end, the KKK launched a campaign of terror in which its members killed thousands of Blacks who worked with poor whites to build a new South. That campaign culminated in the complete defeat of Reconstruction with the Hayes-Tilden Compromise of 1877.

In the 150 years following the founding of the Ku Klux Klan, additional organizations using some variation of the name sprang up. The former Confederacy was always the base of the various Klans, but when the KKK experienced a dramatic revival in 1920, chapters emerged in northern and western parts of the United States as well, including in Connecticut. The remarkable increase in Klan popularity — its membership reached five million during the 1920s — came largely from its branding of its members as nativists defending an embattled pure American white race against Blacks, Jews, Catholics, Bolsheviks and immigrants who came to U.S shores in large numbers in the preceding two decades. Always, though, the Klan's primary animus was toward Blacks.

The KKK Comes to Connecticut

The first reports of individuals in the ubiquitous white robes gathering in Connecticut, as well as of cross burnings (a telltale sign of an organized Klan presence) in the state, date to as early as 1924. The Klan regularly organized field days. One of them held in Greenwich attracted 200 people in 1928. The Klan's membership in Connecticut peaked at an estimated 18,000 in 1920s. The KKK declined in Connecticut as dramatically as it rose, however. By the 1930s, Klan membership had fallen to a fraction of what it had been. Klan activity in Connecticut was virtually nonexistent for five decades until the early 1980s when the Invisible Empire of the Knights of the Ku Klux Klan, one of a myriad of splinter groups, formed. The Invisible Empire established a chapter in and around Meriden, and over the next two years, held a series of actions in that part of the state.

Revival

The most dramatic of these actions was on March 21, 1981, when several dozen robed Klan members and supporters rallied at Meriden's city hall in support of a Meriden police officer who shot and killed a Black man suspected of shoplifting at a nearby mall. A far larger number of anti-Klan demonstrators, however, met the Klan members. The clash resulted in injuries to 20 people, and the arrests of two counter demonstrators.

The KKK held rallies in Meriden on July 4, 1981, March 20, 1982, and April 30, 1983. They also held a rally in Windham on October 10, 1981 that attracted roughly 30 members and supporters. On each occasion, however, crowds 10 to 20-times larger gathered to protest their presence. The Invisible Empire also set up the Klan Youth Corps, a group for young supporters. Leaflets published by the Corps soon began appearing in high schools in the Meriden area. Questions from students prompted the Connecticut Education Association, the union representing many of the state's teachers, to publish a curriculum guide about the KKK. The same article estimated that the Invisible Empire had 200 members in Connecticut in 1982.

Though the Klan's public presence in Connecticut soon waned, it has resurfaced at various times over the years, mostly in the form of flyers attributed to one faction or another. Such flyers appeared in Orange in 2012, and in Milford the following year. According to a 2014 report issued by the Southern Poverty Law Center (SPLC), one Klan faction remains in Connecticut: the Loyal White Knights of the Ku Klux Klan. According to its website, the Loyal White Knights are based in North Carolina and are "the largest Klan in America." Neither the Loyal White Knights or the SPLC provides estimates on how many members or chapters the Knights have in Connecticut, or where they exist. Nor do they provide any insight into member activity.

A Fascist Plot to Overthrow Franklin Roosevelt

In 1933, retired Marine Corps General Smedley Butler was visited at his Pennsylvania home by individuals virulently opposed to newly-elected President Franklin Roosevelt. Butler himself was an enthusiastic supporter of Roosevelt. He took the meeting only because the visitors had told him the purpose was to discuss upcoming American Legion elections. Butler was one of the best-known military men in the country, and had a unique reputation for being popular with everyday soldiers. Unbeknownst to him, it was that reputation that brought the visitors to his doorstep.

Gerald MacGuire

Gerald MacGuire, the Legion's Connecticut commander, was among the visitors. MacGuire was born in Rhode Island on May 10, 1897, served in the First World War, settled afterwards in Darien, and was employed at a prominent Wall Street brokerage house. He and many of the moneyed men he worked with were alarmed at Roosevelt's proposed policies. As the meeting progressed, Butler grew suspicious of MacGuire, especially when MacGuire said he had large sums of money at his disposal to bankroll a run by Butler for the Legion's top post. Butler decided to string his visitors along in order to learn more about their plans.

MacGuire traveled to Italy and Germany in early 1934 to study how veterans' groups helped the fascists come to power in those countries. When he returned, he finally told Butler the whole story. Very wealthy, powerful men had made three million dollars available to him with much more to come — to organize a coup against Roosevelt. The American Legion would be the 500,000-strong vehicle, and they wanted Butler to lead it.

The plan would render Roosevelt a figurehead. Accounts vary as to whether Butler or someone else would be installed as the nation's leader. General Joseph MacArthur and Brigadier General Hugh Johnson, head of the National Recovery Administration (NRA), were also apparently under consideration. That Johnson was considered seems odd given that Roosevelt had just appointed him to head the NRA. But then again, Johnson was an enthusiastic admirer of Italian dictator Benito Mussolini, and his vision of the proposed New Deal was essentially that of a corporate, fascist state.

244

Thomas Lamont, the du Ponts, and Others

Besides MacGuire, Butler met with Robert Clark, an heir to the Singer Sewing Machine Company. Clark confirmed MacGuire's proposal and named other plotters who would soon form the Liberty League. The nefarious group included executives from the du Pont Corporation, among them Irénée du Pont. It also included John Davis, the 1924 Democratic Presidential candidate who was affiliated with the J.P. Morgan financial empire; Thomas Lamont, another Morgan associate and great-grandfather of the current Connecticut governor; Al Smith, the Democratic Presidential candidate in 1928; and Grayson Murphy, MacGuire's boss and a director of Goodyear Tire, Anaconda Copper and Bethlehem Steel — as well as other business and military figures, diplomats and politicians. Weapons and ammunition would be supplied by the Bridgeport-based, du Pont-owned Remington Arms.

Butler revealed the details of the plot to Paul Comly French, a reporter for the *Philadelphia Record*. When contacted by French, MacGuire spoke openly of his desire for a fascist America and steered the reporter to some of his associates. French wrote an expose that was published in both the *Record* and the *New York Post*. Butler, meanwhile, finally told MacGuire his true feelings: "If you get 500,000 soldiers advocating anything smelling of Fascism, I am going to get 500,000 more and lick the hell out of you, and we will have a real war right at home."

Congressional Hearings

Butler told what he knew to various government officials, and Congressional hearings were held in 1934 featuring Butler testifying for many hours. All of those who Butler named as being involved vehemently denied the charge, including MacGuire.

Ultimately, no charges were brought. That was partly due to a lack of concrete evidence, but Roosevelt also intervened to essentially suppress the transcript records of some of Butler's most damning testimony. Several accounts speculate Roosevelt did so out of fear an already divided nation would grow still more divided if the full story of the "Business Plot" — as it became known — was made public.

MacGuire died suddenly in Connecticut of pneumonia on March 25, 1935, shortly after the hearings. Catapulted to national fame, Butler became even more famous when he wrote *War is a Racket* a little while later. In the book, Butler said of his life as a military man, "I spent most of my time as a high class muscle man for Big Business … a gangster for capitalism" who "might have given Al Capone a few hints."

Hailed by many as a hero for exposing the plot, Butler died in 1940. The story of the "Business Plot" has been the subject of documentaries, television programs and a BBC Radio special that implicated another prominent Connecticut man — Prescott Bush. Bush was a Wall Street executive living in Greenwich who later served as a Senator from the Constitution State, and whose son and grandson both became President of the United States. In 2000, Academy Award-winning director Oliver Stone announced he was planning to make a feature film about the "Business Plot," but those plans were eventually scrapped.

17. Resisting Government Repression

Witchcraft In Connecticut

It was one of the most shameful episodes in the long history of Connecticut. It was a period when superstition, patriarchy, a hatred of nature, and religion-fueled repression were bedrock features of colonial life. It lasted fifteen years and preceded the more famous cases of witch-hunts in Salem, Massachusetts by almost five decades. This was witchcraft and witch-hunting in 17th century Connecticut.

Witchcraft as Crime

Witchcraft had been practiced around the world for centuries before the witch scare in Connecticut, It is still practiced today. There is no documented mention of it in the colony of Connecticut, however, until witchcraft became a crime punishable by death in 1642. Historical interpretations and general theories as to why people targeted others as witches tend to focus on the difficulty of life in the New World. Settlers from England had, by 1642, experienced a great deal of hardship that fueled feelings of hostility to the natural world, as well as to anyone within the community who did not strictly conform to harsh social and personal mores.

Epidemics of disease and starvation, as well as winters that were colder and longer than those in England, were among the problems colonists faced. Perhaps more important, though, was the extreme hostility and violence of the colonists toward Native-Americans, which begat retaliatory violence and a constant state of near embattlement.

Patriarchy

Witch-hunting was also very definitely an attack on women. In the guise of attacking select women who did not conform, witch-hunting was a way to terrorize all women into acquiescing to a hierarchical social system that was oppressive at its core. Women in colonial times were regarded legally and morally as second-class citizens. The majority of those executed as witches, both in Connecticut and beyond, were poor women, often single mothers, living on the margins. Although men were overwhelmingly the perpetrators of moral crimes – of crimes of all kinds, in fact – legislation of a moral kind was largely directed at policing the behavior of women. Legislators and religious figures were, by definition, all men, and it was women who bore the brunt of social and religious intolerance. As in our own time, female sexuality was especially contested terrain and it was around the expression by women of any degree of independence and sexual freedom that many of the charges of witchcraft arose.

The great Arthur Miller made these themes – patriarchy, female independence, extreme sexual repression – central to *The Crucible*, his 1953 play about the Salem witch trials. The touching off point for the accusations of witchcraft in the play are multiple violations by women of the mores of the time: secretive bonding, nakedness, communing with nature, dancing. And not just any kind of dancing, but dancing that was uninhibited, orgiastic even, done in the nude and with no need of — in fact no desire for — male partnership. Even the setting for the dancing was an affront to the established order: the forest, far from male supervision and part of the hated natural world where Satan and all kind of other demons were known to live.

There is some evidence that accusations of witchcraft against women were also, at least in part, a money-grab on the part of the powers-that-be. In many cases, for example, the women accused were married, but did not have male offspring, which meant they were in line to inherit their husband's estates should they outlive them. In the event a woman died before her husband, with no male heir, the man's property upon his death would go to the community. Some of these elements came into play in the case of Alse Young, the first person in colonial America to be executed as a witch.

Alse Young

Very little is known about Alse Young (in addition to Alse, she is sometimes referred to as Achsah or Alice). She was born around 1600 in Windsor, Connecticut, married a man named John Young, and gave birth to a daughter named Alice. She was accused of witchcraft in 1647, and hanged in Hartford in May of that year, with her husband surviving her. Thirty years later, her daughter Alice was also accused of being a witch in Springfield, Massachusetts. Although Alice was not hanged, the historical records are sketchy as to what other punishment and ostracism she may have had to endure.

Mary Johnson

In 1646, a Connecticut servant named Mary Johnson was accused of being a witch. Her period of torment dragged on for four years during which time she was tortured by whipping and constantly badgered by the local minister to admit her sins. Under these circumstances, Johnson confessed to being a witch, and more importantly, perhaps, to "uncleanness with men." She was hanged in 1650 after a delay, during which time she gave birth to a child by a man to whom she was not married.

More Executions and Reform

All told, roughly a dozen people in Connecticut were executed as witches, all but two were women. The wives of the two men killed were also executed after trials that ran concurrently. Many more were terrorized, and an untold number fled their homes fearing for their lives, until Governor John Winthrop, Jr., established more stringent evidentiary requirements that brought the worst of the witch-hunting — and one of the most disgraceful periods of Connecticut's history — to an end. Even with Winthrop's actions, it's not difficult to imagine the destructive impact the atmosphere of accusations and executions had for decades afterward on one and all. Although, once again, women felt its effects far more acutely. It seems no stretch to also conclude that the killing of people in Connecticut accused of witchcraft in the middle 1600's established a legal and moral precedent for the more famous Salem Witch Trials of 1692-93— indeed, for all witch-hunting in the colonies that followed.

The "Red Scare" in Connecticut

Eager newspaper reporters dubbed the gathering a "bombology class." Federal agents had targeted a nest of suspected radicals in South Manchester, Connecticut. The site was a small automotive garage where Russian immigrants met on a regular basis. Authorities figured they must be up to no good, learning how to construct "infernal machines," as homemade bombs were then known.

It was November 7, 1919, the first day of the notorious Palmer Raids, named after the U.S. attorney general who led them. A. Mitchell Palmer's Connecticut campaign began a nationwide sweep of thousands of workers, many of them immigrants, designed to rid the country of all dangerous "Reds."

Attacks were launched simultaneously in Bridgeport, Waterbury, Hartford, New Britain and New Haven. The goal, according to one Connecticut newspaper, was to dismantle a "nationwide plot" for a "revolution planned by a reign of terror." Anxiety about the recent revolution in Russia, and fear of growing labor unrest at home, helped fuel this massive crackdown.

Backdrop to the Red Scare

Strict immigration laws and the new Espionage Act gave the government power to criminalize free speech. Demands for wage increases and workplace safety became labeled un-American. Criticism of capitalism's excesses was evidence of "Bolshevik" tendencies. Hundreds faced jail time for simply expressing their opposition to the First World War (some of those arrested were war veterans themselves). Postmaster General Albert Burleson attempted to clarify the law's purpose: "For instance, papers may not say that the Government is controlled by Wall Street or the munitions manufacturers or any other special interests," he explained. Similar city and state laws against "disloyal" speech and publishing soon passed in Connecticut. Individuals became outlaws, not for what they did, but for what they thought.

Authorities secretly planned the Palmer Raids months in advance. Palmer's assistant, the young J. Edgar Hoover, ran the operation. In a number of cases, Hoover planted spies within political and labor organizations. These agent provocateurs then established trust within a group, enabling them to call membership meetings, and thus allowing police to coordinate their raids.

"Bomb-Making Ringleader"

Authorities arrested Mark Kulesch on the night of November 7th, at his home. They considered Kulesch Manchester's bomb-making ringleader

252

since he was secretary of the local Union of Russian Workers. According to some news reports, he was in possession of "two small machine guns" and a "full set of drawings" for more machine gun designs from the Colt Firearms Factory. Classified by federal authorities as an "enemy alien," Mark Kulesch had no right to a trial. It did not matter that the mechanic was a volunteer in the "Americanization" effort to teach English and trade skills to fellow immigrants. Florence Hillsburgh, who led the education program, reacted angrily to his arrest. "This is getting to be a hysteria," Hillsburgh told a reporter. "It seems that all a man has to be to get arrested by federal authorities is a Russian."

After six weeks in the Hartford Seyms Street jail, Kulesch joined 248 other prisoners from across the country placed aboard the USS Buford (nicknamed "the Soviet Ark") and deported to Russia on December 21.

The growing "red scare" atmosphere affected many others in the state — immigrants and citizens alike. Politics forced Edward P. Clarke to resign his position as head of the Employment Bureau, a government job he held for more than four years. His association with the Socialist Party and leading a peace group, somehow proved evidence of disloyalty.

High school student David Sohn faced the threat of expulsion after a report that he made un-American remarks at the school's debating club. When Sohn finally got to speak for himself, he explained what he said — if authorities rounded up radicals, they should arrest industrial war profiteers, too.

At the Seyms Street jail, police arrested visitors when they came to see the prisoners. Palmer explained that the visits were equal to attendance at a revolutionary meeting and proof enough of guilt.

Between November of 1919, and February 1920, authorities arrested and imprisoned 235 Connecticut men and one woman. Nationwide raids on January 2, 1920, led to the jailing of as many as 6,000 alleged radicals. Many spent weeks or months behind bars and held incommunicado. Prisoners did not know the charges against them. Authorities denied some prisoners timely legal counsel or the use of interpreters. Bail costs proved astronomical for these working men.

Support for the Palmer Raids
The Palmer Raids had many boosters among business leaders, politicians and the press. One Waterbury newspaper editorial applauded the effort to "put a leash on violent aliens." Industrialist Clarence Whitney donated $50,000 to stop radical labor influence in Connecticut factories. The American Legion pledged its 12,000 state members to root out non-citizens for trial by a military court and death by firing squad. Retired bicycle maker George Pope called union activists "a new species of plague" to be treated like "brazen traitors." They were "criminals by profession and by heredity," he charged.

Reverend Howard Moss of Hartford's First Methodist Church expressed the underlying cultural and class prejudice that stirred public support for the Palmer Raids. He told his Sunday flock that immigrants were "a sodden, bitter mass of humanity…low living in filth and poverty." If you look a radical in the face, Moss warned, "behold it is the face of a foreigner."

The Palmer Raids were just the beginning of the larger "Red Scare" that continued through much of the 20th century - a broad sweep that disrupted families, cost jobs, caused paranoia in communities and became a weapon against effective union organizing and government reforms. Some alarmists even decried Social Security as a socialist plot.

Exposing Law Enforcement Abuses

The Nation magazine helped lead the fight against the nationwide jailings. The magazine reported on the findings by a committee of well-known, highly respected legal scholars who investigated Palmer's actions. One of those jurists was Felix Frankfurter of Massachusetts (later appointed to the Supreme Court in 1939 by Franklin Roosevelt). Their May 1920 report exposed significant civil and human rights violations. Prominently featured was Hartford's Seyms Street lockup. The committee criticized the use of four particular cells — called punishment rooms — that held the political prisoners. The cells, located directly over the jail's boiler room, often had floors so hot they could burn an inmate's hands or feet. There were no windows and no light bulbs. Prisoners held in these rooms received one glass of water and a slice of bread every twelve hours.

Palmer's methods and intent did not receive universal approval. "The very agencies which should be foremost in preventing (radicalism) have been, and are now, very busy creating it," wrote one Connecticut editorial. The raids used "brutality, torture, forgery, theft - provoking crime in order to detect it," charged *The Nation.*

In retrospect, even the FBI proved unable to defend Hoover's 1919 red scare headhunting. Palmer and Hoover were roundly criticized for the plan and for their overzealous domestic security efforts. The FBI admitted that the Palmer Raids were not a bright spot for the young Bureau.

Congressional Red-Hunters Set Their Sights on Bridgeport

In September 1956, the House Committee on Un-American Activities, commonly known as HUAC, came to Connecticut. The purpose was to hold hearings about activities of the Communist Party in New Haven and Bridgeport. HUAC had been formed in 1938, and was in its tenth year of actively investigating Communism.

Committee members Edwin Willis, Democrat from Louisiana, and Bernard Kearney, Republican from New York, along with several aides, set up shop in the federal courthouse in New Haven. The ostensible reason was to investigate alleged violations of the Smith Act. Passed into law in 1940, the Smith Act made it illegal to teach, advocate or encourage the overthrow of the government and extended to any member of an organization that allegedly did so.

The notion in 1956 that the Communist Party was interested in, let alone capable of, overthrowing anything was patently absurd. The CP's national membership had dwindled to perhaps 10,000 by the time of the hearings in Connecticut. A far cry from its roughly 80,000-member peak in the 1940s. Riddled with divisions and reeling in the face of government assaults, the number of members would soon further dwindle to less than 5,000. Orthodoxy had ultimately defeated a strong tendency that emerged within the Party to scale back its ties to the Soviet Union and reject Leninism in favor of an organic path to socialism. Most of the best organizers left the CP by 1958.

Like HUAC hearings around the country, the majority of those who testified in Connecticut did so in response to a government subpoena – that is, under threat of arrest and imprisonment for noncompliance. As was the case nationally, information about Communist activities was culled from the work of HUAC staff, the efforts of the Federal Bureau of Investigation that included infiltration by undercover agents, and information provided by ex-Communist Party members who had become government informants. Since HUAC knew the names of virtually every Communist Party member in the country, and since they knew very well that the CP was in catastrophic decline, the hearings were, in fact, designed to intimidate activists and dissidents rather than to investigate anything.

Much of the questioning about Bridgeport focused on workers employed at the General Electric factory on Boston Avenue. The first person called was Bert Gilden, a combat veteran of the Second World War who, after the war, had begun a freelance writing career in collaboration with his wife Katya. They had published articles in magazines such as *Collier's* and *Liberty* and would achieve literary success in 1964 with their novel *Hurry Sundown*. They would also write *Between the Hills and The Sea*, a novel published in 1971 based on their experiences in Bridgeport covering the decade between 1946 and 1956.

In addition to his writing career, Bert Gilden had worked at a number of factories in Bridgeport including GE. The committee made much of the fact that he had not included on his application for employment at GE that he was a graduate of Brown University. Otherwise, the bulk of Gilden's testimony was much like what had occurred hundreds of times by 1956: Gilden provided basic information about himself, but invoked the First and Fifth Amendments of the Constitution when questioned about certain activities and associates.

As happened with other witnesses, Gilden was briefly excused while an informant – in this case, Harold Kent — was sworn in. Kent testified that he joined the Communist Party in Bridgeport in 1949. After dropping out, he re-joined at the behest of the FBI and provided the Bureau with information about the Party's activities in Bridgeport. Kent testified that he had seen Gilden and many of those from Bridgeport who had been subpoenaed at Communist meetings.

In addition, Kent testified that Gilden had refused to inform GE about his education at Brown because he and the CP were "colonizing" the workers of Bridgeport. Colonizing is a negative way of describing what Latin American practitioners of liberation theology call accompaniment (*acompañamiento*), in which a person with certain intellectual and professional skills chooses to live and/or work in close proximity to the poor and working classes. It is, in fact, one of the most admirable traits of the American Left and a practice also employed by Jesus Christ, Tolstoy, Gandhi, Archbishop Oscar Romero, and any number of others. Yet, according to HUAC, it was just one more sinister part of a vast criminal conspiracy.

There was a fair amount of interest in the People's Party, the Connecticut chapter of the Progressive Party, which was formed in 1948 when former Vice-President Henry Wallace ran for President on its ticket. Locally, Gilden and several others ran for office on the People's Party ticket, thought it was defunct by 1956. Others like longtime Bridgeport resident Josephine Willard had run for local office on the Communist Party ticket in the mid-1940's when the Party was regarded as less of a threat because of its all-out support of the Allied effort in the Second World War.

The committee repeatedly asked questions about organizations and people linked to the Communist Party, no matter how many times a witness declined to answer. This was done to both try and ensnare witnesses in a legal trap —- and because repeatedly "taking of the Fifth" fueled the perception the witness was a criminal involved in illegal activity. For those subpoenaed, meanwhile, the option of testifying only about oneself had long ago been ruled out legally as an option. So, for example, a witness who stated that he or she was a Communist Party member was not only admitting, according to Supreme Court rulings (rulings that years later were overturned), participation in an illegal conspiracy, they opened themselves up to charges of contempt of Congress if they did not then answer all questions about others they knew to be CP members. This applied even in the case of several from Bridgeport who had left the CP years before. There were undoubtedly any number of others who declined to answer on Constitutional grounds even though they had never been Party members because they believed that the government had no right to investigate an individual's political beliefs, let alone prosecute them for holding them.

Despite the fact that HUAC held in its hands the very real power to destroy careers, and sometimes lives, there were several moments of levity during the hearings. For example, Bridgeport resident Frank Peterson, a tool grinder at GE, introduced himself as "a retired millionaire." And in reply to queries about whether he received orders from or was under the discipline of any organization while employed at GE, Peterson replied that he "received orders all right. I received orders from the company to report there at 7 o'clock in the morning and work until 4 o'clock in the afternoon." GE was "the only organization that disciplined me" to "turn out the work" or else "out you go."

Josephine Willard, who had previously been employed at GE and active in the union there for many years, was another who was subpoenaed. For the most part, her testimony followed the established pattern. However, Willard, who was so concerned about her job that she declined to even state where she was employed at the time she was called (she had left GE in the early 1950's and was working elsewhere), had to face the fact that her photo appeared on the front page of the *Bridgeport Post* the day after her testimony. Such repeated publicity over a period of years often caused people's careers to be pushed back down just as they were recovering from earlier rounds of accusations. Willard, who later in life hosted a show about natural health on WPKN for many years, was so scarred by her experience during the Red Scare that for the rest of her life she spoke about it with extreme reluctance, and then only minimally.

The hearings in Connecticut resulted in no arrests for subversive activity or evidence of any criminal conduct. It is likely, however, that some of those subpoenaed experienced difficulties in their families or at their jobs, as Willard apparently feared. And while no one from Connecticut took their own lives as a result of the pressures, as happened in a number of instances, it is likely some experienced at least short-term physical and mental health problems such as stress, elevated blood pressure, depression and possibly worse. At minimum, many of those from Bridgeport who were subpoenaed likely experienced over many years something akin to Willard: a desire to purge from memory the entire episode by a kind of forced forgetting. Which, of course, meant they were never able to do so.

18. All Connecticut's a Stage: Radical Theater

The Federal Theatre Project's *Macbeth*, With an All-Black Cast, Plays Bridgeport

For five days in the summer of 1936, Bridgeport's Park Theatre played host to one of the most innovative and talked-about theater productions of that era: the Federal Theatre Project's staging of Shakespeare's *Macbeth* with an all-Black cast, as directed by Orson Welles and produced by John Houseman. The play opened in New York City on April 14, 1936 at Harlem's Lafayette Theatre, where it ran for ten weeks before moving to the Adelphi Theatre on Broadway for two additional weeks. Advance word about the production was so great that a reported 10,000 people gathered outside the Lafayette on opening night. *Macbeth* played to enthusiastic audiences, sold-out houses and mostly rave reviews during the twelve-week engagement that lasted through July 18th.

The Federal Theatre Project

The Federal Theatre Project (FTP) was one of five cultural sub-divisions of the Works Progress Administration (WPA) formed in 1935. The purpose of the FTP was to provide employment to actors, directors, playwrights, stagehands and all others involved in theater who had experienced a severe downturn in opportunities with the advent of the Great Depression. A second and equally important goal was to fund Broadway-quality plays, comic acts, children's theater and similar performances in areas of the country where local theater and cultural groups were struggling or non-existent.

Orson Welles

Orson Welles was just 20-years-old when he went to work on developing his idea of a version of *Macbeth* for the FTP. In Welles' version, the story shifted from 11th century Scotland to 19th century Haiti, and featured an all-Black cast. The precocious Welles had been acting on stage in Europe, on Broadway, and in repertory throughout the United States since 1931. He met John Houseman, who was in charge of the FTP's Negro Theatre Unit in New York, and the two worked collaboratively on *Macbeth,* as well as on other projects in the years that followed.

There were conflicts at first between Welles and some cast members who were skeptical of his interpretation of the play, as well as his youth and directorial inexperience. Welles, however, soon won most everyone over with his skills and insights, as well as his around-the-clock work ethic. Canada Lee is probably the best-known actor today from the original cast. In 1936, he was in the early years of a distinguished stage, screen, and radio career that lasted until his premature death in 1952. Despite Lee's initial feelings, he later raved about Welles, going so far as crediting him with making him a real actor.

Jack Carter, Edna Thomas and Canada Lee

While a few of the actors in the huge cast were well-known at the time, many others were relative newcomers. Jack Carter, who was in the original Broadway production of *Porgy* in 1927, played Macbeth during the New York run. He left when the show went on the road. Maurice Ellis was in the title role during the five performances in Bridgeport. Ellis had played Macduff in New York. Edna Thomas, who was living in the Sandy Hook section of Newtown at the time, played Lady Macbeth. Thomas had also been in *Porgy,* and she later appeared in both the original Broadway and movie versions of *A Streetcar Named Desire*. Canada Lee, meanwhile, played Banquo.

In addition to the performances, the production featured striking visual and audio features that captivated audiences and critics alike. The costumes, sets, and lightning in particular, were much-praised. The music that was so vital in establishing the mood of key scenes featured the well-known drummer Asadata Dafora, who also choreographed the show. The witchcraft that plays such a prominent role in the play as written by Shakespeare was replaced by voodoo, giving rise to the production commonly being called "Voodoo Macbeth."

Five Performances at the Park Theatre in Bridgeport

After success in New York, and in keeping with the Federal Theatre Project's mission, *Macbeth* went on the road to eight cities a few days after the final New York performance. Bridgeport was the first stop. Performances took place at the Park Theatre located on downtown Main Street between State Street and what is now Cesar Batalla Way. A building that houses the Aquarion water company stands there today. There were evening performances Tuesday through Friday, July 21-24, and a matinee on Saturday the 25th. Tickets were priced at 50 cents, 40 cents and 25 cents, and were available on a walk-up basis only. Newspaper accounts indicate that the Park Theatre was filled nearly to capacity for all five performances.

Reception by the Bridgeport Public and the Press

The full-house audiences in Bridgeport were apparently overwhelmed by the play. Writing in The Passing Show, a column in the *Bridgeport Post* dedicated to the arts and entertainment, Humphrey Doulens noted that there were six curtain calls at the conclusion of the show on July 22nd. He praised Maurice Ellis and raved about Edna Thomas's "superb performance as Lady Macbeth."

Ethel Beckwith, also writing in the *Post*, was similarly impressed. "Daring, bewildering, full of new and vigorous breath," she wrote of the play, "it gives to the eye a vision into the theater of the future." Beckwith, however, was not so enthusiastic about some of the additions, deletions and changes Welles made to the original. Like Doulens, she singled out Edna Thomas as "a distinctive and most impressive Lady MacBeth."

Bridgeport's other daily newspaper, the *Times-Star*, also praised the production. In the first of two articles, the paper commented on the publicity surrounding the play, its successful run in New York, and how it was making history. The unsigned article also referenced the sheer size of the production, noting that it required 30 stagehands, 750 props, carloads of scenery and a sizable number of costumes.

A review in the *Times-Star* the next day, July 22nd, signed only with the initials "J.E.H.", remarked that the "costumes and settings are ultra-effective," hailed the show as a whole as "stirring and worthy," and singled out Eric Burroughs in the role of Hecate for much praise. J.E.H. found Jack Carter's Macbeth "too mechanical" and had an overall positive, though more mixed assessment, of Edna Thomas's Lady Macbeth than the two *Post* writers.

The *Post* also included comments critical of the play in an unsigned column called "The Last Word." The comments were in response to Ethel Beckwith's review from one-time *Washington Post* society editor Stella McCord, who apparently attended a performance while in Bridgeport for a visit. In addition to *Macbeth*, McCord also raised objections to the WPA, the New Deal and the Roosevelt Administration as a whole.

In a letter published several days later in the *Post*, Bridgeport resident L. Litwin took exception to McCord's criticisms of the WPA. Litwin also referenced the enthusiastic crowds at the performances of *Macbeth* at the Park, and then specifically addressed what it meant for Bridgeport to host such a production. "Those of us who never had a chance to see stage performances before, consider the revival by the government of the legitimate theater in this locality, an achievement," wrote Litwin.

On to Hartford

After two days off for travel and rest, the show opened in Hartford on July 28th for the first of five performances. The eight-city tour concluded in Syracuse on September 25[th,] after which it returned to New York City for twelve final performances at Brooklyn's Majestic Theatre. The conclusion of one performance, apparently one of the shows done at the Adelphi Theatre just before the production arrived in Bridgeport, was filmed and included in a 1937 WPA documentary *We Work Again*. The four minutes of footage can be viewed on YouTube.

Revivals Inspired by Welles's Production

Productions of *Macbeth* that are essentially revivals of or inspired by the one performed at Bridgeport's Park Theatre in 1936 have been done in a variety of places in the years since. The first known major revival was done by the Henry Street Settlement's New Federal Theatre in 1977. In 2012, the National Black Arts Festival in Atlanta and Georgia Shakespeare paid tribute to Welles's production with an all-Black *Macbeth*. The American Century Theatre revived the play the following spring and visual artist Lenwood Sloan did an adaptation titled *Vo-Du Macbeth* in New Orleans in 2015.

The Federal Theatre Project Under Attack

The Federal Theatre Project lasted only until 1939. The House Committee on Un-American Activities (HUAC), is generally associated with the repression of the early 1950s. But it was actually formed in 1938, in no small part to destroy the FTP. The pretext was that many of the FTP's plays were radical. Which was true enough, and perfectly in tune with the mood of the Depression era. HUAC, however, actually cited only a handful of plays during its investigative hearings. A well-reviewed, well-attended all-Black production of *Macbeth* was undoubtedly cause for concern as well for those in Congress who were white supremacists, as well as reactionaries.

While support for artists and the arts at all levels of government continued and exists today in many forms, something important was lost with the destruction of the Federal Theatre Project. Not only was the FTP generously funded, it was decentralized in a way that other such government ventures generally are not. That reality provided for both greater autonomy and greater variety of productions.

It is also worth noting that the very existence of the FTP was directly related to the strength of radical and working class organizations of the time. Such organizations were not strong enough to withstand the attacks on the FTP. Tim Robbins brilliantly captures what that has meant for the world of the theater with the concluding shot of his marvelous 1999 film *Cradle Will Rock*. But the important lesson that remains is that the popular upheaval of the 1930s created space for any number of ventures, including many unanticipated ones. That speaks to both the tasks and the possibilities we face today.

Orson Welles After *Macbeth*

Though Orson Welles was for years a member in good-standing of Hollywood's left-liberal coalition, he apparently never faced in any direct way the career-threatening (and often, as in the case of Canada Lee, career-ending) wrath of HUAC when it again took aim at the arts in the late 1940s. He *had* incurred the wrath of media baron William Randolph Hearst, however, who was outraged at the depiction of his life story in *Citizen Kane,* and perhaps even more outraged at the depiction of Marion Davies, his long-time mistress. The campaign Hearst ordered against Welles was relentless. Movie moguls were at least as cowed by the Hearst empire as they were by HUAC, and probably more so.

Welles's career after *Citizen Kane* was full of missteps, false starts, eviscerated scripts and stalled projects traceable in no small part to the extreme difficulty he faced in getting studio backing. It is testament to Welles that despite all that, he was star, screenwriter, director, and/or producer of so many memorable movies in addition to *Citizen Kane.* They include, *The Magnificent Ambersons*, *Journey Into Fear*, *The Third Man*, *The Lady From Shanghai*, *The Stranger*, *Touch of Evil*, *Mr. Arkadian*, *The Trial*, and *The Long, Hot Summer*. The question "What might have been?" Still hovers over Welles's career. That's fair enough, but there's still an awful lot there.

Cultural Appropriation?

That the key people overseeing the production of *Macbeth* – Welles, Houseman, FTC head Hallie Flanagan – were all white raises the question of cultural appropriation. Such concerns were apparently a part of the tension between Welles and some cast members during early rehearsals. Black people in New York City, especially in Harlem when it was announced the play would open in that neighborhood's Lafayette Theatre, were similarly concerned. One group with a strong base in Harlem, the Communist Party, announced its intentions to picket the opening precisely because the expectation was that the play would rely on the racist stereotypes so common to stage, screen and radio productions of the time.

Compounding any racial analysis of the FTP's *Macbeth* is that it's set in Haiti, a country where U.S. imperialism has wrought as much destruction and suffering as any. Beyond the question of how Black people in the U.S. might view the play is another: how did Haitians view it in 1936, and how do they view it today?

Scholar and performance artist Stephanie Leigh Baptiste is someone who has addressed these and other issues in some detail. While analyzing many aspects of the production, Batiste notes how Black people, particularly in Harlem, anticipated its opening with apprehension. Those apprehensions mostly vanished, replaced by enthusiasm that was often quite joyous, she notes, once the play opened. She cites the large number of Black people who attended and enjoyed the performances in Harlem, as well as positive reviews by Black writers such as Roi Ottley in the Harlem-based *New York Amsterdam News*, one of the best-known African-American publications then, and now. In conclusion, Baptiste writes: "The voodoo Macbeth was a source of social (and financial) relief, of emotional release, and of pride. There was a sense of inclusion and boastfulness in what the voodoo Macbeth and Haiti demonstrated black people could do, and possibly be. " (The reference to *Haiti* is to another FTP play staged in Harlem in 1938) (Shakespeare & Beyond, Folger Shakespeare Library)'

It also speaks well for the FTP's *Macbeth* that prominent Black theater figures like Lenwood Sloan and Woodie King, Jr., and organizations like the New Federal Theatre (which King heads) and the National Black Arts Festival have revived Welles's version of *Macbeth*. In the case of the staging by the National Black Arts Festival in 2012, the organizers specifically commemorated and honored Welles's FTP production.

The Park Theatre in Bridgeport is no more, closed and demolished decades ago. As the reputation and legacy of the FTP's production of *Macbeth* has grown, Bridgeport's association with it speaks well for the city. For it was during the heyday of what might be called "Theater for the People," the city hosted one of the most important stage productions of its time.

It Can't Happen Here

On Oct. 27, 1936, Connecticut theater-goers watched *It Can't Happen Here*, performed by the Federal Theater Project, one of the New Deal's progressive jobs programs. The Nobel prize winner Sinclair Lewis had refashioned his dystopian novel into a dramatic play. It premiered simultaneously in 21 cities across the country, including Hartford and Bridgeport.

Americans in the 1930s were being groomed to accept fascism as a macho solution to the troubles faced by the United States. Lewis's *It Can't Happen Here* was a roadblock to that disturbing movement. A quote attributed to Lewis describes the danger he wanted to capture: "When fascism comes to America, it will be wrapped in the flag and carrying a cross." The play was largely set in New England. Its characters were all home-grown Americans. As Lewis wrote in his novel: "In America the struggle was befogged by the fact that the worst Fascists were they who disowned the word 'Fascism' and preached... Constitutional and Traditional Native American Liberty." (Sinclair Lewis, *It Can't Happen Here*.) The author of *Main Street* and *Babbitt* believed that the real danger lay not from an outside invasion, but from the cynical use by American leaders of patriotism, Christianity and the drive to make America great again.

While some in Connecticut were seduced by fascism, others spoke out forcefully. Rabbi Abraham J. Feldman was a popular orator and the head of Connecticut's first synagogue, Temple Beth Israel. On the celebration of the state's 300th birthday, he gave a clear warning before an audience of hundreds of Christians and Jews. Misguided supporters, he warned, "look hopefully towards Fascism and are willing to play with it and barter away our hard won American ideals." (Steve Thornton, The Shoeleather History Project, *It Can't Happen Here*, 11/22/2016)

Today, there is a resurgence in fascist ideology dressed as Americanism, according to the Southern Poverty Law Center (SPLC). It is called by many names, but it's not monolithic and the groups have some ideological differences. They include the Alt-Right movement, neo-Nazis, the Traditional Workers Party, national anarchists, white nationalists, White Lives Matter and "third position" adherents. They have a racist, anti-Semitic, totalitarian essence in common, heavy on armed resistance (hence their Second Amendment fetish).

In Connecticut, a prime example is the local chapter of the Oath Keepers, now notorious for their leading role in the January 6th attempted coup in Washington, D.C. They claim to be military veterans and police officers. The group pledges itself to a cherry-picked list of Constitutional rights.

Their underlying implication is that they are ready to defend themselves against the immigrant hordes and compliant politicians who plan to rob them of their guns and individual freedoms. While small, this network reaches throughout New England and pops up at town fairs and weekend car shows (especially by collectors of used military vehicles). The Oath Keepers were prominent at the pro-gun demonstrations in 2013 and 2014 at the State Capitol.

These rallies were triggered by the General Assembly's passage of a law banning assault weapons and high-capacity magazines, and the creation of a background check for gun buyers. The Oath Keepers are not the only collection of American fascists that has followers in this state. The SPLC identified 892 hate groups in the United States in 2015, a 14 percent increase over the previous year.

Connecticut has its share of these organizations, including the National Socialist Freedom Movement, the Creativity Movement and the Connecticut Minute Men. These misnamed grouplets don't really foster socialism, freedom, creative expression or an anti-colonial perspective. They hide their hateful nature behind euphemisms, much as the villain in *It Can't Happen Here* created his "Minute Men" paramilitary force.

Ironically, in 1968, an armed group also known as the Minutemen attacked peace activists at the Community for Nonviolent Action in Voluntown. The bullet holes are still on the living room wall of the peace activists' farmhouse. Periodically, monitors report a spike in far-right activity. Under the right circumstances, the unthinkable can happen anywhere.

The Hills of Connecticut, 'Where Life and Theatre Became One'

In 1931, a new theater ensemble was formed in New York City. It was the vision of Harold Clurman, Lee Strasberg, Phoebe Brand, Stella Adler and other key figures in a collective who decided to call themselves the Group Theatre. The Group was committed to both staging plays about the social problems confronting the Depression-era United States, and to utilizing the innovative acting techniques of Constantin Stanislavsky that eventually became known as the Method.

Over the next nine years, the Group performed works by such prominent playwrights as William Saroyan, Irwin Shaw, Sidney Kingsley and Maxwell Anderson. Though he wasn't a Group member, playwright Clifford Odets became a sort of voice for the collective, as the Group staged seven of his plays during its existence. The Group also worked with Martha Graham and others revolutionizing modern dance, most notably Hartford-born Anna Sokolow.

1931: Brookfield

Most members of the Group spent summers together attending workshops and rehearsing plays. They spent two of those summers in Connecticut. The first was in 1931, at a vacation resort in Brookfield five miles north of Danbury in the foothills of the Berkshire Mountains. Twenty-eight members of the Group rented several buildings as sleeping quarters and a barn they used for classes and rehearsals. Though the accommodations were rustic, the grounds also included woods, a swimming pool and a small lake.

In her excellent history of the Group, Wendy Smith writes that the "hills of Connecticut were the backdrop for an exhilarating drama of collective self-discovery" and likens their summer in Brookfield to the magic of a first love affair. Young or old, experienced in the theater or not, there was a strong sense among those gathered that they were embarking on something new and exciting. Brookfield, Smith writes, was "the place where theatre and life became one."

After considering several plays that summer, Group members selected *The House of Connelly* by Paul Green for their first-ever production. Green had won a Pulitzer Prize in 1927 and shared with the Group a desire for a native theater that would stage plays about social issues and everyday people. *The House of Connelly* is the story of an old Southern clan and the conflicts that emerge when the family experiences financial decline. It opened on Broadway on September

29, 1931 at the Martin Beck Theatre (now the Al Hirschfeld Theatre) and had a successful run of 91 performances. Among those in the cast were many who would be Group stalwarts throughout its existence, including Stella Adler, Morris Carnovsky, J. Edward Bromberg, Phoebe Brand, Franchot Tone and Clifford Odets.

1936: Pine Brook

When the Group returned to Connecticut in the summer of 1936, they settled in the Pine Brook Country Club in the Nichols section of Trumbull just north of Bridgeport. Since Brookfield, they had experienced highs such as an electrifying production of Odets' *Waiting for Lefty* and the lows of disdain from influential critics and financial problems. The Group had grown and among those present at Pine Brook were some who had either achieved success in movies or soon would, including Franchot Tone, John Garfield, Sylvia Sidney, Lee J. Cobb, Will Geer and Elia Kazan.

Odets was also present, though he rented a house a few miles away near the Bridgeport town line. He was accompanied by Luise Rainer, fresh off the 1936 Academy Award for Best Actress. Rainer would win the same award in 1937 and become the first person to win for Best Actor or Actress in two consecutive years, a feat that only Spencer Tracy, Katherine Hepburn and Tom Hanks have since duplicated. Odets and Rainer had recently become involved romantically and would soon be married.

Rainer, however, was not involved in any way with the Group. In fact, Group members held her in low regard and made fun of her behind her and Odets' back. The feeling was apparently mutual and Rainer left Connecticut and returned to Hollywood well before summer's end, though her departure was more likely due to the turbulent nature of her relationship with Odets than to any conflicts with the rest of the Group.

The accommodations at Pine Brook were much better than at Brookfield, and nearby woods and Pinewood Lake made for a rather idyllic setting. The Group soon set about reading plays for the fall season. Before long, they settled on *Johnny Johnson*, a musical by Paul Green with strong anti-war themes and a memorable score by Kurt Weill. The play was about the horrors endured by everyman soldiers during World War One. The title and name of the main character were drawn from the fact that 30,000 American soldiers who served in the war were named Johnson, 3,000 of whom were named Johnny Johnson. Both Green and Weill were present that summer at a house near Pine Brook. They worked finishing the play and music while the Group rehearsed the parts that had already been completed.

From Connecticut, *Johnny Johnson* moved to Broadway, where it opened that fall at the 44th Street Theater, before eventually moving to the Mansfield (now the Lena Horne) on 47th Street. Among those in the cast were Phoebe Brand, Morris Carnovsky, John Garfield, Lee J. Cobb, Luther Adler and Elia Kazan. The production ran for 68 performances.

The Communist Issue

The beauty of the Pine Brook surroundings and the optimism of a new play could not mask tensions within the Group, however. Some members were displeased with what had always been a rather hierarchical structure, the theory of collectivity notwithstanding. There was also friction over the inclusion of new and returned members who were seen by some as too closely associated with Hollywood, especially when they were selected for roles over others who had been with the Group from the beginning.

Years later, when he sang like a canary at hearings by the House Committee on Un-American Activities, Elia Kazan claimed that the Communist Party also caused disruptions by attempting to take over the Group. There is little to support that contention. Other Group members who similarly cooperated with HUAC made no such claim. As documented by HUAC with the aid of Kazan and the other cooperative witnesses, most Group members who also belonged to the Communist Party were Party members for only a year or two, including Kazan and Odets, and totaled maybe a dozen over the entire nine years of the Group's existence.

Further undermining Kazan's claim is the fact that the Communist Party was as uncertain as anyone else about the best strategy for the Group, and CP and non-CP Group members were in complete agreement about wanting to stage plays about social issues. Once the CP entered its Popular Front period around 1934, it sought to have such plays reach as broad an audience as possible, much as Clurman and the rest of the Group did. Whatever the opportunism the CP frequently employed, Kazan's claim seems little more than dishonesty designed to curry favor with a government agency that, in 1952, held his suddenly very lucrative career in its hands. Former Group member Tony Kraber, one of the Communist Party members named by Kazan and a blacklistee for many years, uttered one of the most famous quips about the government witch hunt when he replied before HUAC to a question about Kazan, "Is this the Kazan that signed the contract for $500,000 the day after he gave names to this committee?"

A Recurring Problem

The biggest problem the Group faced that summer in Pine Brook, one they had grappled with all along and would never satisfactorily resolve, was how to do the kind of work they wanted to do while also sustaining their venture financially. That problem predates the Group and persists today. Figures as great as Eugene O'Neill and Arthur Miller have lamented it. It was a problem that raised its head especially whenever ticket sales were insufficient to continue a show for any length of time, and one that contributed to the Group's eventual demise in 1940.

That makes it difficult to judge those from the Group who "went Hollywood" harshly. John Garfield and Lee J. Cobb, for example, both said that they would have preferred to concentrate their careers in the theater, rather than in movies. However, by the time each had made it in Hollywood and returned to the stage in the late 1940's without having to worry about making that month's rent, the chill of government and industry repression made it as difficult politically to do the kind of theater they wanted as it had been difficult financially 10-15 years before.

Odets After the Group

The arc of the career of Odets, who could rightly be considered the Group's brightest star, is perhaps the most dramatic illustration of this point. In a remarkable run of creativity over a relatively short time, Odets wrote nine plays including *Waiting For Lefty*, *Golden Boy*, *Paradise Lost*, *Rocket to the Moon*, and *Awake and Sing!* He made several forays to Hollywood before staying for good and was the inspiration for the main character in the Coen brothers' 1991 movie *Barton Fink*.

After 1941, at which point he was only 35, Odets wrote only three more plays that were ever staged, all middling at best. His Hollywood screenplays were also generally middling except for the fine, largely overlooked *None But the Lonely Heart* (1944), which he also directed. Also of note was his co-authorship of the script of *Sweet Smell of Success* (1957), a blisteringly cynical story of a ruthless New York gossip columnist played by Burt Lancaster and his equally ruthless flunky, played by Tony Curtis. Like Kazan, Odets avoided the blacklist by naming some of his former friends as Communists before HUAC. And like Kazan, he was shunned by those former friends as well as by many others until his death in 1963.

Frances Farmer

Others from the Group stood firm against the tyranny of those who sat atop the Dream Factory even as doing so destroyed their careers and their lives. Two of note are Frances Farmer and John Garfield. Though Farmer certainly had her share of personal problems, more than anything, she ran into an impenetrable wall of sexism as she attempted to forge a career both on stage and in movies. She had come up against sexism in the Group, especially in the person of Odets, with whom she was briefly involved romantically, and who treated her abominably.

Farmer fled Hollywood in 1937, after several films and some initial success. Her first love was theater and she had longed to join the Group since reading about it while in high school. Swept to Hollywood at 21 by an improbable series of events, she broke her contract with Paramount because she was unable to abide the totalitarianism of the studio system and what she regarded as vacuous parts in equally vacuous movies.

She traveled east to Connecticut in productions of *The Petrified Forest* and *At Mrs. Beam's* at the Westport Country Playhouse. Odets and Clurman had seen at least one of her movies and, in search of someone to cast as the female lead in Odets' new play, they traveled to Westport to see her in *The Petrified Forest*. Impressed, they immediately offered her the part and she eagerly agreed to star as Lorna Moon in *Golden Boy*.

Farmer soon became involved with Odets while his wife Rainer was away on an extended trip, an affair in which he pursued, and then unceremoniously dumped her just before Rainer's return. Farmer was idealistic about the Group venture and radical politics in general and thus may very well have believed that Odets' attention was an expression of a closer affinity between the two than existed between he and Rainer, especially given the miserable state of his marriage. But she was also appalled and conflicted, as she documents in her autobiography *Will There Really Be a Morning?*, by Odets' constant abuse of her acting abilities and humanity.

Whatever her hopes for the relationship, Farmer was devastated when Odets abruptly broke things off — by telegram, no less. All the worse, she was dropped from the cast when the Group took *Golden Boy* for an extended run in London, replaced by an aspiring actress named Lillian Emerson who was also an heiress to the Bromo-Seltzer fortune, and who essentially bankrolled the London production in exchange for the part of Lorna Moon.

Farmer soon returned to Hollywood, depressed and drinking heavily. She stood up for herself as best she could, demanding better parts, fairer contracts, a healthy work environment, and some say over her work. She had visions of doing Ibsen's Nora; her bosses had visions of making her the next pin-up.

Alone, cut off from any kind of support network, Farmer was no match for the studio moguls or gossip columnists like Louella Parsons and Hedda Hopper (reactionaries both) who prided themselves on their power to make and break careers. She was arrested several times after relatively minor drinking-related incidents, suspended, imprisoned and eventually forcibly institutionalized as her career and life spiraled down rapidly in the 1940's. The horrors she endured from then until her death in 1970 at age 56, including by a number of accounts, an involuntary lobotomy, have been documented in *Will There Really Be a Morning?*, as well as in the 1981 movie *Frances*.

John Garfield

Garfield, the tough guy with a heart of gold who maintained his unbreakable loyalty to his friends to the day he died, tried to help. Especially loyal to friends under siege, he pushed successfully for Farmer to co-star with him in *Flowing Gold* (1940). It was a mostly forgettable film except for the dynamism of the two extraordinarily talented young stars — Farmer, the original Lorna Moon, and Garfield, the actor who more than any other was born to play Joe Bonaparte.

Garfield was not yet a big enough star, however, to intervene with the studios on Farmer's behalf in any serious way had that even been a possibility. Besides which, he was heading toward shark-infested waters himself, though not before he made some of the most memorable films of that or any era.

He was a noir-ish star before noir and when the real thing hit Hollywood big-time after World War II, Garfield did most of his best work. Sick of studio constraints much as Farmer was, he formed Enterprise Productions in 1946, and worked with prominent Hollywood left-wingers Abraham Polonsky, Robert Rossen, James Wong Howe, Canada Lee, Lloyd Gough and Anne Revere on two great films, *Body and Soul* (1947) and *Force of Evil* (1948). He returned to Warner Brothers one last time for *The Breaking Point* (1950), a magnificent film buried under the rubble of the Red Scare that may very well be the greatest forgotten Hollywood movie ever made.

By 1951, Garfield was being hammered by reactionaries from all directions. He knew more than a few Communists including his wife Robbie, had perjured himself in a first go-round with HUAC by denying that he did, and the red hunters were demanding that he name them. It was all a public ritual, of course; HUAC already knew every entertainment figure who belonged to the CP, past and present. The real purpose of the hearings, again, was to intimidate dissidents.

Facing the same career abyss that led Odets and Kazan to sing, Garfield refused to rat out his friends. He returned to the Broadway stage in *Peer Gynt* and then, irony of ironies, a 1952 revival of *Golden Boy*, finally playing the part of Joe Bonaparte he had coveted 15 years earlier and been passed over for. It was an unsuccessful production that closed after three weeks. It was also Garfield's last acting job. He died six weeks after the play closed, literally of a broken heart, with HUAC bearing down ever harder. He was 39.

Morris Carnovsky, the Actors Studio and the Group's Legacy

For each sad tale, however, there are any number of Group stories like that of the ever-resilient Morris Carnovsky. A Communist for many years who was named before HUAC by Kazan and numerous others, Carnovsky endured years on the blacklist before reviving his stage career in the late 1950's. He became

274

a regular on Broadway and returned to Connecticut often at the American Shakespeare Theater in Stratford in productions of *Antigone* (as Creon), *The Three Sisters* (as Chebutykin), *King Lear* (three times, each time as Lear), *Hamlet* (twice, once as Claudius and once as Polonius), *Romeo and Juliet* (as Capulet), *Measure for Measure*, *The Taming of the Shrew*, *King John*, *The Merchant of Venice*, *Twelfth Night*, *Much Ado About Nothing*, *The Merry Wives of Windsor* and *The Tempest*, among others.

Carnovsky and his wife, fellow Group alumnus Phoebe Brand, settled in Easton, Connecticut not far from where it all began for the Group decades before. He died there in 1992, four days before what would have been his 95th birthday. Brand lived to the ripe old age of 96 when she died in 2004.

Similarly, Group veterans Cheryl Crawford and Lee Strasberg were leading figures for many years in the Actors Studio. Their efforts live on in the careers of many of their students including some who achieved monumental success on stage and/or screen like Marlon Brando, Al Pacino and Robert De Niro, on down to Julia Roberts, and even newer actors, writers and directors.

So, though the heady dreams that took shape in the hills of Connecticut in the summer of 1931, like most first loves, didn't last, the Group Theater for nine years did sometimes memorable work in as raucous a decade as the United States has experienced. Along the way, they changed American theater and forged a legacy that is felt to this day.

Theater for the 99%

On stage at Bridgeport's Park Theater in the fall of 1944 stood "Republico, The Little Mechanical Man." He was an empty-headed dummy that the stage barker described as "handy, dandy, and works like a whiz." With his slick hair and neat mustache, the figure looked a lot like Thomas E. Dewey, Franklin Roosevelt's competitor in the presidential race. "He will not break, chip, or take action on any controversial subject," the barker promised, and the audience erupted with laughter. The satire hit home with these FDR supporters.

October 7th was the premiere performance of the "Roosevelt Bandwagon." This 17-act stage revue was backed by unions and organized by actor Will Geer (best known as Grandpa Walton on TV), who had a summer home in nearby Nichols, Connecticut. "Republico" and the musical production traveled to 24 cities from Omaha to Boston. They met with enthusiastic crowds and some controversy; one sketch was banned in Providence.

Featured in the production was Mary Lou Williams, the "first lady of jazz keyboard." Williams, an African American, was a child prodigy raised in Pittsburgh. She wrote tunes exclusively for the show, including "Ballot Box Boogie in the Key of Franklin D." Woody Guthrie and Cisco Houston also performed for the revue.

Bridgeport has been called "an industrial fortress," but the city has a lesser-known distinction as well. Theater, literature and film have flourished there, born from the workplace struggles of everyday men and women. Call it Theater for the 99%, the dramatization of working class life.

Worker-oriented theater dates back at least to 1910, when Bridgeport residents Ben Legere and Matilda Rabinowitz staged a production of Ibsen's *The Master Builder*. The play featured the trials of a wealthy architect, but Ibsen was very popular among those who rejected high society entertainment. Legere and Rabinowitz would soon become union organizers for the Industrial Workers of the World (IWW), the radical labor organization that used song and theater to great advantage in the early 20th century.

In 1936, the groundbreaking Group Theater was spending the summer in the suburban town of Nichols. Their production of *Waiting for Lefty* by Clifford Odets was banned by officials in New Haven despite a very successful debut in New York. *Lefty* is a series of vignettes told by unionized taxi drivers who are anticipating the arrival of their leader. Each man has faced a moral dilemma, sparked by economic or political factors that have brought them together in the taxi cab union hall. To show the absurdity of the ban, the *Bridgeport Sunday Herald* reprinted the entire play in its pages.

The Federal Theater Project, created by Roosevelt's New Deal, provided jobs and popular entertainment during the Great Depression. Many of the plays focused on the social problems of the day. Sinclair Lewis's dramatization of his novel I*t Can't Happen Here* played simultaneously in Hartford and Bridgeport. The plot focuses on the possibility of fascism taking hold in this country in a distinctly American form. The cast included local Bridgeport actors and stagehands who depended on the government project to earn a living.

Macbeth ("the Scottish play") is one of Shakespeare's best-known works. In the hands of 21-year old Orson Welles, the daring production was, as a *New York Times* critic wrote, a drama that "overwhelms you with its fury and its phantom splendor." Welles employed an all-African American cast, and moved the action from Scotland to Haiti. Macbeth played in a handful of cities, including Bridgeport and Hartford in July, 1936.

Not every stage show was dramatic. The musical *Pins and Needles* opened in New York in 1937. This highly successful comedy reflected the real-life experiences of garment workers. It evolved from a union hall cabaret to a full-fledged theater production that toured nationally. In January, 1938, the Park Theater provided Bridgeport's working families with this uplifting, pro-union (and romantic) hit show.

During World War II, the new union federation known as the CIO (Congress of Industrial Organizations) mounted a Broadway-style musical *Marching With Johnny*. It ran at Bridgeport's Klein Memorial Hall in December, 1943. Although the production only lasted two months, it was unique for promoting the idea of cooperation between men and women war workers, in contrast to the common divisive rivalry that prevailed at the time. The musical also featured a song entitled "Crispus Attucks," which told the story of the African-American Revolutionary War martyr.

After the war, military production began to disappear in Bridgeport. So did plays that reflected working class life. Critics and opinion-makers sneered at "proletarian theater." We were all middle-class consumers now, and our biggest struggles were supposed to be which home appliances to buy.

Eugene O'Neill, The New London Influence

For most of the first thirty years of his life, Eugene O'Neill spent summers at the home his family owned in New London, Connecticut. In many respects, the family's house was the closest thing the young O'Neill had to a real home. His father, the noted stage actor James O'Neill, was constantly touring, and when he was on the road he generally took his wife and two sons, Eugene and James, Jr., with him (a third son Edmund died in childhood). When James was engaged steadily in New York City, the family generally resided in hotels. Eugene was born in one such hotel near Times Square in 1888. He died in another hotel a short distance away in 1953, an irony he couldn't help but point out to those close to him in the last hours of his life.

Situated near the confluence of the Atlantic Ocean and Long Island Sound at the mouth of the Thames River, New London has been an important seaport since at least the first European settlement there in the 17th century. The O'Neills actually owned two houses there that were right next to each other on Pequot Avenue. The family lived first in the smaller of the two and then for a longer period in the larger house called Monte Cristo Cottage after the stage production James O'Neill toured in for many years, *The Count of Monte Cristo*.

Beckoned by the Sea

The two houses were located 50 yards from the Thames and two miles from the gateway to the Sound and the Atlantic Ocean. Young Eugene used to sit for hours at a time at water's edge watching the comings and goings of ships of all sizes. When he was 21, he signed on to a Buenos Aires-bound Norwegian ship called the Charles Racine. It was the first of a number of voyages he made.

The influence of New London is apparent in some of O'Neill's revolutionary plays that were set on ships, or in seaports, and often written in New London. The lure and power of the sea is especially notable in early works such as *Beyond the Horizon*, the play that established O'Neill as a playwright and earned him the first of three Pulitzer Prizes for Drama. Seamen were regulars in his plays as well, and he also drew vivid portraits of a vast assortment of waterfront characters in a number of them.

O'Neill came to adulthood during a time of great working class upheaval, and the radical politics of the time influenced him during the years he spent in New London. He knew many socialists, Wobblies and revolutionaries, and radicals appear in a number of his plays. As much as he moved in a revolutionary milieu, O'Neill was ambivalent about the possibility of social transformation. The Wobblies and socialists in *The Iceman Cometh* and other plays, are generally embittered and defeated.

The summer of 1917 was the last that O'Neill spent significant time in New London. He had written four plays by then, but it would not be until the following year that he achieved success with *Beyond the Horizon*. He was also drinking heavily and at odds with his father, who finally asked him to leave Monte Cristo Cottage.

New London in O'Neill's Plays

O'Neill would draw on New London for the rest of his writing career. The text of *Mourning Becomes Electra*, for example, situates the play "on the outskirts of one of the smaller New England seaport towns" and O'Neill stated in interviews that the setting was based on New London. His 1933 play *Ah, Wilderness!* Also takes place in New London and features many characters that are based on real people O'Neill knew. Similarly, *Long Day's Journey Into Night*, written in 1941, and first performed in 1956, is an autobiographical one that takes place in a home drawn on Monte Cristo Cottage.

Aspects of O'Neill's New London even appear in plays that are not set in the city and which, otherwise, have no direct connection to it. Such is the case with the massive elm trees that are described in the stage notes of *Desire Under the Elms,* which were so vividly brought to life in the 1958 movie version of the play. There were, in fact, several similarly large elms on the grounds of Monte Cristo Cottage that survived until the 1980's. Other landmarks, including the foghorn of the New London Lighthouse, appear in both *Long Day's Journey Into Night* and *Ah, Wilderness!*

Museum and Theater

One bit of local irony that O'Neill likely would have appreciated concerns the mansion and sprawling estate of railroad and shipping magnate Edward Hammond in neighboring Waterford. O'Neill and Hammond shared a mutual dislike. The playwright based characters in at least several of his plays on Hammond, characters who were wholly unsympathetic. Twenty-two years after Hammond's death in 1940, and nine years after O'Neill's death in 1953, Hammond's family sold the mansion and it was there that the Eugene O'Neill Theater Center was established in 1963.

The Monte Cristo Cottage, meanwhile, is now a museum that features "a permanent exhibition on the life and works of Eugene O'Neill and an extensive collection of artifacts and memorabilia." The interior is designed to reproduce the house in *Long Day's Journey Into Night* as spelled out in the set directions, and as drawn by the author in production sketches. Many other places in New London that were either a part of O'Neill's early years, or found their way into his plays, await exploration by anyone curious about the Connecticut port city's influence on one of the country's foremost and most innovative playwrights.

The Enduring Importance of Arthur Miller: The Price and The Hook

Seventy years after his initial Broadway success with *All My Sons,* and 12 years after his death, long-time Roxbury, Connecticut resident Arthur Miller continues to cast a long shadow over theater in the United States. His plays are staples of high school drama clubs, college and university theater departments and regional theaters around the country, and his best-known works – *Death of a Salesman*, *The Crucible*, *All My Sons*, *A View From the Bridge* and *After the Fall* – have been revived many times on Broadway.

Miller's influence extends well beyond the United States. *Death of a Salesman*, for example, serves as the backdrop to Iranian director Asghar Farhadi's acclaimed 2016 film *The Salesman*. And it has been said, perhaps apocryphally, perhaps not, that *The Crucible* has played continuously somewhere in the world since its debut performance in 1953.

Hardly a New York theater season goes by without the revival of one of Miller's plays. This summer, the prestigious Brooklyn Academy of Music featured a revival of *Salesman* while earlier this year, the Roundabout Theatre staged a three-month production of his 1968 drama *The Price*. Among many attributes, the Roundabout production featured a stellar cast with Mark Ruffalo, Tony Shaloub, Jessica Hecht and Danny DeVito as the play's four characters. While not as well-known as any number of Miller's works, *The Price* has been revived on Broadway more times – four – than all of his plays except *The Crucible*, which has also had four revivals over a significantly longer period of time.

The Price

Like much of Miller's work, *The Price* is mostly heavy going. As with *Salesman* and *All My Sons* in particular, its main theme is in some ways the lie of the American Dream. Also like those plays, the primary conflict unfolds within a family, in this case between Victor Franz (Ruffalo) and his wife Esther (Hecht) and all the more between Victor and his brother Walter (Shaloub).

The specter of the Great Depression hovers over *The Price* throughout even as the action unfolds three decades later. This, too, is territory Miller has plumbed many times. For Miller, the Depression of the 1930s was only the most extreme expression of the dashing of misplaced hopes for the good life. Its casualty rate was higher and the destruction greater than other low points, but the tragedy of a society in which carving out a comfortable place for oneself through accumulating wealth is the end-all and be-all is the same in 1931, 1968 or 2017. There are always far more losers than winners, for one; and even winners who achieve what we might call upper middle class-dom lose a great deal, including much that can never be re-gotten. Always tenuous, wealth obtained in a society premised on swindling somebody else can vanish very quickly. And as we see in *The Price* in the character of Walter, the psychological and personal costs are often enormous as well.

The 1930s

Miller was 14 when the stock market crashed in 1929. The formative years of his life were those of breadlines, Hoovervilles and the rumblings of fascism, and world war. Those years also marked widespread interest in revolutionary change, including in the arts. Miller, who from the time he was a young man was of the Left, was blown away, in particular, by the early plays of Clifford Odets. Nonetheless, he mostly eschewed the socialist realism, proletarian literature and agit-prop genres, in his own work, that were popular in the 1930s.

Miller, instead, wrote plays one step removed from the battlefield of class struggle. There are no final scenes in his dramas of workers defiantly envisioning coming triumphs with cries of "Strike, strike, strike!" Yet it was he who dramatized the declaration in *Awake and Sing* by the old Marxist Jacob that "life shouldn't be printed on dollar bills" better than anyone — Odets included.

Miller's Influences

Miller's primary influences go back to earlier traditions including Ibsen, whose *An Enemy of the People* he adapted on Broadway in 1950. Miller's staging of *Enemy* was an indictment of the Red Scare and it featured in its cast the left-wing husband and wife team Frederic March and Florence Eldridge, as well as the Communist and soon-to-be blacklisted Morris Carnovsky.

As in a number of Miller's other plays, *The Price* includes Thomas Hardy-esque moments of coincidence or misunderstanding that sharply alter the course of events—a missed phone call, a misinterpreted bit of conversation. A good portion of the play is a sometimes harsh back-and-forth between Victor and Esther about what might have been. When Victor's brother Walter arrives, the great depth of that "might have been" and why it never was, is revealed.

The Price shares with *Salesman* and *All My Sons* the tensions that arise from living by illusions. As he did so expertly so often, perhaps especially in *All My Sons*, Miller blends the impact of big outside forces with the tensions that exist within every individual and family. That we don't always know which ends where is one of the things that make his plays, *The Price* included, so powerful. For Victor, the destructive impact of the 1929 Crash cuts two ways: it ruined his future, while also allowing him to keep at bay nagging thoughts that he, too, had some part in the unsatisfied life he has lived. The arrival of his brother midway upsets the structured explanation he has been telling himself for years, as he learns of heretofore unknown familial betrayal.

While we ache for both Willie Loman in *Salesman,* and Joe Keller in *Sons*, we simultaneously look down on them to a degree for the illusions they harbor. In *The Price*, our sympathies for Victor are less mitigated. So it is with Esther, too, whose finest moment comes when she rallies to Victor's side at the end after laying out his many mistakes for much of the play. All of the tensions and hard feelings are accentuated by Miller's situating the entire play in the confined setting of an attic in an old Manhattan residence. Even with an intermission, the single locale serves to heighten a feeling of claustrophobia throughout, as the brothers in particular, bear down on each other.

As *The Price* approaches its conclusion, anyone seeing or reading it for the first time (or the second or third, for that matter) is likely to anticipate a possibly amicable resolution. There are several points where it seems the brothers may acknowledge the pain each has caused the other, shake hands and go forward as best as possible. Such a resolution, however, was largely alien to the world Miller strove to create, certainly the world of his best work. While the conclusion of *The Price* is not on the scale of *Salesman* and *Sons*, the irreconcilability is final enough.

The Hook

In 1950, eighteen years before he wrote *The Price*, Miller wrote a screenplay titled *The Hook.* It was about corruption on the Brooklyn docks and the impact it had on longshore workers. Much has been written about the genesis of *The Hook,* including by Miller himself, and the story behind it is undoubtedly familiar to many readers. Writing in 2015, James Dacre, who was instrumental in staging *The Hook* in England that year to mark the centennial of Miller's birth, said that the backstory "deserves a screenplay of its own."

At the time Miller wrote *The Hook*, he was still very close with Elia Kazan and the two submitted the story to Columbia Pictures' head honcho Harry Cohn. Miller had had two smash hits on Broadway by then, and Kazan, with several recent Hollywood successes and the original Broadway staging of Tennessee Williams' smash hit *A Streetcar Named Desire* to his credit, had agreed to direct. Cohn initially approved the project, but soon insisted that Miller change the story so that the corrupt union leaders be clearly identified as Communists. Miller refused and the project was dropped. Within a few years, Kazan named names before the House Committee on Un-American Activities, signed a lucrative contract with Columbia, and went on to direct and win numerous awards for another drama set among longshore workers, *On The Waterfront*. Miller, meanwhile, told HUAC where to get off, had his passport revoked, and kept working as best he could, while contending with American Legion pickets at the performances of his plays.

For 65 years, *The Hook* was stashed away where it was read primarily by scholars doing Miller-related research. Then in 2015, Dacre and the Royal & Derngate Theater adapted it for the stage in several major venues in England where it received international attention, garnered rave reviews and was subsequently broadcast as a radio play by the BBC. Despite the success across the Atlantic, however, there has yet to be a staging in the United States.

Pete Panto

While living in Brooklyn Heights in the 1940s, Miller would walk south along Columbia Street into Red Hook through what was then a thriving commercial waterfront. There he saw graffiti, usually in Sicilian, about a dockworker named Pete Panto: *Dov e Panto?* (Where is Panto?). An old-time Sicilian dockworker who was a contemporary of Panto's (as well as my landlord when I moved to that neighborhood in the early 1980s), remembered additional graffiti that asked, *Che ha ucciso Panto?* (Who Killed Panto?)

Panto was a member of the International Longshoremen's Association (ILA), and either a member or close ally of the Communist Party. In the late 1930s, he was organizing fellow workers around democratizing the ILA, doing away with corrupt practices, such as the shape-up, and driving racketeers out of the union. As many as 1,500 dockworkers attended open-air meetings organized by the Brooklyn Rank and File Committee, the group Panto helped form. One evening in 1939, Panto left his home in Brooklyn and disappeared. His body was found two years later in a New Jersey lime pit.

Albert Anastasia and others associated with Murder, Inc. were implicated, but no one was ever charged with killing Panto. A hit man named Abe Reles, who had turned government witness and helped convict several racketeers, was apparently ready to finger Murder, Inc., but went out a sixth-floor window before he could do so. Likely the victim of a hit ordered by Anastasia.

The mostly Italian-American dockworkers carried on bravely despite an atmosphere of intense intimidation that would fester for decades. They formed the Pete Panto Educational Circle (*Il Circolo Educativo Pete Panto*) to carry forward Panto's legacy. Associates of his kept the Brooklyn Rank and File Committee together as best they could. Their meetings were regularly broken up by goons, however, and within a few years, organized rank and file activity had essentially ground to a halt.

A Play for The Screen

The Hook does not attempt to directly tell Panto's story, but it grounds itself firmly in the rough, unforgiving, often violent world of the Brooklyn waterfront of that time. Like so much of Miller's work, *The Hook* is a world inhabited primarily by men. *The Price, Salesman, Sons* and *A View From the Bridge,* are all centered to a great extent around conflicts between fathers and sons, brother and brother, and sometimes, both. Even the extended and often riveting back-and-forth between Victor and his wife Esther in *The Price* feels like prelude to the greater struggle between Victor and his brother.

The relationships between Marty Ferrara, the main character, and the men in his world are central enough in *The Hook* just as in those plays, but there are also differences. There are no father-son or brother-brother tensions, for example. Marty's wife Therese is central to the drama within the Ferrara home to a degree greater than in Miller's plays. Their relationship is rendered with great depth, and reminiscent among other of his plays, only of the love that blossoms between Chris and Ann in *All My Sons*. Their relationship grounds Marty, prompting him to do the right thing at several crucial junctures, and is one of the most effective and moving parts of the story.

Much of the explanation for what makes *The Hook* different from other Miller works lies in the fact that it was written for the screen. There is a greater breadth of locales than is typical of Miller including scenes at work, on the streets, and in the union hall, as well as any number of the many kinds of random spots that fill working class neighborhoods.

Miller seems to have been drawn to film because he regarded it as better-suited to stories that might include more action, faster pacing, outdoor locations and other devices more conducive to the kind of story he wanted to tell. Perhaps, that is why he apparently never attempted to re-work *The Hook* for the stage. Perhaps, too, he knew that it would be virtually impossible in the 1950s to obtain financial backing for a play in which the villain is the profit system. Five years later, when Miller again dramatized Brooklyn Italian-American dockworkers in *A View From the Bridge*, he wrote a very different kind of story. In contrast to *The Hook*, most all of *View* takes place in one location, the Carbone home. Workplace and union concerns are peripheral.

Miller's Audience Today

It's anybody's guess what those who go to these many Miller revivals take away from his plays all these years later. With its obscene prices, Broadway skews toward the better-heeled and it's easy (and true enough) to interpret any number of Miller's plays, *The Price* included, as primarily about unfulfilled lives resulting from missed or stolen opportunities. But one of the great strengths of Broadway, the cost of tickets notwithstanding, is that it still provides a place where artists like Miller can lay bare the darkness at the heart of the profit system. The destruction of illusions can be a harrowing experience and one exits *The Price* (much as I recall exiting the 1984 Dustin Hoffman revival of *Salesmen)*, as needing some time to recover. Yet the right questions are there, and in the story one can uncover much more than troubled family members tearing at each other, a theme that is a great strength, but also often a limitation in the work of both Eugene O'Neill and Miller's great contemporary Tennessee Williams.

Even if those who can afford $150 and more for a ticket are not among those tottering on the brink of economic collapse, the parallels between the devastation Miller wrote about with such insight, and the inescapable sense today of looming catastrophe, is unmistakable. Whatever one can get from any number of modern dramas available every night on HBO and Showtime, one suspects that people return to Miller revivals and similar dramas of theater because there are few places where they can get such an unvarnished look at the modern world. That this past season New Yorkers were also able to see a splendid adaptation of *The Hairy Ape*, O'Neill's most class-conscious play featuring an outstanding performance in the lead by Bobby Cannavale, is further indication that something unsettling is in the air.

Miller would likely be delighted that this past Broadway season also included the opening of *Sweat*, a new masterwork by Lynn Nottage that touches on important themes of economic collapse, and which earned her a second Pulitzer Prize for Drama. Miller knew all too well of Broadway backers' preference for the tried and true and the already familiar and famous, which today often means him. We can only imagine the number of plays like *Sweat* that have been pushed aside in favor of yet another revival, classics marketed as speaking to a specific time that has come and gone. Try as some undoubtedly have, pigeonholing Miller's work in that way is virtually impossible. As much as anything being done today creatively, the best of his plays speak directly to the wreckage of a society in free-fall.

What Next?

Going forward, perhaps someone will bankroll an American production of *The Hook*. That it was well-received in England and provides a fresh Miller work to stage gives hope. Pending that, revivals of a few of Miller's excellent, but somewhat overlooked plays are in order. *A Memory of Two Mondays*, first staged on Broadway in 1955, and not seen in New York since 1976, would be a terrific choice. Another of his plays where the aftermath of the 1929 Crash is front and center, *A Memory of Two Mondays,* shares with *The Hook* a focus on the workplace. Full of people stuck in jobs that barely pay the rent, and that they hate but are afraid to leave, *Memory* is as good a story for the era of Trump as anything around today. It's a short play, however, and thus would likely have to be paired with another work. Imagine if some enterprising soul got the bright idea to pair *A Memory of Two Mondays* with Odets' *Waiting for Lefty,* which, incredibly, has not been seen on Broadway since its initial production in 1935.

Even better would be a revival of Miller's wonderful full-length play *The American Clock,* another Depression-era tale that ran unsuccessfully for a mere three weeks in its 1980 Broadway debut. *The American Clock* could serve as a nice departure from the Miller people know best, with its many laughs and songs that greatly enhance the tragedies and the solidarity at the core of the story. A new staging would hopefully be based on the original and without the changes Miller was pressured to make, changes that seriously weakened the play. The original version has played successfully around the world, as well as in an all too brief revival Off-Broadway in 1997, and is long overdue to be presented on Broadway as Miller intended.

Broadway notwithstanding, regional theaters and high school and college theater departments will likely remain the primary homes for Miller productions. There's no reason to believe that will change any time soon. Given today's political climate, *The Crucible* anyway is likely to remain a big favorite.

19. Art, Media and Culture

Mark Twain: Nation Building at the Point of a Gatling Gun

June 19th marks a significant incident in Connecticut history. Yet no one celebrates it. Not Juneteenth, the African-American community's commemoration of Lincoln's Emancipation Proclamation. Rather, June 19, 1879, was the day Hank Morgan got hit with a crowbar by a worker known as Hercules, a powerful blow that sent Hank back to the sixth century.

The reference is the plot device used in *A Connecticut Yankee in King Arthur's Court,* the 1889 Mark Twain classic. This novel is known as a satire that explores time travel and pokes fun at chivalry, monarchy and gullible human behavior. But *Connecticut Yankee* is much more, and its lessons are especially relevant today. Mark Twain predicts America's international military adventures of the 20th and 21st centuries.

Hank Morgan, a foreman at the Colt firearms factory, finds himself transported to King Arthur's Camelot. As a visitor from the future, he is the smartest man in the world. His contributions to improve the feudal, backward England of 528 A. D. are democracy and technology. But not just any technology– Hank has the experience of mass producing deadly Colt weapons, after all.

Hank recoils from the slave-like conditions of poverty and violence inflicted on peasants by the English gentry. He witnesses the extravagant Gilded Age-style excess of royalty and nobility. In response to this gulf between rich and poor, Hank seeks to create a Republic by bringing this primitive population a new political and economic system based on modern technology. Call it nation building.

Progress comes with a price, however. Hank makes enemies of the Church and the nobility, all of whom have lost wealth and privilege as the result of his reforms. They organize a holy army to drive him out.

Exporting democracy takes a terrible toll on the country Hank wants to save. He resorts to modern warfare to protect the progress he has bestowed on the English peasants. They didn't ask for any of these improvements, or the arsenal he has built, but they have them now.

Hank and his workmen build Gatling Guns (a weapon actually manufactured by Colt firearms) that can spit out as many as 300 bullets a minute – surely the first American weapon of mass destruction. Following the wartime principle of "destroying the village in order to save it," Hank blows up every factory, workshop and mill his Republic has constructed to keep them out of enemy hands.

291

Hank's forces don't fight traditional face-to-face battles, but like today's drone warfare they use remote control. As Hank says, in sardonic Twain fashion, "we shan't have to leave our fortress, now, when we want to blow up our civilization."

Hank's crew creates explosive glass torpedoes and buries them under the sand for use as land mines. Miles of electric fences burn thousands of unsuspecting knights to death so quickly they can't cry out. Hank calls the results his "red terror." This death by electrocution is meant to keep the enemy away, but it also ends up trapping Hank and his followers in their fortified cave, victims of their own technological prowess, in a war they cannot win.

Connecticut Yankee is prescient. It is a narrative that our nation has played out on the soil of many small nations, Iraq and Afghanistan being the most recent.

It's almost like Sam Clemens built himself a time machine.

Carl Sandburg, Poet From the Grassroots, Reaches Connecticut Audiences

At one time, nationally acclaimed poet Carl Sandburg was so popular in Connecticut that even his goats made the news. After his death in 1967, a kennel in Washington, Connecticut, bought some of Sandburg's herd. The goats—Babette, Coty, and Tenu—eventually returned to North Carolina when Sandburg's home became a national historic site. Today, however, if the general public remembers Sandburg, it is only as the white-haired old man who strummed a guitar and dubbed Chicago the "city of big shoulders."

Born in 1878 to Swedish immigrants, Carl Sandburg was a working-class boy who never forgot his roots. His father was a blacksmith for the Chicago railroad who took part in labor causes, including strikes. Sandburg recalled these formative events and considered himself a "partisan" who "took a kind of joy in the complete justice of the strikers" when he was only 10- years-old.

In his 20s, Sandburg was a regular contributor of news and poetry to the *International Socialist Review* (ISR), in addition to other prominent liberal and radical magazines. With his work for the *Chicago Daily News*, he honed his skill as a reporter who wrote in the language of the working class.

In true muckraking tradition, Sandburg exposed the 1915 Eastland steamer tragedy in Lake Michigan. The ship capsized, killing 800 workers on their way to a company picnic. Sandburg discovered that the seamen's union protested the lack of local regulations and quality inspections for years. He further revealed that the "company picnic" was a mandatory event-forcing workers to buy a ticket or potentially lose their jobs.

The College Club of Hartford may have been the first to invite Sandburg to Connecticut. On February 3, 1922, he performed at the Center Church House on Gold Street. His lecture was entitled, "Is there a New Poetry?" Tickets sold for one dollar at Mitchell's Book Shop around the corner from the church. Sandburg recited *"The Windy City,"* which had not yet been published, and sang some of the many folk songs that eventually appeared in his collection, *The American Songbag.*

In January 1932, Sandburg gave readings at Hartford's Weaver High School, Bulkeley High and West Middle School for several thousand students, faculty, and members of the public. He spoke frequently at Wesleyan University and received an honorary degree there in 1940, the year he won his first Pulitzer Prize (for *Lincoln: The War Years*). Sandburg shared the stage in Middletown with Supreme Court Justice William O. Douglas and artist Grant Wood. A few days later, he was in New Haven, receiving another honor from Yale University along with New York City Mayor Fiorello LaGuardia and philosopher Paul Tillich.

The poet's body of work became widely known and celebrated throughout the state; as he completed new books, they immediately moved up the charts at local booksellers. In November 1948, Sandburg's *Remembrance Rock* was on the fiction best-seller list of Hartford's eight bookstores. By the 1950s, Sandburg no longer toured the country, but his works remained as popular as ever. In 1959, Bette Davis and her husband, actor Gary Merrill (who was born in Hartford), performed Sandburg's work at Bushnell Memorial Hall.

A Moral Compass for America

Sandburg supported the Industrial Workers of the World, and his admiration for this radical union frequently appeared in his writing. Sandburg filled his first three published collections, *Chicago Poems* (1916), *Cornhuskers* (1918) and *Smoke and Steel* (1920) with IWW references, along with sympathetic portraits of immigrants, farmers, factory workers, and the poor. He considered himself "an I.W.W. without a red card."

He earned a reputation as a political and moral compass for many people in public life. As Secretary of Welfare in the Kennedy administration, Abraham Ribicoff considered Sandburg's *Lincoln* an inspiration. Connecticut senator Lowell Weicker quoted Sandburg during the Watergate hearings to encourage Richard Nixon to voluntarily testify before Congress.

In addition to the previously mentioned connections to Connecticut, Sandburg also counted a Connecticut governor as his friend. Fellow poet and Wesleyan faculty member Wilbert Snow knew Sandburg for 50 years. Snow became Connecticut Lieutenant Governor in 1945. He served as governor for 13 days when sitting governor Raymond Baldwin resigned to take his newly-elected position in the U.S. Senate. Snow said Sandburg "found poetry not among the rills and rivers of the countryside, but in the smokestacks of the city." Sandburg once told Snow that he "cried for an hour" after he finished writing his six-volume Abraham Lincoln biography. Some years after completing the Lincoln work Sandburg wrote, "Poets cry their hearts out. If they don't, they ain't poets."

An Improbable Connection with Wallace Stevens

Hartford author and poet Wallace Stevens met Sandburg in their early Chicago days. The famously reserved vice-president of the Hartford Accident and Indemnity Company so impressed Sandburg that he dedicated the poem "Arms" to Stevens. In the poem, Sandburg learns that the French impressionist Renoir (who died in 1919) kept a rigorous daily schedule of painting despite arthritis that seriously crippled his hands. In the last stanza, Sandburg writes that when the two poets meet again, "I will ask you why Renoir does it / And I believe you will tell me." This tribute to Stevens was not published until 1993.

Sandburg described Stevens (but not by name) in a newspaper series that recorded his 1932 national lecture tour. "I sat in the home of a Business-man author (there is such an animal!) in Hartford Conn.," Sandburg wrote. He described Stevens as "conservative in his political and economic views" but concerned about how "lady luck" dominated the fate of the middle- and working-class as they struggled through the Great Depression.

Is Sandburg Still Relevant?

Sandburg's early detractors labeled his poetry "propaganda" and chided that a poet had no place focusing on issues of the day. In later years, critics called his work dated and quaint. But many feel there will always be ideas and events that need a poet's anger and passion.

In December 2012, in Newtown, Connecticut, 26 elementary students and staff were shot to death at the Sandy Hook Elementary School. Carl Sandburg, long dead, responded to the killings. Just a month after the shootings, a previously unknown Sandburg poem was discovered. Found by accident at the University of Illinois, the piece is entitled, "A Revolver." It begins:

Here is a revolver.
It has an amazing language all its own.
It delivers unmistakable ultimatums.
It is the last word.
A simple, little human forefinger can tell a terrible story with it.

The poem ends:
And nothing in human philosophy persists more strangely than the old belief that God is always on the side of those who have the most revolvers. (Carl Sandburg Archives, UI Urbana-Champaign, *A Revolver*)

Guns, violence, and war are haunting subjects of Sandburg's poetry. But they are balanced with the courage and hope of people forced to cope with tragedy and hard times. He writes in *The People, Yes:*

> *The people know the salt of the sea*
> *and the strength of the winds*
> *lashing the corners of the earth.*
> *The people take the earth*
> *as a tomb of rest and a cradle of hope.*
> *Who else speaks for the Family of Man?*

Though a native of Illinois who lived in North Carolina, Carl Sandburg made many lasting impressions on Connecticut. His numerous personal and professional acquaintances throughout the state, as well as his touring schedule, made him a regular part of Connecticut life in the early 20th century. In addition, through his words, Sandburg painted timeless portraits of ordinary people throughout the country. The manner in which they still resonate makes them identifiable to readers across generations.

Art Young, Radical Cartoonist

The first two decades of the 20th century were a time of wide-scale dissent from the American dream. It was an era of bohemian salons, such as the one centered around the Greenwich Village apartment of Mabel Dodge. More explicitly political were radicals close to the Socialist Party and the Industrial Workers of the World who supported labor strikes in Lawrence, Massachusetts and Paterson, New Jersey—and, for a short time, the Russian Revolution.

Some straddled both worlds. Their numbers included photographers such as Carl Van Vechten, the novelist Neith Boyce, poets such as Max Eastman, and the painters Charles Demuth and John French Sloan. More than a few served as hangers-on, usually men of comfortable means who spent far more hours chasing a good time than they did engaged in productive labor. Others, such as Big Bill Haywood, Margaret Sanger and Emma Goldman, became outsized characters known and loved primarily as men and women of action, pushing at the outer edges of society.

Perhaps the most prevalent dissenters of the era were the journalists - Lincoln Steffens, John Reed, Louise Bryant and Walter Lippmann, among others. Included in this group was cartoonist Art Young who, even among a crowd known for individuality, was one of a kind.

The Conservative Roots of a Radical Cartoonist

Born in Illinois in 1866, Young grew up in Wisconsin. He proved different from Reed, Goldman and the others in that he embraced conservatism for much of his life and worked in the mainstream for many years, including at the rabidly right-wing *Chicago Tribune*. It was not until Young passed the age of 40 that he embraced socialism, but once he did, it became central to his work as a cartoonist.

Young is known best for the cartoons he designed from 1911 to 1917 for *The Masses*, a left-wing monthly magazine of which he was co-editor. Among his best and most controversial were those critical of US involvement in the First World War. For one cartoon, entitled "Having Their Fling," authorities arrested Young (along with Reed, Eastman and others from *The Masses*) under the newly passed Espionage Act. The magazine staffers initially faced 20 years in prison, but two trials ended in hung juries and authorities eventually dropped all the charges. The trials and ongoing government harassment, however, forced *The Masses* to cease publication.

Art Young's Farm in Bethel

Around 1900, Young purchased a house and four acres of farmland in Bethel, Connecticut. Initially, the house was a country retreat, but shortly after the Espionage Act trials, Young began spending most of his time there. He continued to draw cartoons for a variety of publications including *The Liberator*, a magazine founded in 1918 by his comrades as a successor to *The Masses*.

Both *The Masses* and *The Liberator* featured high-quality art, including covers of color cardstock that proved very striking in style, color and content. Young found his work featured numerous times. Later in his life, he also drew for the *New Yorker*, the *Saturday Evening Post* and *Collier's Weekly*. In his seventies, Young experienced health and financial problems that resulted in his having to sell his Bethel property in 1940. He returned to New York and died there in 1943 at the age of 77.

Before he moved back to New York, Young put many of his original works (6,000 by one account) into storage. Some of those works are on display at the Art Young Gallery, an institution established in Bethel by residents determined to keep alive Young's legacy and relation to the town. The gallery resides just a mile from the house where Young lived. In March 2015, it featured the first exhibit of the cartoonist's work since 1939. The Bethel Historical Society also recently brought out *Types of the Old Home Town*, a previously unpublished manuscript by Young about his years in Bethel and the people he knew there.

Beatrice Longman Breaks the Mold

Connecticut has no shortage of war memorials and statues featuring prominent business and political leaders. The celebration of the state's ordinary working people, however, is almost nowhere to be found. One exception is "The Craftsman" in Hartford.

It is a striking example of a working man, created in 1931 by Evelyn Beatrice Longman, prominently displayed on the campus of the A.I. Prince Technical High School on Flatbush Avenue.

The bronze sculpture portrays a worker sitting and reading. His jacket is thrown across the wooden chair. He is dressed in rough clothes, worn work shoes, rolled up sleeves. His concentration is intense. In one hand is a tool of his trade, at his feet are machine parts. On his lap is a set of schematics. He is concentrating and, perhaps, puzzling out a repair.

"The Craftsman" was dedicated on September 16, 1931 at the Hartford Trade School on Washington Street. The school and the statue moved to Hartford's south end in 1960.

The granite foundation on which the sculpture sits does not include the name of Ms. Longman's work. Instead, the words carved into the stone base read: "Industry, given in honor of the pioneers of industry in the city of Hartford, men whose memory is revered, whose influence survives to inspire succeeding generations."

The subject and the dedication seem like a mismatch. The Craftsman is clearly not a "pioneer of industry;" he is a skilled worker, the kind employed by the pioneers. He is the nameless working man who made the pioneers successful. But the statue was commissioned and paid for by the Connecticut Manufacturers Association, so they had the last word.

In fact, around the time the statue was dedicated, Connecticut was a hotbed of militant union organizing. Leading up to The Craftsman's unveiling, there were a dozen labor strikes throughout the state: textile workers in Putnam and New London, fur workers in Danbury, necktie and shirt makers in New Haven, and laborers in Newtown. Even unemployed workers struck: they were in a city-sponsored relief program at Hartford's Brainard airfield and stopped work until they won transportation, food allowance and a dollar a day raise.

"The Craftsman" is not Longman's only worker-themed sculpture. In 1911, the Triangle Shirtwaist Factory fire took the lives of 146 New York immigrant

299

garment workers, mostly women, some as young as fourteen. The reckless tragedy spurred safety reforms and union organizing. A year after the fire, survivors dedicated the "Triangle Fire Memorial to the Unknowns" for the six victims who could not be identified. The monument's creator was never publicly known, and it was only recently discovered to be Evelyn Longman's work. The identities of the six unknown garment workers were finally determined in 2011.

In 1920, Evelyn Longman moved her New York studio to the campus of Loomis School in Windsor. She had been commissioned to create a piece in honor of Nathaniel Batchelder's late wife. Batchelder was the headmaster at Loomis; he and Longman eventually married. The studio had train tracks running through it so clay and other material could be directly delivered to her workshop.

By the time "The Craftsman" was completed, Longman was firmly established in her field. Besides a variety of local installations (many of which were full of military symbolism including "Spirit of Victory," a Spanish-American War memorial in Bushnell Park), Longman's work was displayed at the 1904 St. Louis World's Fair. She was the only artist for whom Thomas Edison would sit. Around 1920, Longman was asked to work on the Lincoln Memorial. There she created a number of decorative wreaths cut in stone and, it is said, she sculpted the humble rail splitter's hands from Georgia granite.

Anna Sokolow, Modern Dance Pioneer

Anna Sokolow was born in Hartford on February 9, 1910. Her parents Samuel and Sara Sokolowski were Jews from Tsarist Russia. Anna was the third of their four children. Samuel and Sara were garment workers active in both the International Ladies Garment Workers Union and the Socialist Party. Anna's father came down with Parkinson's disease while still a young man, and the family struggled financially throughout Anna's youth.

Sokolow began taking dance lessons as a young girl. When she was 15, she overcame the objections of her parents and dropped out of school to pursue dance in a more rigorous way. The family had moved to New York City where Sokolow was able to earn a full scholarship to the Neighborhood Playhouse at the Henry Street Settlement on Manhattan's Lower East Side.

Transforming Working Class Experience Into Breath-Taking Art

It was a heady, exciting environment for a talented young woman. Sokolow was just 18 when she had her first major dance performance. In the years before her professional breakthrough, Sokolow worked in a factory to sustain herself. The connections she forged with her co-workers, combined with the left-wing milieu of her home, would prove central to the themes of the work she did over the next 15 years.

At the Neighborhood Playhouse, Sokolow studied with Martha Graham. After Graham formed the Martha Graham Dance Company, Sokolow taught choreography there and performed in many of the company's works, most notably *Rite of Spring* in 1930.

At the same time, Sokolow developed her own works that were staged by companies she formed or helped form, such as the Theatre Union Dance Group and the New Dance League. Major turning points were performances of a number of her original pieces in 1936 and a performance on Broadway in 1937. It was a remarkable period of creativity in which Sokolow presented a stunning body of work that made her arguably the second most important figure of modern dance, behind only Graham.

Revolutionary in Both Form and Content

Like many in the 1930s, Sokolow was strongly influenced by radical political ideas. The same was true of others who revolutionized modern dance along with her, including Graham, Sophie Maslow, Jane Dudley and Helen Tamiris. Sokolow's many dances were vibrant, lyrical and thrilling to behold, as she explored serious themes such as death at work in *Strange American Funeral;* youth poverty and aimlessness in *Case History No. —;* fascism in *Inquisition '36;* and war in both *Anti-War Trilogy* and *Excerpts From a War Poem.*

Enthusiastic Audiences Both High and Low-Brow

Some writers and dance critics later sought to decontextualize Sokolow's art. Others like scholars Larry Warren and Hannah Kostrin understood that class struggle and rebellion against oppressive hierarchies were at the heart of her best work. Sokolow's genius lay in the fact that her art was both sophisticated and accessible, as she dazzled workers and cultured elites alike. During her heyday in the 1930s, she performed many works for large gatherings of enthusiastic union members whose backgrounds were similar to hers, and who were her most appreciative audience.

Many Connecticut Performances

Sokolow returned to Connecticut to perform many times. In 1961, for example, she debuted *Dreams* at the American Dance Festival at Connecticut College. A troupe she established, the New Players Project, also performed in the state under her direction. One such event took place in Hartford in 1981 when the New Players Project staged a new Sokolow work, *Variations on a Jewish Theme.*

Sokolow's dance remains timely and is regularly featured in the capital of American dance, New York City, including as recently as March of 2018. On that occasion, the Sokolow Theatre/Dance Ensemble performed a number of her works, including some that had not been done for many years, at the Mark O'Donnell Theater in Brooklyn in a production titled *Moods and Dreams.* The program featured a rich array of her choreography spanning many decades. From *Preludes,* a piece with its roots in the 1930s and accompanied by George Gershwin music — to *Poem,* which Sokolow developed in 1995 when she was 85.

Sokolow was a founding member of the Actors Studio where she taught movement for actors. She returned to Broadway many times beginning in 1947, choreographing shows such as *Street Scene* and *Camino Real.* She also worked briefly on the original *Hair.* She staged many works for the New York City Opera, and remained true to her radical politics with *Time+,* an impassioned 1966 dance piece opposed to the Vietnam War.

Sokolow also taught dance for many years at Juilliard. She died in 2000 at the age of 90.

Bridgeport's Walt Kelly, Creator of *Pogo*

Walt Kelly, the creator of the iconic comic strip *Pogo*, was born in Philadelphia on August 25, 1913. When he was two years old, he moved with his parents Walt, Sr. and Genevieve, and his sister Bernice, to Bridgeport. The Kellys settled in a house at 457 East Avenue on the East End, a short distance from the sprawling General Electric plant, where both his parents soon were employed.

In many interviews he did over the course of his life, Kelly fondly recalled the Bridgeport of his youth as a rich ethnic stew full of colorful characters who, whatever their differences, found a way to get along. In *We Go Pogo: Walt Kelly, Politics, and American Satire*, a book about Kelly published in 2012, author Kerry Stoper wrote about Bridgeport's "colorful dialects, casual tolerance and working class solidarity," themes that Kelly would feature prominently in *Pogo*. Kelly and his parents were supporters of Jasper McLevy, the Socialist who was elected to the first of his twelve terms as Bridgeport's mayor in 1933.

Early Years As Cartoonist and Reporter

It was Kelly's father who taught Walt, Jr., to draw and he developed his skills during the many hours he spent confined to the family home recovering from a series of serious childhood illnesses. At Bridgeport's Warren Harding High School, he honed his art further by drawing for the school newspaper and yearbook. He was also involved in the theater club, an experience he drew on in the skits the characters in *Pogo* performed on a regular basis.

Kelly was also a school correspondent for the *Bridgeport Post* while at Harding, contributing articles to the paper about sports and school news. Not long after graduating high school in 1930, he was hired by the *Post* as a crime reporter. He drew cartoons for the editorial page as well, including a quite detailed comic history of P.T. Barnum, who lived much of his life in Bridgeport. The Barnum motif was another that Kelly used in *Pogo* in the form of a circus impresario named P.T. Bridgeport.

After the *Post*, Kelly worked for a time in the Bridgeport Welfare Department. We can imagine the impact that experience had, occurring as it did in the depths of the Great Depression, and the influence it had on his outlook, and on *Pogo*. Kelly left Bridgeport in 1935, when he fell in love with Helen DeLacy and pursued her to California, where he landed a job at the Walt Disney Studio. He worked on a series of Disney cartoon productions, married DeLacy and returned for a time to Bridgeport where the couple's first child was born in 1942. The Kellys soon moved to New York City where Walt shifted his focus to *Pogo*.

The New York Star

In 1948, Kelly went to work for the *New York Star*, a left-wing daily newspaper that was the successor to Marshall Field's *PM*. Like *PM*, the *Star* was a bold venture: ad-free, pro-New Deal and unstintingly supportive of the old CIO at a time when virtually all of New York City's eight mainstream dailies (nine counting the *Brooklyn Eagle*) were rabidly hostile to labor and wildly enthusiastic about the Cold War and the suppression of domestic dissent. In addition to a wide array of great writers and its revolutionary use of photos, *PM* featured *Barnaby*, a satirical comic strip drawn by Crockett Johnson, whose influence can be seen in *Pogo*. It was in the pages of the *Star* that Kelly made *Pogo*, with its assortment of anthropomorphic animal characters, a regular feature.

Pogo

The main character was an opossum named Pogo, and other regulars were Albert the Alligator and Churchy LaFemme. The strip was set in the fictional Okefenokee Swamp in Georgia. Kelly used it, in part, to send up the powerful and bullies of all persuasions. Animal characters represented easily recognizable figures of the day, such as Senator Joseph McCarthy, who was satirized as Simple J. Malarkey, a blowhard, shotgun-toting bobcat.

Like *PM*, the *New York Star* (and its successor the New York *Daily Compass*) was overwhelmed by the reactionary politics of the time. When it went under in 1949, Kelly syndicated *Pogo* in newspapers throughout the United States. The strip was enormously popular and ran for 26 years. Beginning in 1951, Kelly published the first of over 20 books of *Pogo* reprints.

The Kelly family lived for a while in Darien, Connecticut. Until Walt and Helen divorced in the early 1950's. He returned to New York City, married Stephanie Waggony, and became a regular public speaker who was especially popular on college campuses. During this time, Kelly also maintained close friendships with fellow cartoonists Milt Caniff, the creator of *Terry and the Pirates* and *Steve Canyon*, as well as fellow Bridgeporter Al Capp, creator of *Lil Abner*.

Although *Pogo* had fallen somewhat out of style by 1970, it experienced a revival of sorts when environmentalists organizing the first Earth Day adopted the most famous line from the strip: We Have Met the Enemy and He is Us. Recognizing the sentiment of Earth Day as akin to his own, Kelly illustrated a widely-circulated poster advertising that first Earth Day and its many events.

After his second wife Stephanie's death, Kelly married Selby Daley, an illustrator who carried on with *Pogo* for several years after Walt's death. Kelly was in failing health for some years and died of complications from diabetes in 1973 at the age of 60.

Trouble in the Connecticut Suburbs: *Revolutionary Road*

Connecticut's Fairfield County has for many years been a place of contrasts. It has cities that, even in their bustling heydays, were places where poverty and despair lived amidst booming factories. It has also historically been a place where both the fairly well-to-do and the richest of the rich live in towns that, beginning in the 1940s, came to be known as suburbs. Both the industrial cities and the green suburbs of Fairfield County have been the subject of much literature. Richard Yates's 1961 *Revolutionary Road* is one of the best and best-known novels about the latter.

Set in 1955, the novel tells the story of Frank and April Wheeler, a couple with two children who live on Revolutionary Road in an upscale Fairfield County town. Frank commutes by train five mornings a week to Manhattan, where he is employed as a salesman at Knox Business Machines. While he is paid well enough to afford a lovely home (April is a stay-at-home mom), Frank hates his job, feels diminished by it and never passes up an opportunity to make fun of it.

At first, Frank and April are drawn to living in a nice house on a tree-lined street. Before very long, however, they fall into regularly making fun of their neighbors. They come to see there is something hollow at the core of the suburban dream. It becomes important to both of them to believe that they are better than their surroundings, and also to believe their coming to live on Revolutionary Road was a twist of fate they had no control over.

Paris

Both Wheelers had previously lived for an extended period in Manhattan and enjoyed many good times in Frank's Greenwich Village apartment in the early years of their relationship. That experience in the capital of American bohemia informs the contempt they develop for their suburban town. Out of their unhappiness comes April's idea that they move to Paris so Frank can "find himself."

Their neighbors and Frank's colleagues at Knox greet the Paris idea with shock, skepticism and not a small bit of resentment. The resentment is not so much over the possible loss of friends and a co-worker, but over the fact that the Wheelers, in proposing to chuck it all, make clear what they all seem to know: their well-constructed lives in the comfortable Connecticut suburbs have not produced happiness.

A Kindred Spirit Who's Institutionalized

There is, for example, Shep Campbell. Campbell and his wife Milly are the Wheelers' best friends who echo the jokes the Wheelers make about their other neighbors and their surroundings. The Campbells have made their peace with their lot, however, even as Shep lusts after April and is completely unable to connect with his four television-obsessed young sons. It is only from John Givings, the institutionalized son of local busybody Helen Givings, that the Wheelers receive affirmation for their plan.

Frank is never as enthusiastic about Paris as April. He seems aware in a way she is not, or at least is unwilling to accept, that he has "found himself" and what he is, is a salesman at Knox Business Machines. Events soon cause the Paris plan to unravel. Heated arguments and recriminations ensue, followed, ultimately, by tragedy.

No Escape From Unhappiness

The Connecticut suburbs play a crucial role in *Revolutionary Road*. As they were then and in many ways remain today, any number of Fairfield County towns are held up as the ultimate badge of success for an upper-level professional family. They are places where problems are supposed to be absent or at least easily solved. While it's likely no one ever believed that to be the case, the toll unhappiness takes is greater because of the promise.

At the same time, *Revolutionary Road* is not only about the empty promises of happiness in the Connecticut suburbs. It is easy to imagine similar dramas such as the Wheelers' taking place in Greenwich Village; easy to imagine because they happen there all the time. Yates seems equally to be getting at something bigger about the emptiness of life in the United States at the moment it had attained, within its very real self-defined limits, the best for the most. Fairfield County represents all that the country as a whole aspired to be in the 1950s — and the people in *Revolutionary Road* who live there find it is seriously lacking.

Not so much as we might think has changed and that's why *Revolutionary Road* is still powerful and relevant. Parts of Fairfield County are wealthier than ever, yet unhappiness, perhaps especially among the young, is an ongoing problem. While those problems are not on the scale of young people in Connecticut's poorest cities, problems that are often questions of life and death, they remain a blight on the American Dream.

Other novels of the post-war era set in Fairfield County cover similar ground, most notably Sloan Wilson's *The Man in the Gray Flannel Suit* and Laura Hobson's *Gentlemen's Agreement*. What distinguishes *Revolutionary Road* is that it's an unsparing story that ends in tragedy and defeat. Perhaps for that reason, neither the book or the 2008 film adaptation starring Kate Winslet and Leonardo DiCaprio, no less, were especially popular.

Martha Graham, Connecticut College and the American Dance Festival

In 1948, Martha Graham was the preeminent figure of modern dance. At 52 years of age, Graham danced and fashioned choreography at a pace that those half her age probably had difficulty matching. Just a year before, she introduced two creations, *Errand Into the Maze* and *Night Journey*, that proved among her most innovative and durable works.

It was only natural, then, that when her friend and former student Martha Hill established the School of the Dance on the campus of the Connecticut College for Women that year, she invited Graham to choreograph and dance at the launch of what organizers eventually christened the American Dance Festival (ADF). The 47-year-old Hill studied under Graham and joined the Martha Graham Dance Company in 1929. From 1932 until 1942, she also ran a summer dance school and festival at Bennington College in Vermont that featured Graham, Helen Tamiris, Doris Humphrey and a significant number of others on the forefront of the modern dance revolution.

After retiring from performing, Hill began teaching dance. She was on the dance faculty at New York University and Bennington in 1948. In eventually selecting Connecticut College's New London campus to host the ADF, Hill specifically established the venture in a locale accessible to teachers and dancers in New York City, yet far enough away as to attract new audiences who were not New York regulars.

Combining lectures, instruction and performances over nine days in August, the inaugural event was a rousing success. Administrators reached their initial goal of enrolling 100 students, eventually reaching a total of 119 aspiring dancers. Just as importantly, the combined turnout of aficionados and new patrons also exceeded expectations.

The Martha Graham Company

Unquestionably, the high point was the Martha Graham Company's performance. First the group performed programs from their repertory, including both newer works *Errand Into the Maze* and *Night Journey* and classic pieces such as *Appalachian Spring* and *Dark Meadow*. As well as the audience received those, the highlight that "evoked the wildest enthusiasm," according to one account, was a new work, *Wilderness Stair: Diversion of Angels*, the name of which was soon changed to simply *Diversion of Angels* and became a regular in the Graham Company's repertory.

Hill took on substantial personal debt in the festival's first years, but by 1951, when she accepted a position to establish a dance department at Juilliard, the Connecticut College School of the Dance and the American Dance Festival were well established in New London. As for Graham, she returned in the years that followed to perform and, more frequently, to lecture. She sought to inspire young students of dance in particular, stating in one festival talk in 1954 that dancers were like acrobats of God who were needed "more than you know and more than I ever dreamed."

The list of those who performed at the ADF in the 30 years it was in Connecticut reads like a Who's Who of international dancers, choreographers, musicians and composers and includes (in addition to Graham) Alvin Ailey, Merce Cunningham, Paul Taylor, Twyla Tharp, Isamu Noguchi, José Limón, Doris Humphrey, Sophie Maslow, Louis Horst, William Schuman and Jean Rosenthal. Like Graham, many of those who performed also lectured students enrolled in the Connecticut College School of the Dance.

Despite the wealth of artistic talent it featured, the festival eventually began to suffer financial difficulties. Disputes arose over the monetary obligation of the college to the festival until the ADF board finally accepted a bid from Duke University to relocate to North Carolina beginning in 1978. The ADF continues to attract dancers, teachers and students who are among the most talented in the world. Its success inspired the creation of other festivals that have made a significant contribution to a thriving modern dance scene.

Diversion of Angels Redux

Sixty-seven years after its founding, Connecticut College's dance department remains successful. In 2009, the Martha Graham Dance Company returned to the New London campus to perform *Diversion of Angels*. Martha Hill, meanwhile, continued teaching dance until she was 84. She died ten years later, in 1995.

Four Decades of Radical Radio: An Interview With WPKN's Scott Harris

Scott Harris has been hosting a show at WPKN, Bridgeport's independent, alternative radio station, for a remarkable 42 years. He began in 1977 with a music show which he transformed a decade later to Counterpoint, *a two-hour weekly program chock full of news, analysis, interviews and discussion not heard in corporate media. Along the way, Harris and his colleagues created a second program, the 30-minute award-winning "Between the Lines," that is syndicated to over 60 community radio stations and webcasting outlets.*

Over the years, Harris has interviewed on his shows many well-known radicals and activists including Noam Chomsky, Bill Fletcher, Jr., Phyllis Bennis, Chris Hedges, Kathy Kelly, Leslie Cagan, Richard Wolff, Kim Ives, Michael Albert, Jane Slaughter, Reverend William Barber, Sonali Kolhatkar, Ellen Brown and Paul Street. Visit the Between The Lines *website for more information: https://btlonline.org/. And visit the WPKN website for more information about the station and how you can listen to* Counterpoint, Between the Lines *and other programming: http://wpkn.org/.*

Piascik: What are the origins of your interest in radio and when did you first get involved at WPKN?

Harris: I first became interested in radio growing up in Norwalk, Connecticut listening to New York City talk radio like Brad Crandall, Alex Bennett and Long John Nebel, and I very much loved Jean Shepherd for his wonderful storytelling. Later during the 1960s while in high school I started listening to WPKN as the civil rights movement and anti-Vietnam war movement were rising up. I became very interested in the eclectic music genres and progressive politics which were regularly featured on WPKN.

When I went to college in Massachusetts, I got involved in the student radio station during my freshman year and became manager of the station in my junior and senior years. In 1977, I began working for an activist group, the Connecticut Citizen Action Group, after I graduated from college and got to know some programmers at WPKN. They introduced me to the program director at that time and I was given a regular show on PKN that same year.

311

Piascik: What is the genesis of the two programs you host, *Counterpoint* and *Between the Lines*?

Harris: I started my first radio show at WPKN doing a blues music show featuring older acoustic blues and more modern Chicago electric blues artists. I later mixed in commentary and interviews on a variety of topics and eventually the show transformed into an all-talk format and which I named *Counterpoint*. My slot was originally four hours and I later reduced that to two hours to provide more time for other producers.

An extended trip I made to Nicaragua in 1981, two years after that nation's 1979 revolution, greatly influenced my worldview and politics. Many of my interviews and much of my coverage in the early days of the radio show focused on the Reagan-Bush funded Contra War against Nicaragua's Sandinista government and U.S. support for death squad governments in neighboring El Salvador, Guatemala and Honduras. Several years later, I founded a Sister City project linking my hometown of Norwalk with the Nicaraguan city of Nagarote.

In the days leading up to the Persian Gulf War in 1991, another WPKN producer named Denise Manzari and I, along with other contributors, created *Between The Lines*, a 30-minute show, to probe the causes and conduct of the conflict. After the Persian Gulf War ended, the program's producers continued broadcasting *Between The Lines*, but with a broader focus: providing a platform for activists, journalists and academics generally ignored or marginalized in the corporate media. Like *Counterpoint*, the program's primary focus is to provide a substantive progressive alternative to corporate news obsessed with violent crime, celebrities and "infotainment."

In 2004, we established Squeaky Wheel Productions, Inc., a non-profit organization to distribute *Between The Lines* and other community media projects. In addition to distributing *Between The Lines* to radio stations and websites each week, Squeaky Wheel Productions organizes public education events in the U.S. and internationally.

Piascik: What are some of the issues you've covered?

Harris: For the last 28 years, *Between The Lines* has provided in-depth, timely analysis on a wide range of political, economic and social issues including the history and consequences of U.S. wars in Iraq, Afghanistan, Libya and Syria; growing income inequality in the U.S.; coverage of the global social justice movement and related protests challenging the free trade, corporate-driven policies of the World Trade Organization, World Bank and International Monetary Fund; the post-9/11 erosion of civil liberties; Washington's wars on Central America in the 1980s and attacks on left governments there today; the rise and mainstreaming of white supremacists and political Christian fundamentalism; Palestinian human rights; the struggle for universal health care in the U.S;

international grassroots mobilization to confront global climate change; racism permeating the prison industrial complex; police violence and the Black Lives Matter movement; and efforts to repair flaws in the U.S. electoral system.

Piascik: WPKN began as the radio station of the University of Bridgeport but no longer is. Can you talk about the decision by people at the station to become an independent community entity?

Harris: The decision to become independent was forced upon us when the Reverend Sun Myung Moon's Unification Church was poised to take over the University of Bridgeport board of directors. Awash in debt, directors agreed in April, 1992 to relinquish control of the school to The Professors World Peace Academy, an arm of the Reverend Moon's Unification Church, becoming the first American university run by the church.

Dr. Edwin H. Eigel, Jr., the outgoing, non-Moonie president of the college, gave WPKN an opportunity to break away from the college and we created our own 501c3 nonprofit to which UB transferred the license before the Moon church took over. Eigel also gave us an unlimited lease for our studio space we occupied in the UB building for $1 a year.

Before the Unification Church took over UB, I wrote an article for the local *Fairfield County Advocate* newspaper about how the Unification Church takeover of fishing fleets in Gloucester, Massachusetts negatively impacted that community.

Piascik: You begin each episode of *Counterpoint* by stating that it's dedicated to covering issues not usually discussed in the corporate media and from points of view generally excluded there. Could you elaborate on why this is important and what it means in practice?

Harris: Our station's mission includes the important priority to broadcast sounds and ideas not heard elsewhere, something I take very seriously. Following in the tradition of other producers, I focus on providing air time to progressive activists, journalists and academics who get little time or attention from corporate media. It should be noted that WPKN programmers have an enormous amount of freedom to program virtually anything and everything they want, as long as it doesn't break FCC rules and regulations jeopardizing our license.

When I began airing political interviews in the late 1970s and 1980s, it was rare that any of my guests were also given any attention in mainstream corporate outlets, either newspapers or TV or radio. With the internet now providing many more platforms for progressive journalists and activists, it's much easier to access progressive and radical points of view online. However, while large corporate outlets such as NPR and MSNBC who have brands that supposedly skew to liberal views, most of my guest list still are rarely heard there.

Piascik: Outlets like NPR and MSNBC pay far less attention to people's movements and campaigns such as the wave of teachers' strikes last Spring, the new Poor People's Campaign and organizing against police violence, in favor of non-stop coverage of Trump and Russiagate. Has this created an even greater need for the work you and your colleagues do?

Harris: It has become urgent that independent media outlets cover and place in context the disastrous Trump GOP policy agenda. Russiagate is a sexy story, as it pushes emotional buttons, but meanwhile there is severe damage being done to labor unions, the environment, climate change policy, criminal justice reform, civil rights, the Endangered Species Act, national park and land preservation, consumer protection and safety regulations and of course health care, which isn't being covered with much depth.

Apart from trade issues and some GOP displeasure with his irrational tweets, Trump is for the most part following the decades long GOP playbook on cultivating support for racist, xenophobic immigration policies, opposing universal health care, deregulating corporations to the detriment of the majority of Americans and providing trillions in tax breaks to the wealthiest based on the bogus and disproven trickle-down theory.

There is also the feckless way in which the Democrats fail to effectively challenge voter suppression, voter purges and gerrymandering that makes one feel as though either the Democrats are grossly incompetent or they're secretly in league with the GOP. Corporate media does little to examine the conduct of both major political parties and discuss the extreme flaws in the U.S. winner-take-all electoral system that shuts out third parties and new ideas.

Piascik: You're making an important distinction between what passes for liberal corporate media and real alternative, radical work like what you and others at WPKN do.

Harris: I once spoke to a woman at one of our *Between The Lines* events who said she gets all of her news and views from MSNBC, and didn't think that independent media was that vital anymore. I reminded her that NBC does very little coverage of specific topics that could jeopardize their corporate sponsors like Big Oil, API, the insurance companies. Examples of this include climate change, the Israeli-Palestinian conflict, Saudi Arabia human rights, FCC issues of monopoly ownership of media and net neutrality, to name just a few.

I also told her that a corporation like NBC has a fiduciary responsibility to its stockholders with the main priority of maximizing profit, and if and when the need arises they will fire their hosts, shift their political slant and change formats in a flash. This actually occurred when Phil Donahue was fired for his stand against the Iraq war and primetime host Keith Olbermann was eventually forced out as well.

Piascik: As media ownership is concentrated into the hands of fewer and fewer corporate behemoths, some of which like Sinclair are extremely reactionary, what do you see as the future for shows like yours and stations like WPKN?

Harris: The mindset that all media is "Free" is an enemy of listener supported outlets like WPKN and other non-commercial stations across the U.S. Broadcast media is experiencing a dramatically changed landscape where many millennials listen to their own podcasts they themselves program. Our job is to create radio programming in formats that will be attractive and accessible to a new generation.

Piascik: You and your colleagues regularly host panels at the large Left Forum conference held annually in New York City. Do you see a relationship between journalism and activism?

Harris: Organizing public forums and the like helps us connect with our audience and supporters. Certainly information, discussion and debate is vital to political activism and organizing of all stripes. It's part of our mission to organize events that strengthen the public's understanding of critical and sometimes complex public policy issues.

Piascik: Are you also involved in progressive organizations and campaigns?

Harris: I attend many different political events and support various progressive campaigns but generally attend as a journalist to bring the message and story to our audience on *Counterpoint* and *Between The Lines*.

However, as I mentioned earlier, I am the founder of a sister city project with a town in Nicaragua that we started in 1986, the Norwalk/Nagarote Sister City Project. I'm no longer the president of the group, but still serve on the board of directors. The group began during the Contra War, and since the war ended has focused on youth education projects. We opened a community center that holds regular after school classes and provides scholarships, we have a model organic farm, and are now building a new pre-school. Anyone who's interested can check out our website https://www.sistercityproject.org/.

We're very proud to be one of a handful of Nicaragua sister city groups that continued on beyond the Contra War days when everything about Nicaragua was so politically charged. With the unfortunate current political crisis in Nicaragua, we're trying to find our way through a very dangerous environment in order to limit the harm to our staff and students.

Katharine Hepburn, Hollywood Progressive

Katharine Hepburn is one of the great icons of American movies, regarded by many as the greatest English language film actress. She was born on May 12, 1907 in Hartford to feminist activist Katharine Houghton Hepburn and Dr. Tomas Hepburn, a urologist at Hartford Hospital. Hepburn was instilled with an independent spirit early on and strong encouragement from both of her parents. As a young girl, she attended demonstrations with her mother, who was active in the movements for women's suffrage and to gain easy access to birth control for women, among others.

In 1924, Hepburn enrolled in Bryn Mawr College in Pennsylvania, her mother's alma mater. She graduated with a degree in history and philosophy in 1928. It was at college that she got involved in acting in a serious way for the first time, as she appeared in the school's stage production of *The Woman in the Moon* in her senior year.

Early Career: Broadway and Hollywood

Hepburn moved to New York City immediately after graduating college and landed a lead part in a Broadway production within months. Her stage breakthrough came in *The Warrior's Husband* in 1932. Positive reviews and a run of three months were followed by an offer from Hollywood to appear in *Bill of Divorcement*, which co-starred John Barrymore. The film was produced by David O. Selznick and directed by George Cukor, with whom Hepburn would make 10 films.

Within a few years, Hepburn was one of the leading stars in Hollywood as she had prime
roles in one big film after another: *Morning Glory* (1933), *Little Women* (1933), *Stage Door* (1937), *Bringing Up Baby* (1938), *Holiday* (1938) and *The Philadelphia Story* (1940). She was nominated for the Academy Awards' Best Actress for three of those performances and won for *Morning Glory*. During the same period, she returned to the Broadway stage, most notably for *The Philadelphia Story* in which she starred in the same role she played in the movie.

A New Look For Women

Among Hepburn's striking features were a look, a bearing, and a way of being that was a major departure for women in the movies of the 1930s. The characters she played were almost uniformly strong, independent ones and in sharp contrast to the typical woman in a movie who was invariably not very bright and far more interested in finding a husband than forging a career. Not that her characters weren't interested in men; they were, but only on their own terms. Nor were the women she played incapable of humor, even slapstick. In fact, a number of her movies include some of the best and funniest male-female banter ever filmed.

Her hairstyles and fashions also became quite popular. At a time when it was deemed highly inappropriate for a woman to wear slacks, for example, Hepburn did so without a care to what anyone thought, both on film and in her personal life. One weakness that derived both from her established screen persona and her upper middle-class background, complete with a very noticeable accent: one is hard-pressed to think of any role of hers that could be described as earthy or working class. While it would have been interesting to see what she would have done with such a role, it is perhaps to her credit that she never tried.

Spencer Tracy

Hepburn carried on a 26-year affair with Spencer Tracy, a romance that began on the set of *Woman of the Year* in 1941. Tracy's marriage was rocky and he was mostly separated from his wife, but she refused to give him a divorce. That made it impossible for Hepburn and Tracy to marry, and she apparently never pushed the issue. Instead, they carried on a romance that was an open secret both in Hollywood and to the movie-going public until Tracy's death in 1967. It was Hepburn and not his wife or other family members who attended to Tracy's many needs as his health failed in the last five years of his life, five years in which she was essentially on a leave of absence from the movies.

The Blacklist

While Hepburn was wildly acclaimed for her performances in film after film (her four Oscars are the most of any performer, and her 12 nominations are second only to Meryl Streep), her career waxed and waned throughout. Some of her movies were unsuccessful despite her performances. That may very well be in part because of her insistence on going against the grain in the roles she played. She also experienced some difficulty in the late 1940s and 1950s because of her public opposition to the House Committee on Un-American Activities and the Hollywood blacklist.

It would hard to characterize Hepburn as a radical. When films and plays about social issues were especially popular during the Great Depression, her preference was to let the independent characters she played speak for themselves. Politically, she was an enthusiastic supporter of the New Deal who was a frequent guest at the White House during Franklin Roosevelt's presidency. She was also an enthusiastic supporter of the Screen Actors Guild, the Screen Writers Guild, and of trade unions in general.

When HUAC began hearings in 1947 to investigate Communism in Hollywood, Hepburn was one of the most famous and vocal of a group of actors and actresses to protest their efforts. She helped form the Committee for the First Amendment that made a highly publicized trip from Hollywood to Washington, D.C. to protest the first round of hearings. The Committee for the First Amendment then took up the cause of the Hollywood Ten, ten screenwriters and directors who were eventually imprisoned for refusing to cooperate with the hearings.

Hepburn was among those who stood her ground in the face of a tremendous backlash. Though she had never had anything to do with the Communist Party, she believed a person had the right to be a Communist and that the government had no right to investigate, blacklist and imprison people because of their political beliefs.

Many in Hollywood fully cooperated with HUAC, others did so under pressure. Some from the Committee for the First Amendment, including Humphrey Bogart, angrily disassociated themselves from the group, outraged to discover that some of its members, and all of the Hollywood Ten, were or had, in fact, been Communists. Hepburn never did.

Though it does not appear Hepburn was ever officially blacklisted, her career suffered. She appeared in some movies in the years of the ongoing hearings, but was also passed over for others, very likely because of her opposition to HUAC, and the fact that she never retreated from that position. There were newspaper accounts of audience members in theaters throwing things at the movie screen when she appeared during at least one of her movies. American Legionnaires and other reactionaries regularly picketed her movies well into the 1950s.

Like many of the characters she played, Hepburn persevered. Many of her best performances came in the decades that followed. Perhaps because she had never been a beauty queen or pin-up girl, her career flourished well past the age when those of many actresses end. She won three of her Oscars after the age of 60 and made her last film when she was 87. She also appeared in many plays and television movies. Hepburn was also an enthusiastic supporter of a number of local ventures in her home state including the American Shakespeare Theatre in Stratford, where she performed in a number of plays.

Katharine Hepburn died in Fenwick, Connecticut in 2003 at the age of 96, and is buried in Cedar Hill Cemetery in Hartford.

20. Behind the Prison Walls

Women of the Prison Brigade

On a cold winter morning in March 1919, the "Prison Special" pulled into the Union Place train station in Hartford. Depar63ting from a passenger car were 25 women from all walks of life who had one thing in common—they had all been thrown in jail for demonstrating in front of the White House in support of women's right to vote.

The suffragists riding the Prison Special traveled from city-to-city to rally the public in support of their cause. In Hartford, they spoke first at the Municipal Building and were welcomed by Katharine Houghton Hepburn, the chair of the state's National Women's Party. The group included 75-year-old Mary Nolan and young Lucy Burns, who had been arrested six times in front of Woodrow Wilson's home.

Suffragists Face Prison, Abuse, and Slurs

Local women had also been among those arrested in acts of civil disobedience. Edna Purtell of West Hartford was one of the youngest of the hundreds of suffragists who took part in the actions. According to Purtell, a prison guard broke two of her fingers when she refused to remove her suffragist sash in jail.

Such activity was upsetting to opponents of women's right to vote. Mrs. Daniel Markham, head of Connecticut's anti-suffrage movement, warned that the "suffs" were allied with Reds and were trying to incite class and race hatred. Others predicted "racial decadence" if suffrage was passed.

The U.S. suffrage movement began in the 1840s with Susan B. Anthony and Elizabeth Cady Stanton. By 1914, eleven states had granted full voting rights to women. Connecticut had defeated suffrage in 1917, and was still debating the pros and cons of the vote when the Prison Special arrived in the city.

Dressed in prison garb or in the clothes from countries where women had the franchise, the Prison Brigade walked to the Allyn House for a fundraising breakfast organized by local sponsors. They were greeted by 250 supporters, including a wide range of Hartford women: "colored sympathizers, women munitions workers, Bolshevist and Socialist sympathizers" as one newspaper account put it. The women raised $500 that day. The 19th Amendment to the US Constitution was finally adopted by Congress in 1920. Edna Purtell died in 1985 at the age of 86.

Jail Sit-Down Strike: Prison Rights Are Human Rights

Instead of returning to their cells for the night, 145 inmates at Hartford's Seyms Street jail organized a nonviolent sit-down strike. They were fed up with the poor treatment and living conditions in the 1873-built facility sometimes called the "hell hole."

At 10 p.m. on August 9, 1967, the inmates, all from the maximum security ward, took their stand. Authorities called out the Hartford police, who surrounded the jail; state police were put on alert. The head of the jail rushed in from his home.

Among the 20 demands they delivered to the jail authorities were overcrowding, poor food, lack of medical care and abuse by guards. Eventually they negotiated with a committee of correction officials, a state senator and a newspaper reporter on these and other complaints, including lack of access to bail bondsmen and legal documents, restricted visitor privileges, jail job segregation and no opportunity to exercise (500 men lived in a building meant to house 350 maximum). They were allowed one shower a week with no way to buy toilet paper, towels, soap or toothbrushes. There was no running water in the cells. Sometimes, they got no water from the guards. Lice, roaches and rats moved about undisturbed.

Solitary confinement could be made indefinite at the whim of a correction officer, the inmates said. They were stripped naked when they entered what is called "the hole" and had to urinate and defecate on the floor because there were no toilets, not even a bucket.

Four years after the Seyms Street strike, the Attica prison uprising in September 1971, became the most well-known jail rebellion in U.S. history. Refusal by New York Governor Nelson Rockefeller to meet directly with inmates over their grievances – many similar to those of the Seyms Street strikers – led to an armed raid by authorities. Ten hostages and twenty-six inmates were killed. After much criticism and a (still secret) government report, the state of New York paid $8 million to inmates and their families to settle a lawsuit.

At Seyms Street, the negotiations halted for the night, and after they were guaranteed no reprisals, the inmates ended their brief strike at around 2:30 in the morning. The next day, state officials toured the facility. Some called the conditions "appalling" as they viewed soiled mattresses and smelled the unwashed inmates.

They met David Bradshaw, 22-years-old and already a civil rights veteran from his voter registration efforts in the South. David said he was picked up during the recent disturbances in Hartford's North End. When he arrived at Seyms Street he was immediately put in "Siberia," a section of the jail worse than the rest.

Jail authorities promised some immediate improvements. They argued that other changes could only be made with more state funding.

Seyms Street had been the target of criticism since 1920, and the subject of a legislative investigation in 1938, but very little changed from year to year. In the course of its existence, at least 75 men escaped; too many have committed suicide there.

Although funds were approved by the General Assembly to build a new jail, no suburban town would take it. The jail continued to be the site of protests by local community activists and college students who demanded reforms to the jail's "subhuman" conditions (in the words of a former corrections official). The Attica rebellion spurred local students and others to increase the pressure on the prison authorities.

Seyms Street was finally closed in 1977. Prisoners were transported to the new Hartford Correctional facility on Weston Street. At least 1,000 incarcerated men populated the North End jail.

21. How the Super Rich Live

The Hartford Wheel Club: Disparity in the Gilded Age

In early 1893, the boys at the Hartford Wheel Club had a great idea: they would throw a party and dress up like poor people! The members of the club themselves, of course, were not poor. Being a dues-paying Hartford Wheel Club member was an expensive hobby. Back then, a cycle cost the modern equivalent of $3,800 — half a year's wages for an average workman. The Wheel Club took their cycles to races in other states, which often meant two- or three-day treks (Albert Pope manufactured these "penny farthings," single high-wheeled vehicles, at his factory on Washington Street). Since the work week typically lasted 6 days (and at least 60 hours), only the leisure class found spare time and money to compete.

The party, it seemed, was the perfect occasion for Wheel Club members to reaffirm their place in the social order. On January 20, 1893, they held their "Hard Times Supper" at their club rooms on the corner of Main and Grove Street. The club demanded a strict dress code for the Hard Times event. "Anyone wearing a collar will be thrown out the window," the invitation read. (The detachable celluloid collar was a formal accessory, and only manual laborers walked around without them.) The rules forbade cigars and cigarettes as well. Most of the poor and unemployed were not buying smokes when they could not feed their families. Party-goers smoked crude corn cob pipes instead.

The party's organizers designed the bill of fare to fit the club's poverty theme as well. It is likely the Wheel Club members regularly dined on steak and champagne, but for this meal they were only offered hardtack, dried herring, cold pork and cider. The Wheel Club affair could not compete with spectacles of the very rich, however, such as the dinner party Mrs. Stuyvesant Fish of New York hosted for her dog during which the pet wore a diamond collar worth $390,000 in today's dollars. But what Hartford's young men lacked in ridiculous ostentation, they made up for in mean-spirited fun.

Hartford in the Gilded Age

The fiscal panic of 1893 was no joke, however. It helped give rise to an era of slums, sweatshops and widespread poverty that adversely affected the greater part of Hartford's population. Massive unemployment meant more hobos roaming the city, which spurred the Rev. John J. McCook to lobby for restricting "tramps" to a limited section of Hartford where the almshouse resided.

327

Women unable to find work often began selling their bodies for money (during this period Hartford was home to 12 brothels and roughly 400 prostitutes). The Irish immigrant population lived in poverty in the East Side neighborhood known as "Pigville." The African-American population was small, but widespread discrimination meant that Black families suffered the worst housing and health conditions of any ethnic or racial group in the capital city.

This was life in Hartford during the "Gilded Age," a term coined by Mark Twain and the title of his first novel, co-authored with Charles Dudley Warner. The book served as an exposé of the land speculation, corruption and excess wealth of the period.

"Where are the poor of Hartford?" Mark Twain wrote when he first visited the city. "I confess I do not know. They are 'corralled,' doubtless — corralled in some unsanctified corner of this paradise whither my feet have not yet wandered I suppose."

By the time Twain moved to Connecticut, *The Gilded Age: A Tale of Today* had been published and a stage play based on the book reached theaters in New York and Hartford. Twain championed labor unions as the means to balance the wealth disparity between the "1 percent" of the day and everyone else.

As it turned out, however, even the wealthy Hartford Wheel Club succumbed to the economic hardship of the period. The club failed to pay their rent in October 1899 and their landlord ultimately evicted them and seized their property.

The Shameful Legacy of Samuel Colt

Some Hartford people are pretty desperate for heroes. What other explanation could there be for the recent attempts to glorify gunmaker Samuel Colt? His 19th century factory is now a National Historic Landmark.

Does Colt really deserve all this attention? Or are there others who might better qualify as local heroes in Hartford history?

Interpreting the past is a tricky business, but there are some things we know for sure. Colt started his career by selling hits of nitrous oxide to curious audiences for a cheap high. Eventually he became a "colonel" who never saw battle, and used bribery to secure lucrative government contracts. He sold weapons to both the North and the South in the arms buildup before the Civil War. He sent his last shipment of guns to the South on April 15, 1861, three days after Fort Sumter was fired upon by the Confederate army.

Colt coerced his employees to vote the way he wanted them to, sometimes by stopping the machines and forcing workers to listen to his "suggestions" for which candidates to support. He timed layoffs around elections as a warning to workers that their fate was in his hands. He positioned his secretary at the ballot box where his workmen voted. Colt even kept a secret journal on his employees' political affiliations, and fired workers who were anti-slavery Republicans.

The colonel was described as an "autocratic maniac" who ran his operation like a Southern plantation. "While Colt's workers were not legally enslaved, it was always more a matter of degree than kind," wrote William Hosley in "Colt: An American Legend."

The young, unmarried women who worked for him were employed to produce ammunition, dangerous jobs that Colt kept a safe distance from his precious weapons factory. For this extremely risky undertaking, the women were paid a fraction of what Colt's male employees earned.

But it was Samuel Colt's position on slavery and abolition, the primary moral questions of the day, that became his most shameful legacy. His defenders say Colt actually opposed slavery, citing a vague reference to a speaker who lectured his workers on the subject. But the facts tell a different story.

Colt decried the "Black Republican Devils" he employed, and asked a politician friend to publicly encourage manufacturers to fire employees who supported abolition. Northern business interests "promoted, prolonged and profited from slavery," according to "Complicity," a book written by three

329

Hartford Courant reporters who documented Northerners' dependence on slavery in building financial empires.

This profit connection was made crystal clear on Dec. 16, 1859, at Hartford's city hall. The building was packed with local supporters of "states' rights," a coded phrase that justified Southern slavery. Southern states were being unjustly attacked "from a class of men at the North who constantly harp at Slavery," said one speaker. Another used thinly disguised racist rhetoric to make his point. "Lovers of negroes become haters of white men," former Hartford Mayor William J. Hamersley told the crowd.

William W. Eaton, who later became a U.S. senator, said what everyone was thinking when he addressed the crowd of politicians and businessmen. "Look to your pockets," he told them. "We desire Southern cotton and corn. She is agricultural. She comes to us for her loans, insurance and goods. She is our best customer; and I have yet to learn that a sane business man will kick his best customer out of doors." (Hartford Courant, December 15, 1859).

Samuel Colt was one of the principal sponsors of the mass meeting. Colt joined the unanimous vote to condemn abolition and those who were trying to increase the pressure on the South to end slavery.

There are other men and women who might be promoted in his place as hero of Hartford. One contemporary of Samuel Colt was James Pennington, the Hartford minister who was actually a fugitive slave. Pennington risked his life to escape to freedom, then risked it over and over again by advocating abolition from his Talcott Street pulpit.

We can even look within the industrial empire Colt left after his death for likely candidates. There was William C. Beausang, the Colt employee who led more than 100 machinists on strike in 1912 when the company cut workers' pay in half. And there was Frank S. Cushman, an inspector of .45-caliber pistols in 1918 who was disturbed about the quality of production at the factory. He wrote to his congressman as a whistleblower, and was fired on the same day with no explanation.

Certainly, Rose Santangelo should be considered. Rose was one of 500 workers who, in 1935, risked everything when she went on strike at the Colt factory to win union recognition. With other female strikers, Rose raised funds on downtown street corners and was arrested on the picket line.

And there is Dorothy Rookwood, who left the Jim Crow South to build a decent life in Connecticut. Dorothy and her husband were employees at Colt Firearms and members of the United Auto Workers union in 1986 when they joined 800 co-workers in a walkout that lasted for four years. The National Labor Relations Board declared Colt guilty of unfair labor practices and ordered their reinstatement with back pay. Ultimately, the workers won the longest strike in state history, and ended up buying the company.

Colt supporters can put up as many memorials to the colonel as they want. But let's get the history straight. Thousands of Hartford people built the industry for which Samuel Colt is given credit. They are the ones who deserve to be remembered.

Jay Gould: Octopus of the Wires

"I can hire one half of the working class to kill the other half," Jay Gould is supposed to have said. He was one of the most ruthless "robber barons" of the 19th century. It was not an idle threat. So, why would a handful of Hartford telegraph workers in 1883 take him on?

Gould robbed working people and millionaires alike. He bought his way out of the Civil War draft, issued millions of dollars in phony railroad stock, bribed legislators and manipulated President Ulysses S. Grant in an attempt to corner the gold market. Worst of all, he was a notorious union-buster. Gould bought a newspaper to help his image, kept plainclothes police with him at all times and bomb-proofed his newly purchased New York Western Union office. With good reason, he was the industrialist the public loved to hate, the "Octopus of the Wires" as described by one of his former employees.

Toward the end of the 19th century, three local telegraph offices kept Hartford connected to the rest of the country: Western Union (bought by Gould in 1881), Mutual Union, and American Rapid. Hartford was the largest relay office in New England outside of Boston. Fifteen lines were in constant operation, but the office had the capacity to operate sixty lines at a time. Operators, linemen, battery-men, clerks and message boys were all employed to keep the system running efficiently.

While Western Union's profits had greatly increased over the past decade, telegraph workers' wages had actually been cut and hours increased. On July 19, 1883, a nationwide strike began. Hartford, New Haven and Norwich operators joined the effort.

Telegraph work was arduous, as even the former president of Western Union had admitted to a Congressional committee. William Orton testified that operators could not perform their duties for more than six hours straight without endangering their health. Often working twelve to sixteen hours at a time, workers demanded an eight-hour day. They also pushed for overtime pay on Sundays and a 15% raise for every pay grade to help restore the losses they had been incurring since 1875.

One of the worker demands was quite unusual for the time. The telegrapher union insisted that all workers be paid based on their skill level, not their gender. Women as well as men worked as telegraph operators, took shorthand, and dealt with the public. Women had even run military telegraph offices during the Civil War.

The Brotherhood of Telegraphers of the United States and Canada made equal pay for equal work one of its primary demands (even if its name didn't live up to its aspirations). The union was formed about two years before the 1883 strike when several regional groups came together to form a united organization under the banner of the Knights of Labor. As a Knights affiliate, it accepted women as operators.

One male Hartford operator made the union's demand clear. He told a newspaper reporter that "the clause demanding equal pay for equal work, whether done by men or women, was inserted in the bill of grievances from a sense of justice to the lady operators, who are as much overworked and unpaid in their departments as men." The striker explained that despite the equal effort and skill, women only received half of what men earned, from $25 to $50 a month, compared to $60-$90 earned by male operators (in contrast, house painters and garment cutters earned twice as much as telegraphers).

A local newspaper agreed with the strikers: "[T]he 'woman question' is one that will longest engage the public attention. Equal pay for equal service is a just principle." (Hartford Courant, 1883).

Union leaders met with Thomas T. Eckert, the general manager of Western Union, who rejected all their demands in a manner the unionists labeled "arrogant and disrespectful." They should not have been surprised. Eckert was an officer during the Civil War in charge of communications who passed critical information to Jay Gould just before a Union Army victory or defeat. If the North was about to lose a battle, Eckert would wire Gould and the robber baron would buy gold. If the North was about to win, Gould would switch to dollars. Once, during the Battle of Gettysburg, Eckert failed to pass along the inside information. Gould was furious.

Ironically, when Eckert got his job at Western Union, he issued a sixty-five page list of rules and regulations to all operators. Rule Number 128 read, "All messages whatsoever including press reports, are strictly private and confidential, and must be treated thus by employees of the Company." (Thomas T. Eckert Archives, Huntington Library, San Mareno, CA).

The Hartford strike began promptly at 12:05 on Thursday, July 19th. One operator was in the middle of sending a dispatch when his co-workers walked out; he left, too, with the message unfinished. Twelve of the 13 Western Union operators walked out, leaving only the manager and chief operator. Both American Rapid operators struck as well, as did the lone worker at Mutual. All the linemen at the three companies "dropped their repairing instruments and retired from duty," according to a press report. Railroad and press operators were all told to stay on the job. This meant that the primary impact was on personal correspondence. But a Hartford newspaper reported that "Public opinion here generally seems to sustain the operators in their movement." The operators who kept working "pledged themselves not to interfere in any way with the regular operators' strike.

For the first week, everyone coped. The public stopped coming to the telegraph offices and used the mail instead, since delivery and accuracy was no longer assured. One story circulating concerned three Hartford men visiting New Jersey who wired on a Saturday that they were coming home. When they arrived in the city on Monday, the telegram still had not been delivered. In the meantime, groups of citizens mingled with the strikers at the intersection of Central Row and Main Street to discuss the latest news. The Hartford Knights of Labor office opened its doors so the strikers could meet. When not doing union business, strikers played baseball on a makeshift field in the North Meadows. The Western Union operators faced a team composed of the other two companies for a seven-inning game. The united team won by a score of 15 to 9.

There was plenty of union work to do as well. In order to ensure the local success of the strike, workers had to persuade out-of-town strikebreakers to stay away, such as the female Western Union operator who came into town from a rural office. Approached by the strikers, she listened to their arguments, signed a union card and returned home. Two operators who had traveled from White River Junction in Vermont were similarly initiated into the union by local operators. Two more from Burnside were discouraged from taking jobs as scabs as well. Samuel Adams, a New York lineman sent to American Rapid's Hartford office, was also met by strikers. He signed up and left for New York on the noon train.

Within six days, the American Rapid Company settled with the union, agreeing to 10% wage increases, eight hours for a day's work, overtime pay for hours worked in excess of eight and Sunday overtime. The issue of pay equity was not directly addressed in the settlement. The company also agreed to hire strikers from other companies. But American Rapid was not the biggest target; the strike against Western Union continued.

On August 8th, several thousand union members and their families celebrated the American Rapid victory at their annual Union Grove picnic on Wethersfield Avenue. The event, which lasted until midnight, featured Samuel Gompers, the cigar maker who would soon become the first president of the American Federation of Labor.

The strike raised a fundamental question about ownership of a business that was so crucial to the national interest. Leading newspapers, including those in New Haven, Bridgeport and Norwich, lobbied for a telegraph system that was regulated just like the Post Office. One local editorial writer summed up the public sentiment: "'Let the government take the telegraph,' is the universal demand."

Cracks in operators' solidarity appeared in other parts of the country.

There were reports that some operators who were allowed to stay on the job were doing the work of strikers. In Boston and New York, some returned to work. Desperate acts of sabotage of telegraph lines occurred outside of New York City. There were sporadic attacks on scabs as well. In Hartford, signs were posted on Western Union poles offering a $500 reward for information that would lead to the conviction of anyone damaging company property. "It is not likely that a single reward will ever come to Hartford," a local paper wrote (Hartford Courant, *Sabotage in the Workplace*, August, 1883).

National union leaders tried to meet with Eckert in New York on August 15th, during a meeting of the Western Union executive committee, but he refused. The Western Union strike was called off on August 17th. Some Hartford strikers were rehired and forced to sign "yellow dog contracts" which bound them never to join a union. Others like lineman Walter Clark and a depot office worker identified as Miss Lester were not reinstated. It is reasonable to presume they were blacklisted, a common tactic to thwart future union efforts.

A local newspaper blamed the workers' situation on the union and described it as an "organization which can get its members into trouble but cannot pull them through." In a way, this conservative viewpoint was correct. By deciding which of the operators would strike and which would stay on the job, the union weakened its bargaining position. Jay Gould could be beaten in only one way: by a strong united front.

This lesson was not lost on union organizers. In 1884, a year after the telegraphers' strike, the Knights of Labor organized tens of thousands of railroad workers from a wide range of jobs who struck Jay Gould's Southwestern rail system. And won.

22. Sports

Swinging for the Fences: Connecticut's Black Baseball Greats

Former Negro League baseball player John "Mule" Miles visited Connecticut some years back. He told an audience that despite the adversity African Americans faced playing segregated ball, many persevered for the love of the game. Mule (who could "hit like a mule kicks") reflected on his childhood: "When I was young, my mother would call me to come in and do the dishes," he recalled. "I would ask her, 'can I do 'em later? There's still some sunlight! Please let me play 'til the sun goes down.'" (Steve Thornton, Connecticuthistory.org, 4/6/21, *Swinging for the Fences: Connecticut's Black Baseball Greats*)

If baseball is America's pastime, it has been Connecticut's passion for more than 150 years. Our state can trace the popularity of the game back before the Civil War. Towns, neighborhoods, factories and churches all had their own teams, from the Hartford Dark Blues (one of the first major league clubs), to the semi-pro New Britain Aviators, to the pick-up teams of the young store clerks who, in the 19th century, played in the early morning hours before businesses opened.

The history of this sport, found in a multitude of books and movies, is an important part of American lore. But not that long ago, professional baseball reflected the segregated nature of national life. As the magazine *Sporting Life* put it in 1891, "Probably in no other business in America is the color line so finely drawn as in baseball. (Sporting Life, 1891)"

Despite demoralizing Jim Crow laws, widespread hostility and the physical danger of racism, early Black ballplayers in this state established a proud tradition of excellence in the game. An understanding of America's game is not complete until fans know the names of Frank Grant and Moses Fleetwood Walker (Black athletes who played for Connecticut integrated teams) as well as they know Ted Williams and Mickey Mantle.

Segregated Baseball in Connecticut

In Connecticut, African Americans played organized baseball as early as 1868, when the Middletown Heroes played in Douglas Park against visiting white teams. In 1886, Moses Walker played for the Waterbury Brassmen, one of eight Eastern League clubs. Walker was born in 1857 "at a way-station on the Underground Railroad," according to a biographer. He was the first African-American to cross over to the major leagues, as a catcher for the Toledo Blue Stockings. After baseball, Walker became an author and inventor.

In the Naugatuck Valley, the Ansonia Big Gorhams were part of the short-lived 1891 Connecticut State League. The Gorhams (old English for muddy homestead) also played as one incarnation of the so-called Cuban Giants. None of the players were Cuban, but it was slightly easier to "pass" as Hispanic than Black. Ulysses Franklin "Frank" Grant, called the greatest African-American ballplayer of the 19th century, was a second baseman and power hitter for Ansonia. Grant is credited with the invention of shin guards — improvised wooden protectors against hostile white players who deliberately slid spikes-first into Black players.

That year, the Ansonia team was on the verge of being recruited to Portland, Maine by the New England League. Opposition grew so strong against the transfer of the "colored chaps" that the Portland team signed nine white players instead. "It became very evident that the place for a club of colored players was a league composed of all colored men, and not in a circuit where all the players were white men," explained *Sporting Life*.

Black teams did not often have their own home fields, however, so barnstorming became an important way for them to compete. The semi-pro Corinthians traveled throughout New England before finally settling in Hartford around 1925. Renamed the Hartford Giants, they played their first game against the Manchester Shamrocks. To keep busy, they had to advertise in the local newspaper, calling for any and all teams to face them on the field. Hartford hosted the Colored Stars and the Colored Giants from 1925 to 1934, although these teams were probably reorganized under different names with many of the same players.

Johnny "Schoolboy" Taylor

In 1920, entrepreneurs formed the National Negro League. From that federation of Black clubs came some of baseball's all-time superstars, notably Satchel Paige, Josh Gibson and the young Jackie Robinson. Here again, Connecticut offered its best and brightest to baseball. Johnny "Schoolboy" Taylor was a 1933 graduate of Hartford's Bulkeley High. Experts considered him a phenomenon on the mound, striking out 22 batters in his last high school game. The New York Yankees expressed interest in signing Taylor until the team recruiter discovered he was an African-American. The scout suggested to the pitcher that he join the team as a "real-life" Cuban national, but Taylor refused.

Instead, after his last game with the Bulkeley Maroons, Taylor traveled the semi-pro circuit, pitching for Hartford's Savitt Gems and the Yantic team of the Norwich State League. He pitched his first no-hitter with the Northwest Athletic Club in Winsted. Taylor's first big break came when he signed with the New York Cubans. He went on to play with other Negro League teams and then with the Mariano Club in Havana where he became known as "Escolar" Taylor. There, his manager was the legendary Martín Dihigo. Johnny was the student and Martín was known as "El Maestro." Dihigo is the only player in history to be inducted into the halls of fame in five countries.

Seemingly mirroring circumstances from Taylor's life, the award-winning Broadway play *Fences* by August Wilson tells the tale of Troy Maxson, a former Negro League player too old for the now-integrated major leagues. Angry and bitter, he forbids his son from becoming a college athlete. *Fences* opened on Broadway in 1987, just three months before Johnny Taylor died.

A sports writer actually posed the *Fences* dilemma to Taylor in 1976. "What can you do?" Taylor replied. "You can't live in the past. I've always taken things as they come … I like to think that what we did in the 1930s and '40s by barnstorming with white teams paved the way for the next generation."

Waterbury's Jimmy Piersall: De-stigmatizing Mental Illness

If Jimmy Piersall accomplished nothing else in his long, colorful life, he certainly did a great deal to draw attention to the issue of mental illness. Because he was a major league baseball player, his battles became very public in ways that were undoubtedly quite painful for him. He struggled on, documented his illness and the impact it had on his life in a best-selling book he wrote when he was just 25-years-old age. He went on to have several careers after baseball.

Piersall was not the easiest person to be around. He was prone to vicious outbursts that were often aimed at complete strangers, and in response to things of no consequence. Such behavior was not confined to the times when he was often cruelly taunted on major league baseball fields. They persisted deep into his long life.

His inappropriate behavior notwithstanding, Piersall should be viewed first and foremost as someone who struggled with illness, did so in a very public way, and persevered for 65 years from the time of a public breakdown to his death. The world in which his troubles became public was very different from our own. It may not be accurate to say Piersall was the first person to struggle in such a public way with issues the general population either didn't know about, didn't want to know about, or else had a superficial understanding of. But it wouldn't be far from the truth, either. Whatever his flaws, he did the world a great service for that alone.

Early Life

Piersall was born in Waterbury on November 14, 1929. He was an outstanding athlete from a young age and starred in baseball and basketball at Leavenworth High School, leading the basketball team to the New England championship in 1947. During much of his early life, his mother battled mental illness and was a regular inpatient in mental hospitals. Piersall was a serious, introspective youth. His family's descent into poverty after the 1929 stock market crash troubled him greatly, and undoubtedly impacted his mental health.

Piersall was signed to a contract by the Boston Red Sox in 1948 and played his first major league baseball game in 1950 at the age of 20. After displaying increasingly erratic behavior for a period of months, Piersall suffered a serious breakdown in 1952. He spent time in a mental hospital in Massachusetts, where he was diagnosed as manic depressive and treated with electric shock therapy.

342

He was also prescribed lithium and took it for most all of the rest of his life.

Fear Strikes Out

Piersall made a remarkable recovery and quickly revived his baseball career. In 1953, he became the starting centerfielder for Boston, and was named to play in the All-Star Game the following year; the first of two All-Star appearances. He also began working on a book about his ordeal called, *Fear Strikes Out*. Co-authored with Al Hirschfeld, it was published in 1955. The story was made into a television drama a short time later, part of the anthology show *Climax!* with Tab Hunter playing Piersall.

Two years after the release of the book, a Hollywood movie version of Piersall's story was made. Also called *Fear Strikes Out*, the movie featured Anthony Perkins as Piersall and Karl Malden as his father John Piersall. Though Piersall has written that he did not much like the film, it was successful and well-received, and remains a staple on television channels that feature old-time movies.

Whatever its flaws, the movie was a fairly powerful depiction of a young man struggling with mental illness that was likely seen by hundreds of thousands at the time of its release, in addition to many more over the decades on television. Though any number of movies prior to *Fear Strikes Out* included characters with serious psychological problems, they overwhelmingly were superficial and/or violent, unsympathetic criminals like James Cagney's over-the-top performance in 1949's *White Heat*. Unlike pretty much any mentally ill movie character prior to the 1957 movie, Perkins as Piersall is depicted sympathetically. Scenes like his breakdown during a game remain quite powerful more than 60 years later, even if it was one of the scenes Piersall objected to because the breakdown did not actually occur on the field during a game.

Abusive Fans and Players

Piersall endured a great deal of abuse from opposing players and fans in the years after the book and movie were released. He was even attacked by two fans on the field at Yankee Stadium during a game. Piersall never spoke or wrote much about the taunts and slurs he had to listen to over many years, but he undoubtedly had to tap a deep reservoir of inner strength to withstand them.

Piersall sometimes responded quite forcefully, including several fistfights he had with opposing players. At other times, he displayed a comic touch on the field. In 1963, for example, when he hit the 100th home run of his career while playing for the New York Mets, he marked the milestone by circling the bases backwards. On another occasion when he came up to bat, he doffed his cap and several birds he had hidden under it took flight, to the delight of many in attendance.

While Piersall continued to live in Waterbury through much of the 1950s, he did not maintain a close relationship with his hometown thereafter. He visited the city after moving away while his parents were still living, but rarely did so after their deaths. Given how he wrote about the poverty of his childhood and the mental stress he experienced, themes that are brought to even greater life in the movie version of *Fear Strikes Out*, it's quite possible his memories of Waterbury were mostly painful ones that he preferred to keep at a distance.

Painful memories notwithstanding, Piersall remains one of the best-known Waterbury natives and one of the greatest athletes born in the city. The building where Piersall attended high school in the Brass City still stands, though it is no longer a school. The name of his high school has changed several times, and is today known as John F. Kennedy High School. He is enshrined in the Waterbury Hall of Fame maintained by the city's Silas Bronson Library.

An Elite Outfielder

The fact that Piersall is well-known for his struggles should not overshadow his career as a ballplayer. He was an especially accomplished fielder who won Gold Glove awards in 1958 and 1961 as the American League's best defensive centerfielder. Since the Gold Glove award was not begun until 1957, well after the start of his career, he might have won as many as four more. He is a member of the Red Sox Hall of Fame, alongside the likes of Babe Ruth, Cy Young, and long-time teammate Ted Williams.

While there's no way to quantify Piersall's contribution to our collective understanding of mental illness, the fact of that contribution is undeniable. He was a person whose career unfolded in front of millions and who lay bare a problem that remained largely in the shadows in the 1950s. Everyone who struggles with mental illness or cares about someone who does should be grateful that Piersall was willing and able to confront his problems so forthrightly.

After playing 17 seasons in the major leagues, Piersall worked as a minor league fielding instructor, a broadcaster, and a radio talk show host. He died in Illinois on June 2, 2017, at the age of 87.

SELECTED BIBLIOGRAPHY - BOOKS

EARLY CONNECTICUT: THE 1776 REVOLUTION TO THE CIVIL WAR

Atwater, Dorence. *1845-1910. A list of the Union soldiers buried at Andersonville copied from the official record in the surgeon's office at Andersonville.* New York: Tribune Association, 1866

Gilbert, Amos. *The Life of Thomas Skidmore.* (edited by and with an introduction by Mark Lause) San Francisco: Charles H. Kerr Publishing, 1984

Griffin, Farrah Jasmine. ed., *Beloved Sisters and Loving Friends: Letters from Rebecca Primus and Addie Brown of Hartford, Connecticut, 1854-1868.* New York: Alfred A. Knopf, 1999

Rose, Alexander. *Washington's Spies: The Story of America's First Spy Ring.* New York: Bantam Books, 2006

Welch, Richard. *General Washington's Commando Benjamin Tallmadge in the Revolutionary War.* Jefferson, NC: McFarland, 2014

WORKERS

Asbaugh Carolyn. *Lucy Parsons, American Revolutionary.* San Francisco: Charles H. Kerr Publishing, 1976

Boyer, R. Owen and H.M. Morais. *Labor's Untold Story: The Adventure Story of the Battles, Betrayals and Victories of American Working Men and Women.* 3d ed. New York: United Electrical, Radio & Machine Workers of America, 1979

Dubofsky, Melvyn, *We Shall Be All: A History of the Industrial Workers of the World.* Chicago: Quadrangle Books, 1969

George, Harrison, *The I.W.W. Trial: Story of the greatest trial in labor's history by one of the defendants.* Chicago: Industrial Workers of the World, 1918

Gilden, K.B. *Between the Hills and the Sea.* New York: Doubleday, 1971

Hopkins, Harry L. *Spending to save: the complete story of relief.* Seattle: University of Washington Press, 1972, c1936

Matles, James J. and James Higgins. *Them and Us: Struggles of a Rank and File Union.* Boston: United Electrical, Radio and Machine Workers of America, Beacon Press, 1974

Rosswurm, Steve, ed. *The CIO's Left-Led Unions.* New Brunswick, NJ: Rutgers University Press, 1992.

Simmons, Louise, *Organizing in Hard Times.* Philadelphia: Temple University Press, 1994

Zinn, Howard, *A People's History of the United States.* New York: HarperCollins Publishers, 1999

AFRICAN AMERICANS

Abramson, Doris. *Negro Playwrights in the American Theater 1925-1959.* New York, NY: Columbia University Press, 1969

Douglass, Frederick. *The Life and Times of Frederick Douglass.* Hartford: Park Publishing Company, 1882

Easton, Hosea, George R. Price and James Brewster Stewart, eds. *To Heal the Scourge of Prejudice: The Life and Writings of Hosea Easton.* Amherst, MA: University of Massachusetts Press, 1999

Finkelman, Paul. *An Imperfect Union: Slavery, Federalism, and Comity.* Chapel Hill, NC: University of North Carolina Press, 1981.

Finkelman, Paul. *Slavery and the Law.* Lanham, MD: Rowman and Littlefield, 2002

Keeler, Robert. *Newsday: A Candid History of the Respectable Tabloid.* New York: William Morrow, 1990

Kronenberger, Louis, ed. *The Best Plays of 1953-54.* New York, NY: Dodd, Mead and Company, 1954

Lott, Eric. *Love and Theft: Blackface Minstrelsy and the American Working Class.* New York: Oxford University Press, 1993

Motley, Constance Baker. *Equal Justice Under Law: An Autobiography.* New York, NY: Farrar, Straus, and Giroux, 1998

National Society of Black Scientists. *Edward Bouchet: The First African-American Doctorate*. Hackensack, NJ: World Scientific Publishing Company, 2002

Normen, Elizabeth J., ed. *African American Connecticut Explored*. Middletown, CT: Wesleyan University Press, 2013

Payne, Les. "The Night I Stopped Being a Negro." In *When Race Becomes Real: Black and White Writers Confront Their Personal Histories*. Carbondale, IL: Southern Illinois University Press, 2002

Peterson, Louis *Take a Giant Step: A Drama in Two Acts*. New York, NY: Samuel French Inc., 1954

Williams, Yohuru. *Black Politics/White Power: Civil Rights Black Power and Black Panthers in New Haven* Hoboken, NJ: Blackwell, 2006

Yellin, Jean Fagin, and John C. Van Horne, eds. *The Abolitionist Sisterhood: Women's Political Culture in Antebellum America*. Ithaca, NY: Cornell University Press, 1994

LATINO AND LATINAS
Denis, Nelson A. *War Against All Puerto Ricans: Revolution and Terror in America's Colony*. New York: Hatchette Books, 2016

Fernandez, Johanna. *The Young Lords: A Radical History*. Chapel Hill, NC: University of North Carolina Press, 2020

Morales, Iris, Denise Oliver-Velez and Darrel Enck-Wanzer, ed. *The Young Lords: A Reader*. New York: New York University Press, 2010

Pierson, Charles, "The Day the US Became an Empire," Counter Punch magazine, June 15, 2018

Zinn Education Project, "July 25, 1898: U.S. Invades Puerto Rico," 2020 https://www.zinnedproject.org/news/tdih/us-invades-puerto-rico/

Thornton Steve, "Yanquis or Yankees? Building a New Relationship with Cuba," Havana Times, January 2015,

Campos, Pedro Albizu, *Free Puerto Rico*, Prism Key Press, 2013 prismkeypress. com

RADICAL WOMEN
Brady, Kathleen. *Ida Tarbell: Portrait of a Muckraker*. New York: Seaview/ Putnam, 1984

Coté, Charlotte. *Olympia Brown: The Battle for Equality*. Racine, WI: Mother Courage Press, 1988

Henderson, Robin Légère. *Matilda Rabinowitz, Immigrant Girl, Radical Woman: A Memoir from the Early Twentieth. Century* Ithaca: Cornell University Press, 2017

Nielsen, Kim. *The Radical Lives of Helen Keller*. New York: New York University Press, 2004

Tarbell, Ida M. *All in the Day's Work*. New York: Macmillan Co., 1939

Tarbell, Ida M. *The History of the Standard Oil Company, Volumes 1 and 2*. New York: McClure, Phillips & Co., 1905

Thornton, Steve. *A Shoeleather History of the Wobblies: Stories of the Industrial Workers of the World (IWW) in Connecticut*. Boston: Red Sun Press, 2013

"Planned Parenthood History," Accessed 2015, www.ppct.org.
Reynolds, Michael, *Hemingway: The Paris Years,* W. W. Norton & Company, 1999

McKay, Claude, *A Long Way from Home,* Rutgers University Press, New Brunswick, 2007

Day, Dorothy, *The Long Loneliness: The Autobiography of the Legendary Catholic Social Activist,* HarperCollins, 2009

STUDENTS ORGANIZING ON AND OFF CAMPUS
Gillette, Howard, J. *Class Divide: Yale '64 and the Conflicted Legacy of the Sixties*. Ithaca, NY: Cornell University Press, 2015

PEACE NOT WAR

DeRosa, Ulysses. *The Odyssey of a Conscientious Objector,* unpublished manuscript, courtesy of the DeRosa family

Maier, Thomas. *Dr. Spock: An American Life*. New York: Harcourt Brace, 1998

Mitford, Jessica. *The Trial of Dr. Spock, the Rev. William Sloane Coffin, Jr., Michael Ferber, Mitchell Goodman, and Marcus Raskin*. New York: Knopf, 1969

Spock, Benjamin, and Mary Morgan. *Spock on Spock: A Memoir of Growing up with the Century*. New York: Pantheon Books, 1989

Neale, Jonathan. *A People's History of the Vietnam War: A New Press People's History.* (Howard Zinn, Series Editor) The New Press, New York, 2004

Zinn, Howard; Dana Frank and Robin D. G. Kelley. *Three Strikes: Miners, Musicians, Salesgirls, and the Fighting Spirit of Labor's Last Century*. Beacon Press, Boston, 2002

ENVIRONMENTAL ACTIVISM

Carson, Rachel. *Silent Spring*. Boston: Houghton Mifflin, 1962

Gyorgy, Anna, *No Nukes: Everyone's Guide to Nuclear Power,* Black Rose Books Ltd., Montreal, 1979

Vallianatos, E. G., and McKay Jenkins. *Poison Spring: The Secret History of Pollution and the EPA*. New York: Bloomsbury Press, 2014

Wickenden, Leonard. *Our Daily Poison; the Effects of DDT, Fluorides, Hormones and Other Chemicals on Modern Man*. New York: Devin-Adair, 1955

YOUTH IN REVOLT

Cruz, José E. *Identity And Power: Puerto Rican Politics and the Challenge of Ethnicity*. Philadelphia: Temple University Press, 1998

Morales, Iris, Denise Oliver-Velez and Darrel Enck-Wanzer, ed. *The Young Lords: A Reader*. New York: New York University Press, 2010

STANDING UP FOR FREE SPEECH
Aronoff, Kate, "Industrial Workers of the World campaigns for free speech in Spokane, Washington, U.S.A., 1908-1910," Swarthmore College Peace Collection, 1908-1910

Houchin, John. *Censorship of the American Theatre in the Twentieth Century.* Cambridge, England: Cambridge University Press, 2009

Smith, Wendy. *Real Life Drama: The Group Theatre and America, 1931-1940.* New York: Knopf, 1990

Sova, Dawn B. *Banned Plays: Censorship Histories of 125 Stage Dramas* New York: Facts on File, 2004

Thornton, Steve. *A Shoeleather History of the Wobblies: Stories of the Industrial Workers of the World (IWW) in Connecticut.* Boston: Red Sun Press, 2013

Thompson, Fred, and Jon Bekken. *The Industrial Workers of the World: Its First 100 Years.* Boston: Red Sun Press, 2006

TAKING ON THE KKK AND OTHER TERRORISTS
Archer, Jules. *The Plot to Seize the White House.* New York: Hawthorn Books, 1973

Chalmers, David Mark. *Hooded Americanism: The History of the Ku Klux Klan.* Durham, NC: Duke University Press, 1987

Denton, Sally. *The Plots Against the President: FDR, a Nation in Crisis, and the Rise of the American Right.* New York" Bloomsbury Press, 2012

Spivak, John. *A Man in His Time.* New York: Horizon Press, 1967

RESISTING GOVERNMENT REPRESSION
Burr, George Lincoln, ed. *Narratives of the Witchcraft Cases, 1648-1706.* New York: Charles Scribner's Sons, 1914

Taylor, John M. *The Witchcraft Delusion in Colonial Connecticut, 1647-1697.* New York: Grafton Press, 1908

Tomlinson, R. G. *Witchcraft Prosecution: Chasing the Devil in Connecticut.* Rockland, ME: Picton Press, 2012

Matles, James J., Higgins, James, *Them and Us: Struggles of a Rank and File Union,* United Electrical, Radio and Machine Workers of America, Beacon Press, Boston, 1974

ALL CONNECTICUT'S A STAGE
Batiste, Stephanie Leigh. *Darkening Mirrors: Imperial Representation in Depression-Era African American Performance.* Durham, NC: Duke University Press, 2012

Dowling, Robert: *Eugene O'Neill: A Life in Four Acts.* New Haven, CT: Yale University Press, 2014

Flanagan, Hallie. *Arena: The History of The Federal Theatre Project.* New York: B. Blom, 1940

Leaming, Barbara: *Orson Welles: A Biography.* New York: Viking Press, 1985

Miller, Arthur. *Timebends: A Life.* New York: Grove Press, 1987

Papa, Lee, ed. *Staged Action: Six Plays from the American Workers' Theater.* Ithaca, NY: ILR Press, 2009. (https://digitalcommons.ilr.cornell.edu/cgi/viewcontent.cgi?article=1053&context=books)

Smith, Wendy. *Real Life Drama: The Group Theatre and America, 1931-1940.* New York: Knopf, 1990

ART, MEDIA AND CULTURE
Anderson, Jack. *The American Dance Festival.* Durham, NC: Duke University Press, 1987

Black, James Eric. *Walt Kelly and Pogo: The Art of The Political Swamp.* Jefferson, NC: McFarland, 2016

Edwards, Anne. *A Remarkable Woman: A Biography of Katharine Hepburn.* New York, NY: William Morrow & Company, Inc., 1985

Fitzgerald, Richard. *Art & Politics: Cartoonists of the Masses and Liberator.* Westport, CT: Greenwood Press, 1973

Graff, Ellen. *Stepping Left: Dance and Politics in New York City, 1928-1942*. Durham, NC: Duke University Press, 1997

Hendrick, George, and Willene Hendrick, eds. *Billy Sunday and Other Poems*. Harcourt Brace & Co., New York, 1993

Kosstrin, Hannah. *Honest Bodies: Revolutionary Modernism in the Dances of Anna Sokolow*. London: Oxford University Press, 2017
McPherson, Elizabeth. *The Contributions of Martha Hill to American Dance and Dance Education, 1900-1995*. Lewiston, NY: Edwin Mellen Press, 2008

Soares, Janet Mansfield. *Martha Hill and the Making of American Dance*. Middletown, CT: Wesleyan University Press, 2009
Soper, Kerry D. *We Go Pogo: Walt Kelly, Politics, and American Satire*. Jackson, MS: University Press of Mississippi, 2012

Twain, Mark. *A Connecticut Yankee in King Arthur's Court*. New York: PenguinRandom House, 2004

Warren, Larry. *Anna Sokolow: The Rebellious Spirit* New York: Routledge, 1998

Young, Art, and Heywood Broun. *The Best of Art Young*. New York, NY: Vanguard Press, 1936

Yates, Richard. *Revolutionary Road*. Boston, MA: Little, Brown, 1961

Zwick, Jim. *Confronting Imperialism: Essays on Mark Twain and the Anti-Imperialist League*. Conshohocken, PA: Infinity Publishing Co., 2007

BEHIND THE WALLS OF PRISONS
Nichols, Carole. *Votes and More for Women: Suffrage and After in Connecticut*. New York: Institute for Research in History, Haworth Press, 1983.

HOW THE OTHER .0001% LIVES
Dulles, Foster Rhea and Melvyn Dubofsky. *Labor in America, A History 5th rev. ed*. Harlan Davidson, Illinois, 1993

Josephson, Matthew. *The Robber Barons*. New York: Harvest Books, 1962

Schechter, Harold. *Killer Colt: Murder, Disgrace, and the Making of an American Legend.* Random House, New York, 2010

SPORTS

Arcidiacono, David. *Major League Baseball in Gilded Age Connecticut: The Rise and Fall of the Middletown, New Haven and Hartford Clubs.* Jefferson, NC: McFarland, 2009

Golenbock, Peter. *Fenway: An Expurgated History of the Boston Red Sox.* New York, NY: Putnam, 1992

Piersall, Jim and Al Hirshberg. *Fear Strikes Out: The Jim Piersall Story.* Boston: Little Brown, 1955

Rice, Ed. *Baseball's First Indian: The Story of Penobscot Legend Louis Sockalexis.* Lanham, MD: Rowman & Littlefield, 2019

Wilson, August. *Fences, A Play by August Wilson.* New York: Penguin Group, 1986

OTHER SOURCES

Thornton, Steve, 2014. *Josephine Bennett: City Mother.* Accessed April 17, 2020, https://connecticuthistory.org/hartfords-city-mother-josephine-bennett/

Working Man's Advocate, 1929, New York, Accessed April 17, 2020, https://popularfreethought.wordpress.com/browse-by-title/working-mans-advocate-1829-1836/

"Connecticut's Longest Labor Strike," Shoeleather History Project, 2017, Accessed January 15, 2020, https://shoeleatherhistoryproject.com/2017/02/23/connecticuts-
longest-labor-strike/

Royce, Jon, *The Execution of Henry Wirz,* University of Missouri Kansas City School of Law.

Price, George R., "The Easton family of southeast Massachusetts: The dynamics surrounding five generations of human rights activism 1753--1935" (2006).

Graduate Student Theses, Dissertations, & Professional Papers. 9598. https://scholarworks.umt.edu/etd/9598

S.S. Stewart, *Catalogue and Pricelist,* Philadelphia, 1893. Accessed January 1, 2018, piccoloplace.org

"Hicks Georgia's Minstrels," *The Mercury,* Tasmania, 1879, Accessed January 20, 2018, https://trove.nla.gov.au/newspaper/article/8976430#

"Broadside - The Fugitive Slave Law." Hartford, CT, ca 1850. Library of Congress, American Memory

"Newspapers of Connecticut: Charter Oak (ca. 1838-1848) - Digital Newspaper Archive." Connecticut State Library, 2016
"Research Guide to Materials Relating to Slavery in Connecticut." Connecticut State Library, 2016

Federal Bureau of Investigation, "Malcolm Little (Malcolm Little)," 1925-1965, HQ files 1-27. Accessed https://vault.fbi.gov/malcolm-little-malcolm-x

Swarthmore College Peace Collection, Accessed 2018, swarthmore.edu
"Clamshell Alliance: Legacy." Accessed July 3, 1997, https://www.clamshellalliance.net/legacy/category/labor/

"Historic Timeline of Connecticut's LGBTQ Community," Connecticut Historical Society, accessed 2019, https://chs.org/lgbtq/

Langness, David, "Did Rock and Roll Integrate the Races?" June 7, 2016, https://bahaiteachings.org/did-rock-n-roll-integrate-the-races/

Baer, Cheryl LS, "Concurrent Revolutions: Rock and Roll and the Civil Rights Movement," Masters Thesis, Humboldt State University, May, 2005, Accessed 2019, http://humboldt-dspace.calstate.edu/bitstream/handle/2148/31/CBaer.pdf?sequence=1

Spivak, John. "Wall Street's Fascist Conspiracy: Testimony That the Dickstein Committee Suppressed" *New Masses*, January 29, 1935

"The Influence of 'The Birth of a Nation,'" Facing History and Ourselves, https://www.facinghistory.org/reconstruction-era/influence-birth-nation

"Are We Headed for a New Civil War?," CT Mirror, August 21, 2017, https://ctmirror.org/category/ct-viewpoints/a-new-civil-war/

Stinnett, Graham, "The Ku Klux Klan, Rebel Pride, and Anti Klan Resistance," UConn Human Rights Archives, https://blogs.lib.uconn.edu/humanrights/2015/07/08/the-ku-klux-klan-rebel-pride-and-anti-klan-resistance/

Hale, Swinburne, "Act-of-Hate Palmer," The Nation, June 12, 1920, hathitrust.org, Accessed 2013, https://babel.hathitrust.org/cgi/pt?id=mdp.39015060789552&view=1up&seq=935

Heitman, Danny, "The Workingman's Poet," Humanities: The Magazine of the National Endowment for the Humanities, March/April 2013, Vol. 34, Number 2 "Evelyn Beatrice Longman Batchelder," Connecticut Women's Hall of Fame, 1994, https://www.cwhf.org/inductees/evelyn-longman-batchelder

"Standard Minimum Rules for the Treatment of Prisoners,"
Adopted by the First United Nations Congress on the Prevention of Crime and the Treatment of Offender 1955, American Civil Liberties Union, May, 2014, https://www.aclu.org/files/assets/UN%20Standard%20Minimum%20Rules%20for%20the%20Treatment%20of%20Prisoners.pdf

Wallach, Alan, "Col. Colt's Ambiguous Legacy; or When I Hear the Word 'Revolver,' I Reach for My Culture," American Quarterly, Vol. 50, No. 3 (Sep., 1998)

Thornton, Steve, "Would Sam Colt Be Considered a Good Businessman Today?," Hartford Business Journal, August 11, 2014, https://www.hartfordbusiness.com/article/would-sam-colt-be-considered-a-good-businessman-today

Thornton, Steve, "Some Hero," Hartford Courant, September 24, 2006

PHOTO ATTRIBUTIONS

FRONT COVER:

(Women on strike) Photo by Steve Thornton

(In red) Photo by Nick Lacy

(Clapping) Photo by Nick Lacy

(Newsboys) Lewis Hine, 1909. National Gallery under Creative Commons Zero (CC0) "Users may download and reproduce—free of charge and without seeking authorization from the National Gallery—any digital image of a work in our collection that the we believe is in the public domain. These digital images are being released by the National Gallery under Creative Commons Zero (CC0)."

INSIDE PHOTOS:

(Twain mural) Photo by Steve Thornton

(Matilda Rabinowitz) Courtesy of Robbin Legere Henderson

(ILGWU garment) Courtesy of Kheel Center for Labor-Management Documentation and Archives, Cornell University Library. Public domain.

(Hartford Federal) Hugo Gellert, 1943. Courtesy of Congrees of CT Community Colleges

(The war criminal) Creativecommons.org/licenses/by-sa/4.0

(Stand against klan) Photo by Christine Breslin

(Roving Bill) Independent 53 no. 2764, Nov. 1921. Courtesy of Hathi Trust.

(Malcolm X) PICRYL public domain media "Permission for use, re-use, or additional use of the content is not required. GetArchive believes there are no usage restrictions or limitations put on content in the U.S. Get Archive LLC does not charge permission and license fees for use of any of the content on PICRYL, however, upon request, GetArchive can provide rights clearance for content for a fee."

(Vieques arrest) Photo by Steve Thornton

(Eugene Debs) Shoeleather History Project

(Vietnam peace) Courtesy of District 1199NE/SEIU

(Women of prison) Ms. Magazine,3/5/20. Feminist Majority Foundation. Public domain.

ABOUT THE AUTHORS

Andy Piascik is a long-time radical activist and award-winning author whose work has been published in numerous publications and websites. His previous book is the novel In Motion. He can be reached at: andypiascik@aol.com.

Steve Thornton is a retired union organizer and writes for the Shoeleather History Project.com, exploring the stories of working people. He has been a labor educator, tenant organizer, and nonviolence trainer for 45 years and is the author of three books.

TITLES FROM HARD BALL PRESS

A Great Vision: A Militant Family's Journey Through the Twentieth Century, Richard March

Caring: 1199 Nursing Home Workers Tell Their Story, Tim Sheard, ed.

Fight For Your Long Day, Classroom Edition, Alex Kudera

I Still Can't Fly: Confessions of a Lifelong Troublemaker, Kevin John Carroll (Winter 2018-19)

Love Dies, A Thriller, Timothy Sheard

The Man Who Fell From the Sky, Bill Fletcher Jr.

Murder of a Post Office Manager, A Legal Thriller, Paul Felton

New York Hustle: Pool Rooms, School Rooms and Street Corner, A Memoir, Stan Maron

Passion's Pride: Return to the Dawning, Cathie Wright-Lewis

The Secrets of the Snow, Poetry, Hiva Panahi

Sixteen Tons, A Novel, Kevin Corley

Throw Out the Water, Sequel to Sixteen Tons, Kevin Corley

We Are One: Stories of Work, Life & Love, Elizabeth Gottieb, ed.

What Did You Learn at Work Today? The Forbidden Lessons of Labor Education, Helena Worthen

With Our Loving Hands: 1199 Nursing Home Workers Tell Their Story, Timothy Sheard, ed.

Winning Richmond: How a Progressive Alliance Won City Hall , Gayle McLaughlin

Woman Missing, A Mill Town Mystery, Linda Nordquist

THE LENNY MOSS MYSTERIES, TIMOTHY SHEARD

This Won't Hurt A Bit

Some Cuts Never Heal

A Race Against Death

No Place To Be Sick

One Foot in the Grave

Slim To None

A Bitter Pill

Someone Has To Die

All Bleeding Stops Eventually